Workflow Modeling

Tools for Process Improvement and Application Development

Workflow Modeling

Tools for Process Improvement and Application Development

Alec Sharp
Patrick McDermott

Artech House
Boston • London
www.artechhouse.com

Library of Congress Cataloging-in-Publication Data
Sharp, Alec
    Workflow modeling : tools for process improvement and application development/
Alec Sharp, Patrick McDermott.
        p.   cm.—(Artech House computing library)
        Includes bibliographical references and index.
        ISBN 1-58053-021-4 (alk. paper)
        1. Reengineering (Management).   2. Organizational change.   3. Industrial
    management.   4. Information technology.   5. Workflow.   I. McDermott, Patrick.
    II. Title.   III. Artech House computer library.
        HD58.87.S53   2000
        658.4'063—dc21   00-050811
                                                                                CIP

British Library Cataloguing in Publication Data
Sharp, Alec
    Workflow modeling : tools for process improvement and application
    development.—(Artech House computing library)
    1. Workflow   2. Reengineering (Management)   3. Organizational change
    4. Industrial management   5. Information technology
    I. Title   II. McDermott, Patrick
    658.4'063
    ISBN 1-58053-021-4

Cover and text design by Darrell Judd

© 2001 ARTECH HOUSE, INC.
685 Canton Street
Norwood, MA 02062

International Standard Book Number: 1-58053-021-4
Library of Congress Catalog Card Number: 00-050811

20 19 18 17 16 15 14 13 12 11

For Karen and our family—AS
For Lilian—PM

Contents

10 Questions and Difficulties **171**

Part IV
Understanding the As-Is Process **183**

11 Techniques for Modeling the As-Is Process. **185**

Part I
The Convergence of Process
and Systems

1

Why We Had to Write This Book

Fosdick's thesis

Just when process orientation has become mainstream thinking for business people and systems people alike, it seems that the flow of process-oriented literature has pretty well stopped. So here we are, thousands of us, up to our necks in process improvement and information systems projects, finding that there is a real shortage of practical, how-to information. The irony of this situation was described in Howard Fosdick's terrific 1992 article, "The Sociology of Technology Adaptation."[1] Our book isn't a book about technology, but there is a connection—the article dealt with the adoption of new technologies, and this book deals with the adoption of new methods and approaches for solving business problems.

The article begins with the observation that when any significant new technology appears on the scene, it receives widespread publicity in the information technology (IT) arena. This attention could be displayed graphically (see Figure 1.1) in a publicity vector measured by such attributes as: the number of articles on the technology in the trade press, the frequency of conferences on the topic, how many industry analysts discuss the technology, to what degree vendor sales pieces and ads employ the

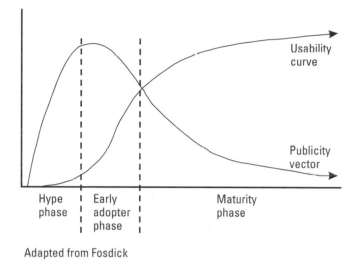

Adapted from Fosdick

Figure 1.1 Publicity versus usability for new technologies.

technology's terminology, and similar measurements. This curve initially rises steeply, but the high degree of publicity received by the technology is completely disproportionate to the usability of the technology and the number of people and organizations doing anything more than just talking about it. However, if the new technology takes hold and becomes widely used, as depicted by the rising usability curve, it seems to fall off the collective radar screen of the various publicity machines, and the publicity vector moves back towards zero.

This happens, of course, because it's no longer a hot, new topic. Bluntly put, once the technology is widely installed, it is evidently time to focus on the next big thing—the consultants and IT advisory services have made their money, and the vendors have a revenue stream in place. The consequence is that just at the point when the most people need practical information on the technology, the attention paid to it in publications becomes negligible. We always, it seems, are provided with a glut of material on the *next* big thing, and not enough on how to make the *last* big thing actually work. Or, as Fosdick put it, "Ironically, once the technologies achieve full maturity, supporting hundreds or even thousands of shops on a daily basis, they receive much less attention in the media and other publicity forums."

Process reengineering: the rise...

Fosdick made his case using examples such as relational databases and expert systems, but the relevant example in our case is, of course, the emergence of business processes and business process reengineering (BPR) as important topics. The first references to cross-functional business processes appeared in the mid-1980s, and by the early 1990s, BPR was without question the next big thing. It was attracting the attention of executives, managers, consultants, pundits, academics, IS professionals, and, of course, writers of books and articles from both business and IS orientations. These first publications covered the problems encountered by functionally oriented organizations, the justification for becoming process-oriented, a few soon-to-be-familiar examples, some introductory process concepts and terminology, and if we were lucky, some actual how-to advice. Some of this how-to-do-it material was really just an attempt—sometimes sincere, sometimes a bit cynical—to capitalize on BPR by recasting older methods such as business systems planning or information engineering with a process-oriented spin. This was a familiar pattern, and as usual, the results were not terribly useful. The other how-to material really tried to describe the new BPx[1] approach, but in the end provided little more than a high-level or broad-brush outline. The focus was on *what* had to be done, but the method was unproven and there was precious little guidance on *how* to actually do it. Practitioners the world over read about identifying the core business processes, mapping the as-is process, or creatively rethinking the process, but when they tried to put this guidance into practice, all manner of issues and problems arose.

However, those early works *did* serve a purpose. In fact, they were invaluable. They paved the way for widespread adoption by promoting process orientation with a key audience of early adopters—executives and other decision makers—and making it familiar and acceptable to the rest of us. Besides, how much practical advice could we realistically expect? At that point, there simply wasn't a large enough base of experience to draw on, and without those books and articles to promote the concepts, there might never have been.

---

1. There are several variations of the term "business process reengineering." We like the one given in a presentation by Jerry Huchzermeier of ProForma Corp.—he refers to "BPx" where "x" is "engineering," "reengineering," "design," "redesign," "improvement," "innovation," and so forth.

...And fall and rise

By the mid- to late 1990s, the term "reengineering" had fallen out of favor (for reasons we'll review in the next chapter), and what had been a deluge of BPR articles and books was now all but dried up. At the time of this writing, it has become a mere trickle, but e-commerce and e-business articles are in full flood. One could reasonably suppose that no one cares about business processes anymore, and the whole process phenomenon was a flash in the pan. In fact, the opposite is true—everyone cares about business processes. Enterprises of all sizes and types—commercial, government, and not-for-profit—are making major investments of time and resources in the redesign of their core processes and in the implementation of information systems to support them. More and more often, the order is reversed—an enterprise acquires a major new information system or enterprise application, and then redesigns its processes to take the best advantage of it. Either way, the same conclusions follow:

- ◆ For both businesspersons and technologists, process orientation has become mainstream thinking.

- ◆ Whether you're business-oriented or systems-oriented (note: we hate to even separate them, because the best IS organizations *are* business-oriented), BPx and information systems are inseparable; it has been years since we saw a process redesign project which didn't involve major information systems effort, or conversely, since we witnessed the implementation of a significant information system that didn't also involve redesigned processes.

Finally, the stakes are higher than ever, for at least two reasons. First, in some industries, effective and flexible core processes have shifted from being a competitive differentiator to being the price of admission—they're a mandatory requirement just to stay in business. Second, with the rise of e-commerce, the complexity and visibility of processes are rising because they now do not just span functional boundaries *within* an enterprise, but cross the boundaries *between* enterprises. For instance, in the area of supply chain management, it's not unusual to see a business process with activities performed by the customer, the supplier, and the supplier's supplier. We note with some glee the number of organizations that are belatedly realizing that having a well-designed and implemented business process is essential for success in the e-commerce arena.

The need for guidance

The current state of affairs is that many thousands of professionals from both business and IS disciplines are engaged in the design and implementation of new business processes and systems. And, just as Fosdick predicted, the available literature simply hasn't kept pace. That is precisely why this book is needed and why we have received so much encouragement to write it from practitioners in the field.

The need has been demonstrated in two particular ways. The first is simply that in our consulting and educational assignments, we are continually asked by people working on process redesign and application implementation projects if we can suggest a reference book that will get past the theory of process and into the practical matters they are struggling with. Those professionals have searched, and so have we. The answer, evidently, is "No." The books on BPx provide concepts, an overview, and some encouragement, but don't get into the details of process identification, modeling, and analysis that practitioners are looking for. On the other hand, there are lots of IS-oriented books on the business modeling techniques that have become standard practice for understanding a business and conducting requirements (or systems) analysis. A host of techniques are covered, including various forms of process modeling, data modeling, state transition analysis, event analysis, data flow diagramming, and object modeling. Many of these techniques at least appear to address process, so do these books fit the bill? Again, the answer is "No." They take a more limited scope with respect to business processes than practitioners are looking for—they focus more on the analysis of individual steps or rules than on dealing with a complete business process. What people are looking for is a book that addresses the issues they encounter when studying a complete business process, and then makes the transition into the systems analysis techniques that these books cover so well.

The second kind of evidence of the need for this book comes from troubled projects. Many of our consulting engagements come about because a project has run into problems, often verging on outright failure. The assignment, should we decide to accept it, is to determine what's gone wrong and set it right. The same mistakes show up so often that we have to conclude there isn't any reference material available to help people avoid these recurring problems. Here are five common examples over the life of a project that have serious consequences.

1. Right from the earliest stages of a project, the wrong body of work is identified as a business process. This is common to virtually every troubled project we encounter. The "process" might be some activities that are actually just a piece of a process; the work performed by a specific department; or an area such as Customer Relationship Management that comprises many processes. The result is that the scope balloons, the project drifts, and the potential benefit associated with improving a specific, complete business process is never realized.

2. Once the team begins to map or model the current ("as-is") process, the work gets bogged down in detail while, ironically, missing important participants and steps. In extreme cases, so much time is wasted on as-is modeling that the project is canceled before any improvements can be identified, much less implemented. In any case, an inaccurate picture of the existing process is developed, which has negative consequences down the road.

3. The assessment of the current process, if it is performed at all, doesn't consider all of the major factors and important stakeholders. This leads to incorrect assumptions about what aspects of the process need to be improved. By default, it is usually assumed that the goal is to make the process faster and cheaper. We have a host of case studies where speed and cost were not the important variables, and new processes that met the fast and cheap criteria ended up failing.

4. Process "improvements" are implemented which are *detrimental* to the overall process. Two common reasons:

   • *All* of the factors that constitute a successful business process—the enablers—aren't considered.

   • A single task or stage of a process is optimized by imposing constraints on the flow of work from or to adjacent tasks and phases.

5. Processes are designed and redesigned without taking into account what a good information system could do. The result: the wrong activities are automated, or a system is developed which supports individual tasks but doesn't expedite the entire process.

Our response

Obviously, there is a need—the frameworks and techniques that we now use are not widely known. In fact, we had to piece them together ourselves, drawing on multiple sources and experimenting on the job. We are grateful to our clients and associates for helping us develop our methods, by trial and error, on real projects. In return, we will preserve their anonymity. As we said, much of our experience comes from dealing with projects that had gone off the rails. We will refer to these cases throughout, because people learn just as much from the stories of what *not* to do. However, we will not refer to any organizations by name, and in some cases we will even disguise the industry or build an example that is an amalgam. We do not want one of our clients to read this and suddenly realize in horror, "Oh, no! They're talking about *my* project!" If you were worried, you can breathe a sigh of relief and get back to reading the book!

After the methods had stabilized and proved themselves on projects, clients started requesting a workshop to transfer skills to more of their staff. Sensing a revenue-generating opportunity, one of us (Sharp) obliged by developing a two-day workshop—Workflow Process Modeling—that became very popular with clients. Participants recommended it to their friends and associates, and the most positive feedback came from people currently working on projects—they said it addressed the real issues that caused real problems. Those were the most gratifying comments of all, because the intent of the workshop, like this book, was to provide practical hands-on guidance for members of a project team.

An interesting development has been the way the mix of workshop participants has evolved. Even though the class was originally developed for information systems professionals (analysts and project leaders), the participant mix has become much broader and multidisciplinary. Business managers, subject matter experts, internal and external consultants, business analysts, individual process contributors, trainers, and others take the class alongside the core audience of systems analysts. In the last couple of years, there has often been a 50/50 split between participants with a business background and those with an IS background. And again, the feedback was along the lines of "I can put this material to work tomorrow" or, more commonly, "I wish I'd had this course four months ago." That pretty much sealed it—it was time to write a book.

What to expect

We had a good idea what sort of book we wanted it to be—a practical exposition of what works, by practitioners for practitioners. Alec still remembers how useful the classic textbook *Structured Systems Analysis* [2] was in 1979 when he was coping with his first major analysis assignment. He'd go through a chapter or two in the evening, and put the material to work the very next day. The next night, another chapter, and the day after that, more progress on his project. And, wonder of wonders, the project was very successful. That is the model we aspire to—a handbook that will guide you through a successful project. The book follows the flow of a typical project, and the entire approach is summarized in Chapter 3, "The Approach in a Nutshell." After you read this, you will be able to read a chapter, immediately apply it to your project, read the next chapter or two, apply them, and so on.

Like the workshop on which it is based, we have tried to make the book suitable for a broad audience that includes nontechnical people responsible for improving their business processes, and systems personnel working on a development or implementation project with a process focus. We have often joked that our topic is "Application Development Meets Process Reengineering," in the same vein as the cartoon *Bambi Meets Godzilla*. Actually, we're aiming for the intersection of three topics:

1. Workflow process modeling;

2. Business process improvement;

3. Application development.

The three are inseparable nowadays, and they need to be brought together between two covers.

In closing, a caveat—we describe an overall methodology and the details of specific steps, but this isn't a cookbook. Every project we have ever worked on has unique issues, and yours will be no different. So use this as a starting point, but please adjust and experiment as you see fit—that is how we developed many of our methods and continue to evolve them. Remember, though, that experience shows unequivocally that if you skip entire phases, like "framing the process" or "characterizing the to-be process," you will regret it—"adjust and experiment" does not imply "short-circuit and eliminate."

Before we cover more about these techniques in Chapter 3's overview, let's have a brief history lesson, and learn how the world came to be process-oriented.

References

[1]   Fosdick, H., "The Sociology of Technology Adaptation," *Enterprise Systems Journal*, Sept. 1992.

[2]   Gane, C., and T. Sarson, *Structured Systems Analysis: Tools and Techniques*, New York: Improved Systems Technologies, 1977.

2

A Brief History of Process

If I have seen farther it is by standing on the shoulders of giants.
                                                    —Isaac Newton

Those who are ignorant of history are condemned to repeat it.
                                                    —George Santayana

Learning from the past

Within a single decade, a focus on the assessment and improvement of business processes— so called process orientation—has become standard practice at organizations all over the world. But it wasn't always so — for most of the past 100 years, there was virtually no discussion of the concept of business processes.[1] At the dawn of the century, the scientific management revolution[2] began the quest to find the best way to design

---

1. Deming is a notable exception, but his seminal work on quality was largely ignored (except in Japan) for decades.

2. By Frederick Taylor and others. See Robert Kanigel, *The One Best Way: Frederick Winslow Taylor and the Enigma of Efficiency* (New York: Penguin Books, 1997), for a good story about the dawn of management consulting.

manufacturing processes, but the focus was on individual tasks, not on improving the entire end-to-end process. This focus on individual tasks remained in place for most of the century, and didn't start to change until the mid-1980s, when the first references to cross-functional business processes appeared. Then, in the early 1990s, business process reengineering (BPR) burst onto the scene with an explosion of interest in processes. Coincidentally, we also saw a massive transfer of wealth from large enterprises to BPR consulting firms. And then, almost as quickly, BPR went from "silver bullet" to "goat" status. Apologetic books and articles appeared. Reengineering fell off the lists of hot topics. Suddenly, organizations that had positioned themselves as leaders of the reengineering charge were distancing themselves from the term. Nonetheless, even though you don't hear the term "reengineering" very often now, the legacy of process orientation, both good and bad, remains.

One aspect of this legacy is that business process, or simply process, has taken on a specific meaning—"a complete end-to-end set of activities that together create value for a customer."[1] End-to-end means that the process is wide—it crosses organizational and functional boundaries, encompassing activities all the way from the initiating event right through to the result expected by the customer.[3]

So what's the big deal? To take everyone's favorite example, wasn't it *obvious* that there was a *process* that began when a customer placed an order, and ended when it was delivered and paid for? How could this simple discovery have been a breakthrough in the organization of work and the cause of a virtual revolution in management thinking? To understand, we need to take a brief, simplified look at the history and forces that led to the reengineering revolution, and the advances that have been made since then. There was no problem identifying processes before the Industrial Revolution, so we'll start then.

The Age of the Craftsworker

Before the Industrial Revolution in the mid-eighteenth century, most products were produced by craftsworkers to whom process and product

---

3. Although the customer may be internal or external to the organization, and stakeholders other than the customer might also expect a specific result from the process, the basic concept is clear.

were the same thing. It was possible to stand at one spot in their workshops and observe the construction of a product in its entirety. In fact, one person often accomplished the entire process—and not just the manufacturing, but the marketing, sales, design, and service as well. Today, few workers are directly involved in making the products or delivering the services their companies provide, and those few typically see only a small part of the process. For many products made today, you would have to visit several continents to view the process that had been visible from one spot in the craftsworker's shop. Since the task was the product, measuring the work measured the result. This began to change with the Age of the Factory.

The Age of the Factory

In 1776, Adam Smith heralded the Industrial Revolution in *The Wealth of Nations* [2]. Watt's invention, the steam engine, provided power that only a new industrial organization could harness. This new organization called for the division of labor into specialties. Before this advance, pins, made individually by individual workers, were such expensive luxuries that money for frivolities was called "pin money," since only people with money to squander bought pins. Smith described in detail how the manufacture of pins was divided among many workers, each performing specialized tasks: "One man draws out the wire, another straightens it, a third cuts it, a fourth points it, a fifth grinds it at the top for receiving the head; to make the head requires three distinct operations; to put it on is a peculiar business, to whiten the pins another; it is even a trade unto itself to put them into the paper." This allowed a fantastic increase in the number of pins produced per worker, making pins available even to the most frugal.[4] Such success led to further division and narrower specialties, ushering in the Age of the Specialist.

The Age of the Specialist

As the successes arising from the Industrial Revolution took hold, organizations required growing numbers of specialists, not just in

---

4.   Smith notes how 10 men, none of whom could make even 20 pins in a day, were collectively able to make not 200, but 48,000 pins in a day by dividing the labor and specializing.

manufacturing, but in areas such as finance, accounting, legal, personnel, marketing, and sales. More sophisticated products and customers necessitated growth in other areas, such as research and development, engineering, purchasing, logistics, and manufacturing planning. Equally important was the emergence of professional managers to, as management is often defined, "plan, organize, and control" all that other activity. Specialization had worked spectacularly well on the factory floor, so why shouldn't it also be applied to the growing field of office work? Consequently, white-collar (professional, technical, and managerial) employment levels rose steeply, with a corresponding decrease in the proportion of employees actually doing the work that produced the product. A cynic might argue that many, if not most, white-collar workers were concerned with increasing the efficiency of the few remaining blue-collar workers, but that misses the point. While the resulting bureaucracy has often been criticized, it was the glue that allowed large organizations to come into existence and thrive.[5]

How was this new breed of professional managers going to manage all of this new work? Well, it's easier to manage people and their activities if they are grouped into specialized fields or "functions" such as finance, engineering, and manufacturing. The path of least resistance led to the "functionally oriented" organization that went on to dominate most of the twentieth century.

Take a moment to think about the functions of your organization —what are the specialties that make up the whole? Make a list. If you're like most of the people in our workshops, you will respond with a list of the major divisions or departments that make up the higher reaches of your organizational chart. The functional organization is so ingrained that most people think of organization and function as synonymous, but they aren't.[6] An organization is a structure for grouping people and other resources to achieve a common purpose. A function, on the other hand, is a field of endeavor involving work of a similar nature, employing particular skills and knowledge. These definitions provide an important clue to the central problem with organizations based on functional specialties—what *was* the common purpose that these functional organizations sought to achieve?

---

5. Although our discussion so far has centered on manufacturing organizations, the same happened in service-providing organizations—banks, insurance companies, hospitals, utilities, government agencies, and so on.

6. We often ask our workshop participants what a function is, and they invariably (and collectively) respond that it is an organizational unit within an enterprise.

The downside of functional organizations

In general, workers and departments in a healthy organization do the best they can to contribute to the organization's success, so they optimize the work they do. But optimizing the individual parts does not optimize the whole. For one thing, if you can't see the whole, you might inadvertently be damaging the end result when optimizing a piece of the process. What's good for, say, accounting, might not be best for the company. Operational considerations such as getting the goods out the door conflict with financial considerations such as "collect all necessary information to cost and bill the transaction." Consider the steps of the process to fill an order for a customized widget, illustrated in Figure 2.1.

Take Order should collect all the information to Make, Ship, and Bill the widget, even if it slows down taking the order. Manufacturing must be tracked in sufficient detail to bill costs to the customer and to analyze the process for improvement, but wouldn't that also introduce delays? Billing and Shipping might prefer to batch transactions for efficiency, but that might not be best for the customer or the enterprise. So the limited perspective of each part might lose us the opportunity to improve the whole.

In many cases, the reward system causes dysfunction. Promotion is a key aspect of the reward system but too often, what gets someone promoted is often *not* what's good for the corporation. Managers' salaries are largely determined by the number of people they manage, leading to empire building, bloated staffing levels, duplication of effort, and even people working at cross-purposes.

To summarize, specialization yielded huge efficiency gains, but brought problems as well. Many have been documented, but they are usually variations of these three:

* The overall process became so fragmented that is was no longer visible, and thus couldn't be measured or improved. Remember, the process was always there, it was just hidden by a focus on functions and specialties. No one could see the big picture, and narrow

Figure 2.1 Main steps in the "Fulfill Order" process.

specialization often led to narrow-mindedness. The common terminology for functional departments—the "functional silo" or "functional stovepipe"—graphically conveys an image of a vertical structure that you can't see into or out of.

- Activities and methods benefited the function to the detriment of the process. The common purpose driving organizational units (divisions, departments, and so on) became inwardly focused—it was assumed that if the individual divisions and departments were doing well, then so was the entire enterprise. In fact, work in one area often negated work done elsewhere, or produced no value for the process' customer, other stakeholders, or the enterprise.

- As a work item or transaction winds its way through the fragmented process, the handoffs between specialized individuals and groups cause delay, errors, and expense. For the function to handle a work item as efficiently as possible, it was common to batch them up before they entered the function, or to transform them in some way, for instance, by reentering data into another system. This had a negative impact on the overall process.

Over two centuries, the pendulum had swung too far from generalization toward specialization, which led, not surprisingly, to a reaction. That reaction was business process reengineering. Just as the Age of the Craftsworker gave rise to the Age of the Factory, the Age of the Specialist led to the Reengineering Revolution.

Enter reengineering: 1985–1993

The insight of reengineering was that by identifying, making visible, rethinking, and radically redesigning end-to-end business processes, they could be dramatically improved. The process-centered organization would focus on the whole and see accumulated inefficiencies and irrationalities eliminated. Measurement would shift from individual tasks, such as checking the most forms or stamping the greatest number of fenders, to the achievement of value, such as the timely delivery of a high-quality product or service, or overall customer satisfaction. The application of both common and advanced information technologies was a crucial factor.

The "shot heard 'round the world" of the Reengineering Revolution[7] was Michael Hammer's article, "Reengineering Work: Don't Automate, Obliterate."[3] Hammer called reengineering "undoing the Industrial Revolution," because it undid overspecialization and re-unified tasks into coherent, visible processes. This was, as Martha Stewart would say, "a good thing." But not so fast! The Industrial Revolution brought some incredible benefits. Even though the functionally oriented organization is widely criticized, wasn't it the source of the wonderful things we've come to expect as consumers? Could it really be true that a large proportion of workers were deadwood that added no value to the enterprise? Did moving work to an outside contractor actually reduce the total work or cost? Questions like these brought a backlash to reengineering when the dark side of process emerged.

Exit reengineering: 1994–1995

As it turned out, process redesign was easy, but implementation was difficult. Reports of high-profile failures spread. There was shock in reengineering circles when articles appeared [4] citing a failure rate among BPR projects of 70% to 80%! The downside of achieving buzzword status was at least partly responsible for the high reported failure rate—everything became reengineering. For example:

• "I reengineered my department by putting our forms on an imaging-based workflow system," or worse;

• "I reengineered by laying off most of my employees and outsourcing their work."

Reengineering became a euphemism for the thoughtless application of IT, for slash-and-burn downsizing, restructuring, and outsourcing. Reengineer went from something you *do*, to something that's done *to* you, as in "I was reengineered out of my job."

---

7. Actually, reengineering was well under way before the term was coined, packaged, and marketed by consulting organizations. For example, the auto industry was using concurrent engineering and team-based assembly long before BPR burst onto the stage, but Michael Hammer in particular performed the invaluable service of identifying the technique, describing it, and moving it into the limelight. After that, the improved performance of early adopters drove home the point that process orientation solved many problems.

Because of these negative connotations, the term reengineering is now used infrequently. In fact, at some organizations it is a forbidden word. The irony is that although the term has fallen into disfavor, more enterprises than ever are focused on process redesign, and the success rate is going up. Process orientation is part of the organizational landscape, and part of the reason is that "best practices" and a balanced perspective have emerged. Part of that balanced perspective is the realization that all of the stages that preceded process orientation had strengths in addition to their more widely publicized weaknesses.

A balanced perspective

In the rush to embrace the new, writers and consultants often fail to take note of the benefits of whatever they're rushing away from. This was certainly true during the heyday of reengineering, when there was a steady stream of commentary about the flaws of functional orientation, and the virtues of process orientation. With the benefit of the perspective that several years of experience provides, it is now clear that just as functional orientation also has benefits (could it have prevailed for most of the twentieth century if that wasn't the case?), process orientation has some difficulties.

A process is a way to organize work, and each of the ages or eras we've looked at represented a different approach to organizing work. In the Age of the Craftsworker, work was organized around a multiskilled individual who accomplished the entire process. In the eras of the factory and the specialist, work was divided among individual and organizational specialties. Finally, the reengineering era saw work organized to expedite its flow among the various contributors to the overall process. Each of these was an advance over the previous era, although each had both strengths and weaknesses. Here is list of positives and negatives from the various ages that is useful because:

- Successfully redesigned processes exhibit the positive characteristics from all eras.

- If you are aware of the downsides of process orientation, you can avoid them.

The Age of the Craftsworker was characterized by an expert individual performing most or all of the activities comprising a process, and exhibited the following:

Positives:

- It was clear to "everyone" (the worker) who the customer was, what the product or service was, and what the goal was.

- There was a single point of contact for the customer.

- The craftsworker knew the whole process from beginning to end.

- Products and services could be customized relatively easily.

- There was no miscommunication or handoffs between specialties.

Negatives:

- There was a single point of failure with no backup or synergies.

- Quality could be erratic, because the individual was not necessarily expert in all aspects.

- There was very limited output, and scaling up was extremely difficult.

- The work essentially stopped during the transitions from one task to another.

- There was no entry-level workforce available—a new craftsworker required an extended apprenticeship.

The next eras (the Age of the Factory and the Age of the Specialist) saw progress through the specialization of individuals and then organizations. This specialization has been widely condemned, but it wasn't all bad, and the large enterprises of the twentieth century simply couldn't have emerged without this style of organization:

Positives:

- It vastly increased output and economies of scale with a consistent and surprisingly high level of quality.

- It was easier to manage personnel ("birds of a feather" doing a specific kind of work).

- Specialization leads to very high skill levels and evolution.

- It scales up or down relatively easily (add, subtract, or reassign specialists).

- It is built around recognized fields; therefore, educational institutions supply an entry level workforce who then have a career path.

- It ushered in professional management, rather than owner management.

Negatives:

- The focus is on tasks and local efficiency at a cost to the overall outcome.

- Loss of customer visibility can lead to complacency and deterioration of service.

- Cross-functional communication is hampered or nonexistent.

- There is a lack of communication, or even outright conflict, between functions.

- Customization or change requiring cross-functional cooperation is much more difficult.

- It lowers individual accountability and requires proportionally higher management (a "bureaucracy") to manage the divided labor.

- Jobs can get bo-o-o-ring.

- Issues that span functional boundaries are difficult to resolve and require executive involvement.

Ultimately, BPR drove the adoption of process orientation, which exhibits many well-publicized advantages but also some drawbacks:

Positives:

- Appropriate focus is on the customer and on outcomes.

- Repeatability of a defined process means it can be measured and improved.

- There is much greater overall efficiency through streamlined flow and elimination of unnecessary or counterproductive work.

- Less bureaucracy is needed (flatter organization structure), so a higher percentage of work goes into fulfilling customer needs.

- There is greater individual ownership and accountability for the outcome versus the tasks.

- It provides richer and more fulfilling jobs (the craftsman redux).

- In a competitive environment, it often means jobs are preserved, when the alternative is the company failing.

Negatives:

- It is harder to manage the diverse personnel who comprise a process.

- Individual jobs are broader and more demanding, so:

  An entry-level workforce isn't available, coupled with higher turn-over because multiskilled people are in demand.

  Constant training and skills upgrading are needed, leading to stress and shortages, while those who "can't cut it" are dislocated.

- It is difficult to implement, and harder to scale up.

- Constant change (often associated with process) brings about inefficiency (e.g., "who's doing this now?") and higher levels of stress and burnout.

- It often requires huge technology investments in order to replace or rearchitect functionally oriented systems.

- The focus on process for process' sake—everyone implements a process—makes it harder to do business with them.

The reengineering aftermath: 1996–present

The aftermath of the reengineering revolution is, all in all, a pretty good state of affairs. Like many worthwhile management trends before it, process orientation has settled in and there is general awareness that business process thinking is fundamental to organizational performance. The economic success of the late 1990s is probably at least partly attributable to improvements made during the reengineering boom. Rather than proclaiming that they are "doing reengineering," organizations understand that dealing with their business processes is normal behavior—we have arrived at "process without slogans."

One of the best aspects of this de-sloganizing has been that explicit reengineering has given way to "process orientation" or "process management" (see Figure 2.2) which is the merging of business process reengineering and continuous process improvement (CPI). CPI, and its cousin total quality management (TQM), is an outgrowth of Deming's work, especially in Japan, and is what the Japanese call "kaizen."

Kaizen

Kaizen [5] is the concept of continuous improvement. Its central tenet is that you must continuously improve your processes to keep a quality product in production. Not just because you can always get better, but because "better" is a moving target. When the Bureau of Labor Statistics tracks price changes for the Consumer Price Index, it attempts to measure changes in price, not quality. They try to factor out any nominal price change attributable to quality improvement. For many years, when the retail price for a particular make of automobile went up, the manufacturers explained the increase as a quality change: "This year's model is bigger than

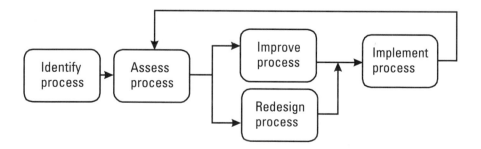

Figure 2.2 Merging process reengineering and continuous process improvement.

last year's!" Reasonable enough. But then came the gas crisis, and the manufacturers explained the subsequent price increases as quality changes: "This year's model is *smaller* than last year's!" At first blush it sounds absurd, but it actually makes sense. For many years "bigger is better" was the guiding principle, but conditions changed and "small is beautiful" became the new cry. Continuous improvement is necessary to even stay in the same place.

When reengineering first emerged, there was a certain tension between the reengineering and kaizen (or CQI or TQM) communities. The reengineers wondered why their kaizen-oriented counterparts were improving processes that ought to have been scrapped. And those who espoused kaizen found the reengineers to be rash and destructive, often throwing out the baby with the bathwater. Now the two have been de-sloganized and brought together under the milder term "process management." If reengineering a process is done once (or periodically), then improving it (kaizen) goes on forever. Kaizen and BPR have become less state of the art and more standard practice, like many other business innovations and management concepts with merit:

- Management by objectives (MBO);
- Management by walking around (MBWA);
- Customer focus;
- Total quality management (TQM);
- Empowered work teams;
- Identifying core competencies;
- Communicating mission and values.

Although these might at one point have appeared to be little more than fads, as each burned out we were able to reemerge from the ashes stronger. New trends build on the last, so in the end we incorporate the best ideas from each into our way of doing business. In a sense, no one is doing reengineering (or quality, or MBO) anymore because everyone is doing it. As with new managerial developments, technical fads and silver bullets also come and go, but the good ones leave a lasting impact—nobody does structured programming anymore, everyone does.

BPR and IT—joined at the hip

Just as BPR proponents were at loggerheads with kaizen aficionados, they also ran into conflict with IT professionals. In many cases the reengineers clearly felt that the systems folks were uncommunicative and insensitive to business issues, while the IT staff was convinced that the BPR consultants had some clever slogans (and nice suits!) but never had, and never would, actually implement anything. Now they're inseparable. In fact, often they aren't identified as separate "process redesign" or "application development" initiatives—an effort to improve business operations will have both aspects to it, and will simply be referred to as a project. After years of being treated as a support organization, IT is now a full partner in developing business strategy and implementing new processes.

Process has been integrated into the fabric of IT in other important ways.

- Many of the major commercial applications include facilities for automating and managing process workflow.

- Workflow systems, especially in the document management and imaging areas, have been a staple of the IT scene for years.

- The study of workflow—"who does what, when"—has emerged as a critical component of systems analysis and design methodologies and the tools that support them.

In a similar vein, the design or redesign of business processes is no longer the exclusive purview of consultants and specialists—everyone is involved. Successful efforts invariably involve a variety of disciplines—management, performers, consultants, and specialists from IT, human resources, training, facilities, and other areas.

Nirvana at last?

This isn't to say that everything's perfect. One dark spot is that jobs are becoming so complex and demanding that one wonders if "mere mortals need not apply." Stress levels are rising, and it's no wonder that the "simplicity" movement is attracting so many converts. Reengineering emerged as a response to the problems of functional specialization; what will emerge as a response to the high demands placed on individual contributors? We don't know what it might be, but continued change is a certainty. Whether we plan for it or not, kaizen seems to be at work in our management and technical techniques. In the next chapter, we'll look at how kaizen has brought us to the intersection of process improvement, systems development, and workflow modeling.

References

[1] Hammer, M., *Beyond Reengineering: How the Process-Centered Organization Is Changing Our Work and Our Lives,* New York: HarperCollins, 1996.

[2] Smith, A., *An Inquiry into the Nature and Causes of the Wealth of Nations,* London: W. Strahan and T. Cadell in the Strand, 1776.

[3] Hammer, M., "Reengineering Work: Don't Automate, Obliterate," *Harvard Business Review,* July–Aug. 1990. At the same time, Tom Davenport and James Short published the other seminal article, "The New Industrial Engineering: IT and Business Process Redesign," *Sloan Management Review,* Summer 1990. In 1993, Hammer's article was expanded with James Champy into the now-classic book *Reengineering the Corporation: A Manifesto for Business Revolution* (New York: HarperCollins, 1993), and Davenport published *Process Innovation: Reengineering Work Through Information Technology* (Boston: Harvard Business School Press, 1992).

[4] Hall, G., J. Rosenthal, and J. Wade, "How to Make Reengineering Really Work," *Harvard Business Review,* Nov.–Dec. 1993.

[5] Imai, M., *Kaizen: The Key to Japan's Competitive Success,* New York: McGraw-Hill, 1989.

3

The Approach in a Nutshell

This chapter and beyond...

This chapter summarizes the overall methodology employed by successful process improvement and application development projects. This approach—a process for process improvement—is organized into four phases:

1. *Frame the process*—includes identifying a business process, clarifying its boundaries, performing an initial assessment, and establishing goals for the redesigned process.

2. *Understand the current (as-is) process*—includes modeling its workflow, and performing a more specific assessment.

3. *Design the new ("to-be") process*—includes devising potential improvements, assessing them, selecting the main characteristics of the process, and finally designing the new workflow.

4. *Develop use case scenarios*—makes the transition into system requirements analysis by describing how process actors would interact with a system to complete tasks.

This chapter also introduces the various modeling techniques and frameworks that are employed by this approach. Process workflow modeling is the central technique, but the others are necessary to establish context for the process, to ensure that other critical factors in addition to workflow are addressed, and to define information systems requirements.

This is your guide to the rest of the book—a one-chapter summary of everything else we will cover, intended to clarify how the individual parts make up the whole. After some brief notes on the method and the intended audience, we will get into the specifics.

Why it works

This methodology works because it uses modeling techniques, frameworks, guidelines, phases, and steps that make it complete, repeatable, and learnable. Just as important, it is a practical response to where projects *actually* go wrong rather than a theoretical exploration of how things *ought* to be done. Many process improvement projects stumble badly or fail outright, and key lessons from these experiences have been incorporated in this approach, and verified in practice. The methodology is conceptually similar to many others, but it differs substantially in four important ways:

1. It includes frameworks and guidelines to ensure that real business processes are identified with clearly delineated boundaries—failure to do so is a common denominator of troubled projects.

2. It uses a process modeling technique that is simple to read and highlights the role played by individual participants—this increases participation, buy-in, and accuracy.

3. It includes methods for addressing all of the factors (enablers) that support a process, and the environmental factors that constrain it—otherwise, projects tend to zero in on the obvious enablers, workflow design, and information technology.

4. It integrates process-oriented and IT-oriented efforts by including techniques such as use case scenario analysis that support the transition from process improvement to requirements definition activities.

Whom it's for

We developed and organized this material specifically for people *working on or responsible for* a process improvement project, including:

1. Business analysts, consultants, and project leaders, whether internal to the organization or employed by a consulting firm;

2. Systems analysts defining IT requirements;

3. Business managers with a mandate to fix their processes;

4. Other professionals with an interest in the topic, especially those participating in executive M.B.A. or continuing education programs.

Many of the examples are drawn from medium to large enterprises, but there is nothing in the material that prevents using it in smaller organizations—some of our most successful projects with this approach have been in companies with fewer than 40 people. On the topic of examples, we have avoided including one big case study and instead have drawn upon a variety of illustrations. We did this because a single example cannot represent the range of issues encountered in practice, and tends to encourage a focus on the specific example rather than the general message. Besides, a life-size case study would be too large for the book, and our feedback was that the reader would quickly tire of a simplified example.

The book concentrates more on how-to and less on justification, case studies, or management issues. The book will not, however, cover everything that goes into a complete process improvement undertaking. Issues such as the design of organization structures, developing compensation schemes, and managing change are beyond our scope. Others have already done a fine job of covering subjects like those.[1]

This chapter, once again, is an *overview* of the rest of the book. It introduces various concepts, methods, frameworks, and tools, but at the core is the business process, so we will begin with a definition.

---

1. One book that does an excellent job of addressing some of these issues is *Improving Performance: How to Manage the White Space on the Organizational Chart* by Geary A. Rummler and Alan P. Brache, New York: Jossey-Bass Publishers, 1995. This is an essential title in the library of anyone interested in improving business processes.

Processes—results, not work

The term "business process," or simply "process," is used in many contexts, with varying meaning. Our definition is "a collection of interrelated work tasks, initiated in response to an event, achieving a specific result for the customer and other stakeholders of the process." It's awkward, but it includes the main elements in establishing the scope of a process—the event at one end, and at the other, the result and the customer expecting it. Do not be confused by the term "customer"—it doesn't just refer to a customer purchasing goods or services. The customer of a process could be a government agency, a supplier, an employee, a trade association, or any internal or external person or organization expecting a result from a process.

The result is the most important part of the definition—without a result or output, what reason is there for a process to exist? And the result is not a vaguely defined service or condition—individual results must be specifically identifiable and countable. For instance, a client called to report problems with his company's process improvement project. The team was having trouble controlling scope, and could not seem to get all of the activities into a single process model. The root of the problem was that the scope was the logistics process, which violates the rule about specific, countable results—it is impossible to identify specific occurrences of logistics, or answer a question like "How many logistics did we do today?" because logistics isn't a process, but a function that participates in multiple processes. Deliver Shipment, however, is a manageable process because you can identify each specific shipment delivered, count how many have happened, and identify the process's customer.

Without a clearly defined process or subprocess as its scope, a project will suffer "scope creep," or implement improvements that do more harm than good. A more precise definition of business process is in Chapter 4, and techniques for process identification are in Chapter 5. The essence, though, is a triggering event, a defined sequence of tasks and decisions involving multiple actors, and a countable result for the primary customer and each of the process's other stakeholders.

"Event—tasks—result" is a framework for defining a process, one of several frameworks employed in this methodology.

Frameworks in general

A framework is a structure for discovering, organizing, and presenting ideas or information. They are as simple as the two-by-two matrices loved by consulting organizations for categorizing products, or as complex as a multidimensional structure for financial analysis. Ours are typically straightforward—a set of categories to be filled in or questions to be answered. For example, the simple framework we use to state clear and actionable objectives is the three Ts—topic, target, and time frame. Improve customer service is a fine overall goal, but vague, until the framework is used to break it into measurable objectives:

- Topic: telephone hold time for calls to the customer service line;
- Target: 60 seconds or less 98% of the time;
- Time frame: within 45 days.

Frameworks manage complexity by reducing vague or complex topics to a set of simpler questions. They organize work, maintain focus during interviews or facilitated sessions, ensure coverage of all aspects of a topic, and provide a standard format to document the findings. One of the most important frameworks is the one we use to consider all dimensions of a process.

A framework for process enablers

We defined a process as a set of tasks, but there is more to it than that, specifically the important concept of enablers. An enabler is a factor that helps a process to achieve its intended results and meet performance targets within the applicable constraints. The two that we are most concerned with are workflow design and IT support, but the framework employed here includes a total of six, as illustrated in Figure 3.1:

1. Workflow design;
2. Information technology;
3. Motivation and measurement;
4. Human resources;

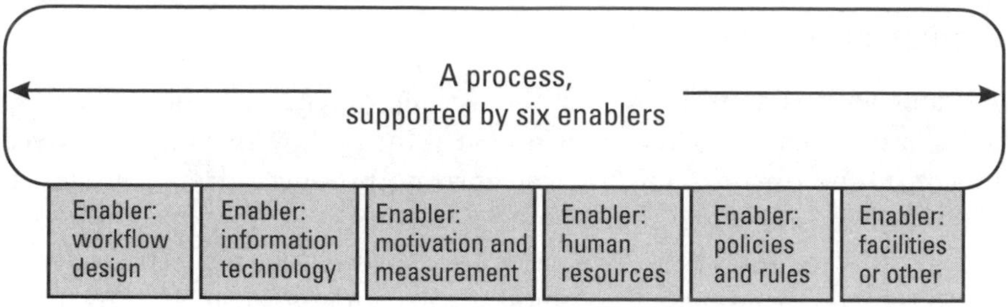

Figure 3.1 A process is supported by six enablers.

5.   Policies and rules;

6.   Facilities design (or some other categories appropriate to your situation).

Collectively, enablers are how we make the process work, and no process will work optimally until all of the enablers are acting in concert. For instance, improvements in workflow and IT will have little impact if personnel are untrained, or motivated by inappropriate measures to do the wrong things. Each enabler addresses a specific aspect of the total process.

Workflow design

The process workflow design is the work plan for responding to an event. It shows the sequence of steps, decisions, and handoffs carried out by the process's actors between the initial event and the final result.

Information technology

IT includes systems, information, computers and other devices, telecommunications equipment, and the networks they comprise. Our focus is on information systems—applications and databases that perform specific functions, and that are managed and referred to as a whole, such as the personnel system or the purchasing system. Information systems enable a process by automating or supporting steps, capturing or presenting information, or managing and expediting the workflow. Later, we will look at a framework for breaking systems down into manageable components.

Motivation and measurement

Motivation and measurement encompass the explicit and implicit reward systems of the organization. Their concern is how people, organizations, and processes are measured and assessed, and the associated consequences—reward and punishment. Experience shows that people do what they are measured on, and if the measures do not align with the goals of a redesigned process, failure is virtually certain.

Human resources

The human resource enabler covers the knowledge, skills, and experience of the workforce, training, organizational structure, job definitions, and so on. A process requires the right people in the right job with the right skills.

Policies and rules

This includes the rules and policies established by the enterprise to guide or constrain business processes, as well as applicable laws and regulations. Clearly, a policy such as "any requisition over $1,500 requires approval from a vice president" has a substantial impact. In practice, many processes include work to enforce rules or regulations that are obsolete, contradictory, or overly complex.

Facilities

Facilities are the workplace design and physical infrastructure such as equipment, furniture, lighting, air quality, and ambient noise. There is a growing trend to recognize the importance of facilities as enablers to effectiveness, productivity, and well-being. This may not be of concern in your process, and might be replaced by other, more relevant, enablers.

All too commonly, we see new processes with a well-designed workflow and supporting information systems fail because other enablers, especially motivation and measurement and human resources, were not adequately considered.

A framework for putting processes and systems in context

Information systems are of particular interest in this book, and we use a framework for putting the analysis of business processes in context with analysis of information systems requirements. We will build this framework up progressively, beginning by recognizing that neither processes nor systems exist in isolation—their sole purpose is to support the aims of the enterprise. Once the enterprise has clarified its mission, strategy, goals, and objectives, business processes that support them can be developed. In turn, information systems can be developed or acquired which support the aims of the business processes. Thus, we arrive at the following three-layer framework for organizing analysis and design activities:

> Mission, strategy, and goals
>
> Business process
>
> Information system

Conversations about the top layer are often ambiguous because the most commonly used terms—mission, strategy, goals, and objectives—take on multiple definitions. We attach a specific meaning to each:

Mission: The mission articulates the essential nature of the business—it states the products or services provided, and the markets or customers served. Generally, there is also an indication of the "style" of the enterprise—how it wishes to be perceived by stakeholders such as customers, employees, investors, and the community.

Strategy: This term is used to describe everything from a specific action plan through to the competitive space the enterprise wishes to occupy. We use a definition closer to the latter, in which strategy describes how an enterprise differentiates its products and services (e.g., low price, customization, and so forth), and therefore, why a customer would choose it over alternatives. As we will see, this concept is just as applicable in government agencies or internal services where there doesn't appear to be a choice.

Goals and objectives: The overall improvement directions established by an enterprise are its goals, backed up by measurable performance targets, which are its objectives.

Individual processes have their own mission strategy and goals, which should align with their enterprise counterparts, and which provide important guidance when making design decisions. Other factors, such as culture and core competencies, are also important. Collectively, we refer to these as the environment within which a process operates. Chapter 7 expands on the topic of a process's environment.

In practice, we use a five-layer framework, which we arrive at by expanding on the information system layer. Information systems are not monolithic, but are themselves made up of layers (tiers) of interacting components. In the three-tier information systems architecture, these layers are named according to the service they provide—presentation services, application logic services, and data management services:

Presentation

Application logic

Data management

This is probably the most widely used framework in the world of systems analysis and design. If we take this three-tier framework, and use it in place of the simpler information systems layer in the preceding framework, we end up with this five-tier framework:

Mission, strategy, and goals

Business process

Presentation

Application logic

Data management

This five-tier approach is at the heart of the methodology we employ for studying business processes and information systems requirements. Each tier in the three-tier systems architecture bears further explanation.

A closer look at the three-tier architecture
Presentation
A system (or any automated device) requires mechanisms to capture data and instructions from a person (e.g., for an ATM, "Withdraw $200 from the checking account for this customer/password combination") and a way

to convey information back to that person (e.g., "Sorry, insufficient funds in account."). This is the service provided by the presentation layer, also known as the user interface, or UI. It includes any mechanisms by which people (or other systems) interact with an automated system. In our context, the user interface is usually a graphical use interface (GUI) running on a desktop, like the familiar Windows, Macintosh, or Web browser interfaces, but it could be just about anything—a character-based computer terminal, an interactive voice response (IVR) system, a kiosk's touchscreen, a bar code scanner, a badge reader, a hand geometry scanner, or some new device technology just over the horizon. We can also consider it to include printed output, such as receipts or reports. The presentation layer for an ATM includes a variety of mechanisms— a display screen, command buttons, a numeric keypad, a card reader, an envelope taker, a cash dispenser, a receipt printer, and a security camera.

Application logic

Everyone seems to have a different name for this layer—process logic, application, business logic, business rules, and transactions, among others. Whatever the name, the concept is the same—programmed transactions containing logic to enforce the rules of the business and properly update files and databases.

In the withdraw cash example, application logic receives a message from the presentation layer and then checks that the PIN is valid for the account number, verifies that the account has adequate funds, determines applicable service charges, and so on. It also coordinates updates to the data management layer, updating the account balance and logging details of the transaction. Depending on the technology, the programmer might implement the logic in programs called stored procedures, methods, components, or modules. As analysts, our concern is only with defining the business rules and data updates.

A major strength of the three-tier architecture is that the same transaction (programmed application logic) may be invoked by different presentation mechanisms. For instance, the same transfer cash functionality may be accessible via an ATM, via a terminal at a teller's workstation, over the telephone via an IVR system, or over the Internet via a Web browser. This gives us the flexibility to add or modify user interfaces without reprogramming transactions, or to change the rules of a transaction without having to change all of the user interfaces.

Data management

The major strength of most computers in a business setting is not in the computing they perform, but in their ability to store and retrieve data. The data management layer provides this service, maintaining the records of people, places, things, events, and so on that are necessary for an enterprise to operate. Commonly, a relational database management system (DBMS) is used, but any of a number of database or file system technologies could be employed. Since business computers are primarily data processors, and since processes act on objects that are represented as data, data is considered throughout our analysis.

Each of these three tiers, as well as business processes, is analyzed and documented using specific modeling techniques. Before introducing these, we offer a few observations about models in general.

Models in general

A model is an abstraction or representation of some subject matter, and is one of two types. An aircraft mockup used for wind tunnel testing, like an architect's model of a building, is an iconic model—it resembles the physical object it represents, except that it is smaller and simplified. A mathematical model of the economy is a symbolic model—a representation of some physical (i.e., the weather) or conceptual (i.e., a budget or a project plan) subject matter that isn't intended to look like that subject. Symbolic models often represent concepts that can't actually be observed. Our workflow models are made up of boxes, lines, and text that bear no resemblance to the people, documents, and in-boxes that they represent.

Whatever the type, useful models generally meet the following criteria:

- They highlight facets of interest while masking unnecessary detail, and employ conventions for adding progressive amounts of detail.

- It is more convenient, less expensive, and safer to manipulate a model than it is to manipulate the corresponding real-world objects. In our case, a process workflow model supports understanding and assessing a process design without actually implementing and then observing it.

Modeling is not an end in itself, and people frequently need to be reminded to stop modeling when the purpose has been achieved. An as-is workflow process model is used to understand why the current process behaves the way it does—modeling should stop as soon as that understanding has been reached. On the other hand, a model of the to-be process is used to guide implementation, and will continue to be maintained through implementation and revision, and therefore requires much more detail and precision.

The modeling techniques we employ

As noted, there are associated modeling techniques for each of the lower four tiers of the five-tier framework.

Business process: process workflow models

Process workflow models (or workflow process models) as illustrated in Figure 3.2 are known by many names, but because of their appearance are most commonly referred to as "swimlane diagrams." A swimming pool might be divided lengthwise into swimlanes for racing or swimming laps. Just as each swimmer is expected to stay in his or her swimlane, each "actor" with a "role" in the process has his or her own swimlane. A box

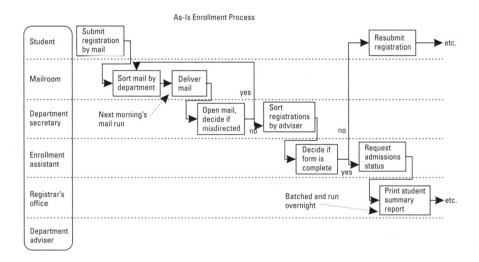

Figure 3.2 A workflow process model or "swimlane diagram."

represents a task or step in the process, and is placed in the swimlane of the responsible actor. Arrows connecting the boxes indicate the sequence and flow of the steps. This type of diagram can be used to show both current (as-is) and proposed (to-be) process workflow, from a simplified overview down to very detailed steps. This particular form of workflow process model[2] has become the de facto standard for depicting business processes because of its merits:

- They are self-explanatory. While other techniques may require considerable training before they can be read, swimlane diagrams are immediately understandable by almost everyone. (That's not to say they're easy to build, but that's what this book is for.)

- They show individual actors, and emphasize their tasks and interactions with other actors. Participants can identify with the model, so it's easier to produce a complete and accurate representation.

Several chapters are devoted to process workflow models, beginning with Chapter 8.

Presentation: use case scenarios

Eventually, while we are designing the to-be process, we begin considering how information systems will help an actor complete a task. Swimlane diagrams are not appropriate for this kind of detail, so we switch gears and employ "use case scenarios," a variant of the popular "use case" technique. Essentially, a use case scenario models a dialogue—the back and forth—between an actor and a system for a particular scenario. The scenario is like a single test case, with defined actors, conditions, and data values.

Why is this necessary? Well, think of all the times you've used a system and wondered, "What in the world were they thinking?"—Web sites with torturous navigation, interactive voice response systems that never get where you want to go, and ATMs that take you through 15 steps before concluding that you made a mistake in the second step and must start over. By depicting the interaction between actor and machine *before* the system is designed and developed, use case scenarios help us avoid this sort of problem.

---

2. This modeling style was popularized by Rummler and Brache in *Improving Performance*.

Use case scenarios are introduced in Chapter 16, along with information on how they are used as a springboard into more detailed analysis.

Application logic: various techniques

This is the most complex of the three layers to analyze, requiring a number of techniques including event identification, state transition modeling, and transaction specification. The key points are covered in Chapter 16, in the context of use case analysis.

Data management: data models

The heart of a data model is an entity-relationship diagram (ERD) made up of three types of components:

1. The distinct things ("entities") about which information is needed (e.g., Order, Customer, Facility, Product, Part, Supplier, etc.);

2. The associations ("relationships") among those entities (e.g. "Part is used in Product," "Product is requested on Order," and "Order is placed by Customer");

3. The facts ("attributes") about each entity that must be recorded (e.g., the attributes of Part include Part Number, Description, Unit Weight, and Unit Price).

A definition is produced for each entity, to ensure consistent interpretation by all project team members. The first time you go through this step, you'll be amazed at the different interpretations for common terms like "product" or "customer." This makes data models a powerful tool early in a process-oriented project—they improve communication and consistency, because the entity names and definitions provide a standard vocabulary for the things the process deals with. Later in the project, data models are essential for database design and for describing data-oriented system requirements such as user interface behavior or program logic.

Examples can be seen in Chapter 15, which is an overview of data modeling.

Five-tier thinking

To summarize, this framework encapsulates the essence of our approach—it organizes the analytic techniques we employ on all process improvement and application development projects. It lets us look at a business, including the processes and systems that support it, as a whole. As we have noted before, processes and information systems are inseparable, and both exist to support the aims of the enterprise.

We have found this five-tier approach very useful for explaining the analysis steps that a project will undertake. Often, during a project kickoff, we will present a variation on Figure 3.3, and review each layer while making the following points:

An enterprise has a mission, strategies, and goals

...which are supported by business processes. Actors in a business process are in turn supported by information systems that they interact with via

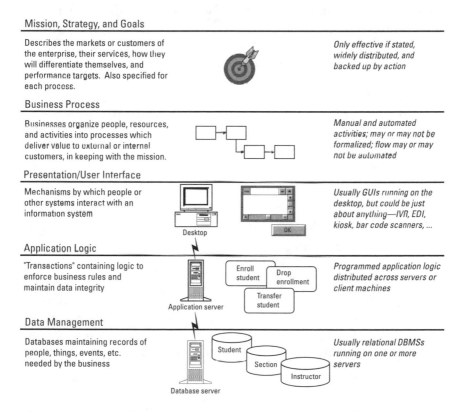

Figure 3.3 A five-tier framework for business analysis.

...the presentation layer, which communicates commands to the

...application logic layer, which enforces business rules and coordinates updates to the

...stored records in the data management layer.

Participants, from senior executives to technical specialists, consistently express support for this framework because it shows the interrelationships between their respective areas of interest.

A workflow-driven methodology—the process of studying processes

Finally, let's review the methodology we will explore in the remainder of the book. We describe it as a starting point, because there are unique aspects to every project—the world of business processes is filled with politics, sensitivities, conflicting goals, old habits, seemingly unshakable paradigms, resource constraints, and a host of other pitfalls, so you'll probably have to tailor the approach to your environment.

As outlined earlier, the approach proceeds through four phases:

1. Frame the process;

2. Understand the current (as-is) process;

3. Design the new (to-be) process;

4. Develop use case scenarios.

This approach is summarized in Figure 3.4.

Frame the process

This is arguably the most important phase, because, while quick, it prevents many common problems later. When we are called in to assist with a project that is in trouble, we invariably have to go right back to the beginning and work through framing the process. This includes:

* Identify a set of related processes, including the target process to be improved, by developing an overall process map. This clarifies what's in and what's out of scope by showing the process to be studied, plus touch points to other processes.

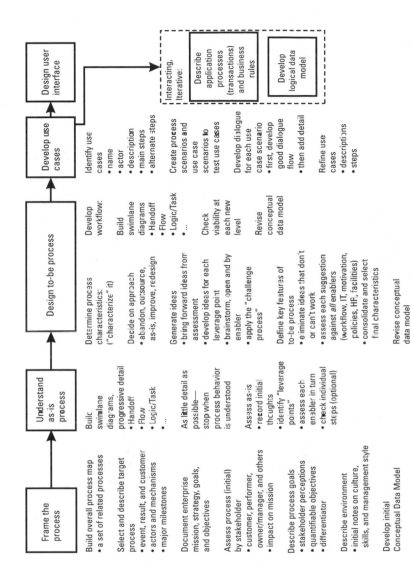

Figure 3.4 A workflow-driven approach.

- Establish the scope of the target process, using a framework for identifying a process and its boundaries:

  Process name, initiating event, customer and result, other stakeholders and the result they expect, approximately five to seven milestones within the process, actors, timing, and frequency.

- Review or document enterprise mission, strategy, and goals.

- Perform an initial process assessment:

  Stakeholder-based: customer, performer, owner/manager;

  If necessary, consider other stakeholders: supplier, regulator, and so forth;

  Summarize in the process case for action.[3]

- Determine process vision and performance objectives:

  Describe how different stakeholders will perceive the new process, and specify the improvement dimension;

  Summarize in the process vision.

- Develop glossary of terms and definitions (the start of the data model);

- Summarize—construct and distribute a poster;

- Optionally, begin documenting noteworthy observations of culture, core competencies, and management systems.

Understand the as–is process

Now that the goals for the process are clarified, you will need to understand why those goals are not being met—many so-called improvements are implemented that don't actually improve anything because other factors are the root cause. The key here is not to exhaustively document the current process, but to understand it.

- Map the current process workflow to show who does what, when:

  Develop swimlane diagrams;

---

3.   This phrase was introduced in Hammer and Champy's book.

Use progressive levels of detail (we will define them later), stopping when process behavior is understood—don't get bogged down in detail!

- Investigate all other enablers (current use of IT, motivation and measurement, and so forth).

- Record initial thoughts on strengths and weaknesses of the current process, especially leverage points where significant improvement is possible.

- Perform an enabler-based final assessment of the as-is process:

  Enablers: workflow, IT, motivation and measurement, policies and rules, HR, facilities (or other).

  At this point, you will also start to collect ideas for the to-be process, so in a way, you have a foot in both camps—the as-is and the to-be.

- Optionally, assess each individual step (e.g., is it necessary, is it done by the right performer, and so forth).

- Document important aspects of culture, core competencies, and management systems.

Design the to-be process

We divide this part into two stages. The first, characterize the to-be process, determines a set of improvements or design characteristics that will work in concert to achieve process goals. We do this stage specifically because teams often leap into the design of a new workflow that incorporates "improvements" that actually work at cross-purposes or are inconsistent with other enablers. Once the team is satisfied that it has identified a cohesive, effective set of characteristics for the new process, the second stage begins—design the to-be workflow.

A) Characterize the To-Be Process

- Decide on direction—abandon, stay as-is, improve, redesign, or outsource?

- Develop ideas for characteristics or features of the new process. Techniques include:

  Identify improvements that would address leverage points;

  Challenge assumptions underlying process steps;

Brainstorm by enabler (this may, in effect, have been done during assessment).

* Assess promising ideas in context (with respect to other enablers) using a matrix format (e.g., a change in workflow may require a change in job definition that may in turn require changes to recruiting and training, as well as changes in compensation and performance measurement).

* Based on the assessment, select the key features of the to-be process.

* Develop/revise conceptual data model.

B) Design the To-Be Process Workflow

This is actually quite straightforward if all the previous steps have been worked through.

* Draw the to-be workflow:

  Progress through the different levels of detail;

  Assess and check viability at each level;

  Revise, or move on to the next level of detail;

  Iterate.

Analyze use cases

With use cases, we make the transition to looking at how systems can support the process.

* Identify use case scenarios:

  Review the to-be process workflow to identify individual use cases.

  Identify a set of process scenarios (usually around 5 to 10) that will exercise the main paths through the new workflow.

  For each process scenario, identify the individual use case scenarios (typically 7 to 15), and document the preconditions, major decisions, and outcomes for each.

* Develop individual use case scenarios:

  First pass—focus on the dialogue;

  Second pass—add data, transactions, and interface objects.

From use case analysis, we can proceed to other activities such as detailed data modeling, business rule specification, and user interface design. A detailed treatment of these is beyond the scope of this book.

Applications of the approach

Our approach could be characterized as process-focused and workflow-driven, but should you *always* use a process-focused, workflow-driven approach? Here's a short answer—a tautology, in fact. If work flows at all, you should *consider* using workflow, and if it flows far, you *must* use workflow. Let's clarify that.

Anytime the application or business improvement project under consideration involves multiple actors (e.g., job titles or organizational units), and the handling of an event flows between them, workflow should be considered. It may not be essential until at least four or five actors are involved, but you can always give it a try. If you are able to develop a good workflow process model easily, without any significant discoveries or major issues arising, it probably was not necessary, but you won't have wasted much time.

In other cases, the problem at hand is entirely transactional—an event is handled almost completely by one or two actors in a single transaction. These types of projects are becoming less common, but in those cases a workflow-driven approach may not make sense. An example is an application to automate the basic transactions of a video store—place a reservation, book a rental, and so forth. In this case, there is not a multistep, multi-actor process, so we'd define the scope and objectives and then jump right into data modeling and use case analysis.

Finally, there are other cases that we have not alluded to where elements of this approach have proven to be extremely useful. So far, we have described a method in which a new process is designed, and then a supporting information system is developed. Often, this is not the sequence of events. Instead, a major information system is acquired, such as:

- An enterprise resource planning (ERP) application (e.g., from SAP, PeopleSoft, or Oracle);

- A customer relationship management (CRM) application (e.g., from Siebel, Clarify, or PeopleSoft via their Vantive acquisition);

◆ A supply chain management (SCM) application (e.g., from i2 or Manugistics).

Recent experience shows that when these implementations don't take a business process orientation, the result is often disastrous. One approach is to develop process workflow models for your desired (to-be) business processes to use in selecting and configuring a purchased application. Alternatively, many commercial applications are designed around an ideal (best practices) business process. If the necessary expertise (usually from the vendor or a consulting firm) is available, a model of the process the application supports can be developed. This will clarify whether a particular offering supports your goals and objectives, and assist you in identifying the changes necessary to implement it.

We have also used these techniques when integrating enterprise applications with preexisting legacy and custom applications. A new field called enterprise application integration (EAI) provides methods and technology for doing just that. The application of EAI is much more effective when coupled with process-oriented approaches. Some of the available EAI tools focus specifically on expediting business processes, which of course requires that the processes be identified and mapped. This is such a critical aspect of EAI that we feel the field should have been named "enterprise *process* integration." A particularly important use of EAI is in e-commerce applications, where it is used to coordinate existing applications in support of a Web-based front end. As of this writing, two good sources for EAI information are www.eaijournal.com and www.eaiquadrant.com.

One of the hallmarks of a powerful tool, technique, or approach is that it proves itself useful in a wide variety of situations, some of them quite unexpected by the originators. The process-oriented approach and the techniques that come with it fall into this category. Armed with this overview, let's dive into the details and see how it can work for you.

Part II
Framing the Process

4

Just What Are Processes, Anyway?

The trouble with "process"

We've said it before, and we'll say it again—identifying the wrong collection of activities as a process is the most common, and arguably most serious, problem we encounter. A business process is not just a random collection of activities—it meets certain precise criteria. Time and again on consulting assignments, when a development or process redesign project is in serious trouble, we find that a true business process was not correctly identified or its scope was not clearly defined. Jumping into a process without putting it into context with other business processes or confirming that you have, indeed, initiated work on a true business process is sure to lead to trouble. Some of the problems will show up fairly early as difficulties in constructing a workflow model. Others will arise later, perhaps not until your new process is implemented and performance turns out to be worse instead of better.

Consider three examples:

1. Senior management specifically instructed a project team to develop cross-functional business processes during the implementation of a large, purchased information system. With the

assistance of an international consulting firm, the team determined what their processes were, and began mapping and assessing them. After a month's work, the team sensed that all was not well, and we were called in to provide some assistance. We had the team use our guidelines and methods to identify a set of processes. This made it very evident that the processes the team had already identified were anything but cross-functional. In fact, the processes had *exactly the same boundaries as the existing organization structures*. We advised the team that they were not going to achieve the benefits that their executives were expecting unless they proceeded with the set of cross-functional processes they had just identified. The project managers, however, opted to continue with the original processes because of the work that had already been done. A year later, the problems from this decision were apparent to everyone, and the team had to go back and redo most of the work of the past year using the "real" cross-functional processes. Moral: It's the Process, stupid.

2. A project team attempted to model the workflow for a major area they had improperly described as a single process—Supply Chain Management. Eventually, the effort collapsed amidst finger pointing, frustration, and missed deadlines. Their process model became too confused to follow (or complete!). The reason was clear. Because their scope actually included some five processes, it was impossible to express in a single diagram. There was no clear beginning point—there were many—and there was no clear ending point—there were many. It was impossible to trace a path (a workflow) through all of the included activities, especially because of timing issues. Some tasks were part of transaction-oriented processes that happened hundreds of times per day, others were part of ad hoc processes that occurred several times a month, and others still were monthly or quarterly. Try getting all that on one diagram, and then improving it! Moral: Too many Processes spoil the broth.

3. One organization enthusiastically embraced process improvement, with good reason: customers, suppliers, and employees found the company's processes slow, inconsistent, and error-

prone. Unfortunately, they were so enthusiastic that *everyone* defined his or her own work, or the work of his or her small department, as a process. Of course, each of these was in fact a function within a small number of overall processes. You can guess what happened. Within the boundaries of each of these processes, work was efficient *from the perspective of the performer.* However, these mini-processes were efficient largely because they had front-end requirements that made work easier for the performer, but imposed a burden on the customer. The attendant delay and effort meant that the real processes behaved even more poorly than they had before. Moral: One department's improvement is another department's bottleneck.

Our goal is to be sure your project gets off to a good start and avoids problems like these by defining a project scope that is equal to a complete business process—as we will define the term. This maximizes the potential benefits, and is easier to work with. If all projects are defined in this manner, then overlap, under-lap (gaps), and duplication will be apparent and avoided.

On the other hand, your intent may not be to work with a complete business process—your scope may be some other set of tasks, like the work done by a particular job function, or perhaps it is just a stage within a process because you lack the sponsorship or resources to take on the whole thing. That's fine, and is in fact the most common situation, but understanding what constitutes a process is still important. Otherwise, you might optimize a part of a business process only to cause a deterioration of the whole. There are ways to avoid this, but only if you recognize the situation in advance.

In this chapter, we will give some very specific guidelines on what constitutes a business process. In the next chapter, we will put those guidelines to work with specific techniques for discovering business processes and clarifying their scope.

The trouble with terminology

The early part of your project, and this book, is concerned with defining business processes properly: not too small (by task), not too big (an area), not by specialty (a function), and not by organizational structure (such as a division or department). Along the way, we'll use some common English words, such as "process," "function," "task," and "activity," that have multiple and overlapping meanings. These terms have taken on a specific interpretation in the context of process and workflow analysis, and business in general, so we must carefully distinguish among them so as not to confound the concepts.

English words—dictionary definitions

Except where noted, definitions are from [1].

A *process* is a particular course of action intended to achieve a result (synonym: procedure) [2]; a series of actions or operations conducing to an end; *especially*: a continuous operation or treatment especially in manufacture.

A *function* is a professional or official position: Occupation.

An *activity* is a natural or normal function: as a process (as digestion) that an organism carries on or participates in by virtue of being alive; a similar process actually or potentially involving mental function; an organizational unit for performing a specific function; *also*: its function or duties.

A *task* is a usually an assigned piece of work often to be finished within a certain time; a duty or function.

So a task can be a function, and an activity can be a process or a function. To further complicate things, the word "procedure" shows up too. It usually means a defined series of steps and decisions to accomplish some task or activity. Yikes! About the only thing we can conclude is that some work (or is that activity?) is involved!

But if the English terms are confusing, information systems jargon is downright contradictory.

Information systems terms

In the later part of our project, we will become increasingly concerned with information systems, as automated implementation considerations come to the fore. Then business terms can become confused with computer jargon, which uses some of the same terms in a different way. At that point, we will really need to be precise in the meanings of these terms. Let's look at some computerese.

A *process* is an executing program. A process consists of the program code (which may be shared with other processes which are executing the same program), and some private data [3].

A *function* is a computer subroutine; *specifically*: one that performs a calculation with variables provided by a program and supplies the program with a single result [1]; or a set sequence of steps, part of larger computer program: subprogram, procedure [2].

So processes are programs, which may incorporate functions. But the terminology for the information engineering methodology introduces another scheme: functions are composed of processes, and an activity is either a function or a process [4]. In another scheme, functions are composed of processes which are composed of activities which are composed of tasks. In yet another, activities are composed of processes. A process can even be "a generic term that may include compute, assemble, compile, interpret, generate, etc." [5]

Similar conflicting definitions can be given for the other terms: tasks can compose, or be composed of, processes, and if we cared to bring in procedure, operation, or, worse yet, system, we could easily construct a huge circular definition that would require a computer to process—and you can be sure we'd become confused in the process.

So what is a process?

Business process terms

You keep hearing "make sure your business processes aren't functions," which, using normal English or computer definitions, doesn't make sense. But we will precisely define these two terms such that it does make sense, and provides guidance on how best to scope your project. The definition of business process is meant to be prescriptive, not descriptive: you should strive to make your project focus on a business process as we will define it. Addressing a complete business process offers the potential for greater benefits, and is easier to analyze using tools like workflow modeling. And even if you can't take on a complete business process, recognizing the actual process boundaries can save a lot of grief, so let's try to precisely define our terms.

Essentially, a process is a way for an enterprise to organize work and resources (people, equipment, information, and so forth) to accomplish its aims. Historically, an enterprise would organize its work and resources into specialties or functions. Nowadays organizations try to organize work and resources to achieve a specific output—a result—for a specific customer. This is process orientation, and gives rise to this definition:

"*A business process* is a collection of interrelated work tasks, initiated in response to an event, that achieves a specific result for the customer of the process." We will look at each phrase in the definition, but not in the order they appear. Surprisingly, even though the first reference is to work tasks, they are the least important aspect of a process. Far more important are the result, the customer, and the event. Let's take Stephen Covey's sage advice, and "begin with the end in mind:"

...that achieves a specific result...

The only reason a business process exists is to deliver a specific result. That result might be goods, such as the products requested on an order, or services, such as information in response to a query. The all-important guideline is: The result must be individually identifiable and countable. The processes Develop New Product, Resolve Service Problem, Fulfill Order, and Hire Employee all conform to this guideline. You can identify the specific new products that are developed, and count them. In other words, it is possible to count how many times the process Develop New Product was completed. Similarly, it would be possible to identify and count the service problems that were resolved, the orders that were fulfilled, and the employees that were hired. However, you cannot count how many Research and Developments, Help Desks, Telemarketings, or Human Resources were completed because those are departments or functions, but not processes. A good process name clearly indicates the result or end state of the process—new product is developed, service problem is resolved, and so on.

...for the customer of the process...

This is critical: A customer is the recipient or beneficiary of the result produced by the business process. This customer may be a person, an organization, or even a broad marketplace, but the customer can be identified and can pass judgment on how satisfactory the result and the process are. The customer might be internal to the organization, such as the employee whose service problem was resolved, or the department that receives the newly hired employee.

Taking the customer's perspective helps identify and name processes accurately. At a Motor Vehicle department, a process called Handle Application Form would not pass the customer perspective test, because the application form is not what the customer cares about. Would you be satisfied knowing that your form had been handled—taken, copied, sorted, sent, bent, folded, spindled, stapled, and mutilated? No, you expect some result like a driver's license issued or a vehicle registered, so the appropriate processes are Issue Driver's License and Register Vehicle. Also note that while the business process must provide a result to the customer, it likely has to provide a result to other stakeholders, notably the organization itself. The classic example: Most customers would probably be happier if you did not bill them for the result they receive, but since you would go out of business if you did that for long, the process result includes collecting the payment.

...initiated in response to a specific event...

You must be able to trace a process back to the earliest event that triggers or initiates it. Think of the process as a machine that is inactive until the on switch is flipped. In other words, the event is what makes it go. Effectively, the event is a specific request for the result the process produces. Develop New Product begins in response to the event "market opportunity is confirmed," which is a request for a new product that will satisfy the market opportunity. Resolve Service Problem begins in response to the event "customer reports service problem," which is a request for the service problem to be resolved. Identifying the earliest event is not always easy. Does Fulfill Customer Order begin in response to the organization's receipt of an order, or customers initiating an order, or customers realizing they have a need? Sometimes, there are multiple events that can initiate a process. In any case, the effort in determining the event(s) is worth it— once you have an event and a result, it is far easier to trace the sequence of tasks that transforms the former into the latter.

...work tasks...

The business process is a collection of actions, activities, steps, tasks, or whatever you want to call them. Generally, we will use the term "step," but they are all identifiable pieces of work, typically done at a point in time (in one sitting) by a single actor, or multiple cooperating actors. An actor may be a person playing a specific role, a job function, a department, or even an automated system. A step in the initial workflow model will likely divide into more and finer steps during development of more detailed models. Just think of a work task as any activity an actor needs to accomplish in the course of a process. A more precise definition is not necessary at this point.

...a collection of interrelated...

The steps in the process must interrelate—they are not just an arbitrary collection of work. For instance, we do not want to end up analyzing Joe's job or the human resources (HR) department. Joe does a variety of tasks, from taking orders to handling customers' problems. The HR department does a variety of things from hiring and firing to benefits and reimbursement of training costs. In both cases, the only relationship among the steps is that the same performer does them all. That may be interesting, but it is not a process. Joe and the HR department probably participate in many processes. In a process, the steps are interrelated through sequence and flow—in simple terms, the completion of one step leads to (flows into) the initiation of the next step. Just as important, the steps are interrelated by dealing with the same work item, such as a specific service order, or benefit enrollment, or whatever the process deals with. Further, all of the steps are interrelated by being traceable back to the same initiating event. For example, when Joe finishes taking one customer's order, he may return to resolving another customer's service problem, but in process terms the two are unrelated—they deal with completely different work items and are part of the response to completely different events.

...a business process is...

Throughout this book, the terms "process" and "business process" refer to this definition, which is consistent with the basic principles that made BPx such a phenomenon—a process delivers a result to a customer.

So what?

It might be occurring to you that this definition is self-evident. That occurs to us on a regular basis, too. Most companies already know they need to focus on their business processes, and they know that these processes transcend specialties and organizational structures. But it is surprising that with all the exposure process orientation has received, many, if not most, businesses still cannot state what their major processes are, much less describe how they should, or even do, operate. How can this be? The answer, it turns out, is that the concepts of organizational structure, specialization, and, more than anything else, function, are so embedded in the organizational psyche that it is amazingly difficult to break out of functional orientation.

Business process versus function

Perhaps the most common error in defining business processes is to mistake a function for a business process. In this discussion, we are defining function as an occupation or department that concentrates skills. A function is a kind of work, or a field, which typically involves similar skills and tools, and has its own language. Customer service, research, engineering, manufacturing, logistics, marketing, sales, human resources, finance, shipping, billing, collections, and accounting are all functions, not business processes.

Since the Age of the Factory, organizations have been traditionally organized around functions. Education, job titles, and careers are all based on function, so functions take on such an importance that it is easy to mistake a function for a business process. "Hey, processes are important, and my function sure is important, so I guess my function must be a process." Well, functions are important—in fact, we will go against the prevailing wisdom and say that being process-oriented doesn't mean dismantling your functions. But differentiating your functions and your processes is paramount. Let's look at the differences.

In the case of an order for a customized widget, multiple functions are involved. You must take an order (Direct Sales), orchestrate the flow of materials (Logistics), make the widget (Manufacturing), pack and ship the widget (Shipping), invoice it (Billing), collect the money (Collections), reflect the transactions on the company's books (Accounting), and deal with various issues along the way (Customer Service). If your business process is defined as just one of these functions, you are likely to cause or perpetuate problems. Work methods will be defined for the benefit of the individual function, not to optimize the manner in which work flows through the functions. The idea that functions are self-contained units that

impede the flow of work has given rise to the prevailing terminology—
"functional silos," "functional stovepipes," or "functional castles": strong
walls that keep the outside out and the inside in. Functions are described
as "vertical," like a silo, and processes as "horizontal," cutting *across*
functions.

Recently there has been a different sort of problem: defining cross-
functional work (which is good!) that doesn't yield a business process
(which is bad!). These structures are "areas" or "horizontal silos." For
instance, Customer Relationship Management is a popular term (along
with Supply Chain Management and Demand Chain Management), and
is often referred to as a process, as in "our CRM process." It *is* cross-
functional, the way a business process should be, but it is not countable, so
it's like a function. You cannot say how many Customer Relationship
Managements you did yesterday. And if you try to map, assess, and
improve Customer Relationship Management, you might find it to be a
very frustrating endeavor following all the paths. The underlying problem
is that the CRM area includes multiple cross-functional business processes
such as Secure New Customer, Resolve Customer Inquiry, and Complete
Customer Communication, each of which can be studied as a separate
process.

Other business process characteristics

So, we have established that a business process begins in response to an
event, proceeds through a sequence of tasks, and ultimately yields a result
for the customer of the process and the other stakeholders. Let's add a few
more characteristics to the definition:

Measurable

We must be able to measure the business process in whatever way is important to the stakeholders. Customers may care about the effort they have
to invest and the total time until they receive the result. The organization's
performers may care more about training time or the impact on their
own productivity statistics. The owner or manager will want to track
cost, overall customer satisfaction, and other variables. A well-defined
and well-designed business process must satisfy the demands of all
stakeholders.

Automation

In looking at individual tasks within a process, automation may or may not play a role. A task could be totally manual, for example, "interview client." However, nowadays almost all processes are at least partially automated, and with the emergence of straight-through processing (STP), many processes, such as executing a trade order on a stock exchange, may be completely automated. In that example, the initiating event could be the detection of a particular condition, such as a preset stock price limit being reached, and the result could be the deposit of funds in the client's account. Essentially, this means that automation is a nonissue when deciding whether or not a step belongs within a process—a step could be totally manual, partially manual with automated support, or fully automated. We mention this because it emerges as an issue. Unbelievably, within the past year, we were told by one group of reengineering consultants that process models should only include steps that involved people, and by another "guru" that process models should only include automated steps. Obviously, neither approach would lead to a full understanding of the process.

Levels

Processes can be described at various levels. Initially, simply identify the process, as in Resolve Service Problem. Next, identify the milestones within the process, and then map the process workflow to increasing levels of detail. Any number from two (the business process and its milestones) up to five or so is reasonable, depending on the situation. There are no widely used terms for the various levels of the processes, or the steps within them, although we will define three levels of swimlane diagrams in Chapter 9. We can continue breaking the process down until we are describing individual interactions between people and systems, which means we have gone too far—that is what use cases are for.

Customers: internal and external

Every process has a customer, the person or organization expecting the primary result that the process delivers. Obviously, customers must be identified so we can obtain their assessment, and ensure that the process design meets their expectations. Another reason to focus on the customer is that in many processes, there is no overall responsibility—no one in the organization makes sure the process is completed. So we must focus on the customer because the customer is the glue that holds the process together, and must retrigger the process to move it along. A recent example is that one of us had a major appliance fail, and had to "walk" the warranty claim from the dealer to the manufacturer to the local service organization to the appliance repair agency to which they subcontracted the job. The moral: Sometimes only the customer sees the entire process from beginning to end, so identifying the customer is essential to understanding process behavior.

We sometimes distinguish processes depending on whether the customer of the process is internal or external to the organization. Figure 4.1 shows an example of each type of process.

Processes that serve *external* customers are typically why the business exists, so they are often referred to as core processes. Most businesses have only about seven to ten core process clusters or process areas in total. These are the horizontal silos. Examples are Market Research, Customer Acquisition, Product Development, Supply Chain Management, Order Fulfillment (which includes manufacturing in a build-to-order environment), Customer Relationship Management, and Customer Service. These areas are useful for high-level presentations and to get people "into the ballpark," but not specific enough to analyze and improve. When it gets down to actual workflow process modeling, you have to get down to real processes.

A process focused on an external customer is ideal for a project, because it's so much easier to demonstrate that the bottom-line performance of the company is being improved. But for some business processes, there is only an internal customer. HR-oriented processes such as Enroll in

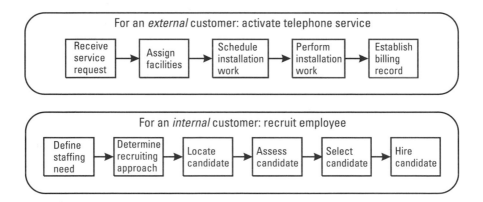

Figure 4.1 Processes with external and internal customers.

Benefit Program or Resolve Contract Issue are definitely internal. Some experts say focus only on the external customer—we disagree. How you treat your internal resources inevitably translates into how your customers are treated. If you treat your employees poorly, you may soon lose them all and go out of business. Logistics win wars—you need to support the fighters if you expect them to win. Just be sure you don't arbitrarily redefine the process to use an internal customer when there really is an external customer.

Processes that serve *internal* customers are sometimes referred to as supporting processes, and within this category we have seen them further subdivided into technical supporting and social supporting. Technical supporting processes provide or enhance infrastructure, and they almost always serve other business processes. Examples include Provide Facility, Deploy Application, and Develop Business Process. Social supporting processes provide or enhance people, for example, Recruit Employee, Hire Employee, Train Employee, and Provide Employee Benefits. Your scope will generally be smaller than the major business processes we have used as examples here, but the pattern of core and supporting will scale down and still be useful.

All processes are important, so don't use this as a way to decide which processes are more or less important, as some experts do. This classification scheme is useful because it helps avoid drifting out of a process's natural boundaries. For instance, if you are mapping a process within Product Development (core), and you find yourself including training activities (social supporting), you may be mixing two different processes, which can get very confusing.

Closing advice

Keep two key points about the nature of business processes in mind when defining process boundaries:

1. Processes are hidden within your organization.

2. There is a tendency to define business processes too small.

Processes are hidden
Business processes are usually not evident, because they are hidden by organizational structure, jobs, and systems. Don't be surprised or

disappointed if your organization has trouble identifying its processes and gaining consensus. In some cases, it is easier for customers to define the business process because they are the only ones who see it all. That was the case at a telecommunications company. They were quite sure that there were four processes, corresponding nicely to the organizational boundaries illustrated in Figure 4.2.

1. Capture Service Order;

2. Assign Facilities;

3. Install Service;

4. Update Customer Records.

The customers, of course, did not care about the organizational structure of the phone company—they just wanted their telephone service activated. The real process that was eventually identified was Activate Telephone Service. Remember, even if the organization doesn't recognize it, the process is there—somehow, the initiating event eventually makes its way to a result. It's hard for companies to identify their processes because of years of conditioning in looking at things organizationally.

Bigger is (usually) better

Business processes coordinate their elements: people, resources, systems, and *work*. Without business processes, everything would be done on an ad hoc (and probably uncoordinated) basis. In a well-designed process all of these elements are well coordinated, including the individual work steps.

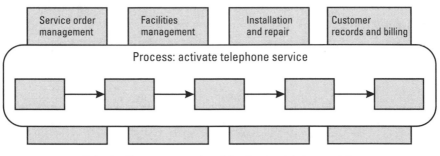

Notice that this process passes through four departments before completion

Figure 4.2   Process and organizational structure are often confused.

You should walk the process backward from any point in the process until you find the customer (internal or external) that generated the earliest event that kicked off this work, backward and forward from the cog to find the other wheels, until you reach a customer on each end.

If you take a single "natural" process, like our Activate Telephone Service example, the odds are it will perform better if designed as a single larger process than if the same result was achieved through five smaller processes as illustrated in Figure 4.3. But why should this be so, especially if each of the small processes is well designed? Let's go back to the notion of coordination to answer that.

In an ideal process, the inputs and outputs of the individual steps are well coordinated. That is, the output from one step flows smoothly and uninterrupted to become the input of the next step in the process. That is the whole notion of workflow. Process designers often accomplish this within the boundaries of a process, but are not usually as successful at the process boundaries. That is because there is a strong tendency, when trying to achieve optimization within their process, for designers to put constraints on work entering and leaving their process. Rekeying of data, batching of inputs, transport to a separate location, and fixed processing schedules are some obvious examples. Processes often require their customer—whoever precedes them in the flow—to reenter data into a format that is optimized for the receiving process. This makes the receiving process internally optimal, but the overall (natural) process is slowed by

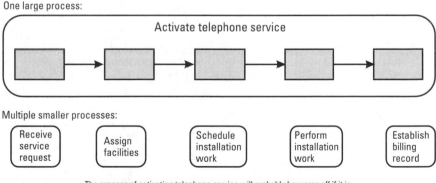

One large process:

Activate telephone service

Multiple smaller processes:

Receive service request → Assign facilities → Schedule installation work → Perform installation work → Establish billing record

The process of activating telephone service will probably be worse off if it is handled as five smaller processes instead of one larger one.

Figure 4.3 With processes, bigger is usually better.

the additional work. Worse yet, errors will be introduced during the re-keying of data that will ultimately cause even longer delays. Batching introduces similar problems. The idea behind batching is that a process will handle individual work items most efficiently when they are grouped into batches of like items. The process performers can then get set up to handle that type of item most efficiently. It appears that the process is very efficient, but *only within that process for those performers*—the natural process is less effective. Individual work items might spend a lot of time waiting for their batch to get big enough, or for their turn to come.

This phenomenon was described by Eliyahu Goldratt,[1] and it leads to this conclusion: Processes should be defined as large as possible, because multiple, small processes each tend to strive for internal efficiency; local optimization leads to overall suboptimization. This really is not surprising, because it is essentially the same problem as functional organizations putting constraints on the entry and exit of work.

Well-meaning process improvement teams can unwittingly make a large process less effective by locally optimizing a subprocess. This leads to an important corollary: If you know that your project scope is less than a complete business process, *be sure to focus attention on expediting the flow of work into and out of your process.*

Putting the definition to work

Everything we have covered in this chapter boils down to defining a process by discovering the earliest event and the delivery of the final result to a customer that signals the complete handling of that event. It still isn't easy, though, as evidenced by the difficulty organizations have in discovering their true business processes. In the next chapter we will look at some techniques for putting the material in this chapter to work defining the boundaries of your processes.

---

1. See *The Goal* by Eliyahu Goldratt, which describes this and other important process improvement concepts in the context of an entertaining novel.

References

[1]   By permission. From *WWWebster Dictionary*, copyright © 1999 (based on *Merriam-Webster's Collegiate® Dictionary, 10th Edition*) at Web site http://www.m-w.com by Merriam-Webster, Incorporated.

[2]   WordNet 1.6, copyright © 1997 by Princeton University. All rights reserved.

[3]   The Free Online Dictionary of Computing, http://wombat.doc.ic.ac.uk/, Editor Denis Howe, copyright © Denis Howe, 1993–1999.

[4]   Texas Instruments, *A Guide to Information Engineering Using the IEF: Computer-Aided Planning, Analysis, Design*, Plano, TX: Texas Instruments, Inc., 1988, pp. 14–15.

[5]   Sippl, C. J., and R. J. Sippl, *Computer Dictionary and Handbook*, Indianapolis, IN: Howard W. Sams & Co., Inc., 1980, p. 402.

5

Establish the Process Boundaries

Business processes and project scope

All projects, especially process improvement projects, require a clear scope. Disastrous consequences ensue when a project team jumps in and starts drawing swimlane diagrams and use cases right off the mark. The project spirals aimlessly, implements improvements that actually make things worse, or any of a host of other problems. To avoid this, it is essential that you begin by accurately specifying a business process, its boundaries, and some important facts about the context in which you will be studying it. We refer to this as "framing the process," and it is arguably the most important phase of your project.

More often than not, when we see a process modeling effort that has gone off the rails, it is because the up-front steps of defining the business process and establishing its scope were not given adequate attention: the process was not framed. In *The Reengineering Revolution*, Michael Hammer identifies process identification and analysis as the second and third top mistakes in reengineering: "*Moral: Only (business) processes can be reengineered. Before you can reengineer processes you must identify them.*"[1] Let's use what we learned about business processes in the last chapter to identify genuine business processes, and establish the boundaries for the process your project will study. Three key lessons from the previous chapter must be kept in mind at all times:

- A process has an event at the beginning, and a countable result at the end, produced for a customer (who quite likely triggered the initiating event).

- Most business processes cross departments and functions.

- Bigger is better.

Guidelines are fine, but what exactly will the project that you are working on encompass? This is sometimes referred to as the scope of the project—exactly what you will include, and just as important, what you'll exclude. This can be a tricky area, because your scope should be small enough to master, yet large enough to make a difference. If you include too little—a subset of a process—the project will probably be ineffective because you will not be addressing enough of the problem to make any real difference. Your improvements might even make the overall process worse. But if your scope is too broad, you risk dissipating effort or overextending and thus not achieving your goals. Koulopoulos warns that your project scope probably should not extend beyond the authority of your sponsor [2]. If it does, you should seriously consider changing your scope, or enlisting the support of a higher level sponsor (which, of course, will lead to negotiations and scope changes). If you cannot do this, at least be aware of the dangers so you can keep an eye out for problems developing outside the scope of your authority.

It is perfectly reasonable to have project boundaries that do not correspond to business processes—just make sure you don't damage any processes, and don't expect the benefits that come from improving a cross-functional process.

The dilemma

You and your organization are convinced—process focus is the way to go. But dilemmas remain:

- You might say, "I know what a business process is, and I know what one isn't, but the theory and rules aren't helping. I need some step-by-step techniques to help me identify *my* business processes."

+ Most of the time, you will be handed a project that was defined from on high before you even heard about it. Probably, almost certainly, the boundaries won't correspond to a proper business process. You'll start with something like "Fix our logistics processes" or "Move our customer-facing processes to the Web." You need to either scope or cope—adjust project scope, or adjust to the situation.

A way forward

Many errors arise in drawing process boundaries, but three are especially common. The first two are the "Goldilocks errors"—the scope is too large, or too small, but not just right. Boundaries often become too large through scope creep, where your project grows to unmanageable proportions one small piece at a time, until it's so large that forward progress is impossible. This in turn is often caused by a project scope that is actually a function or department that plays a role in many processes. When the project team starts following workflows that cross the boundaries (they will, because processes do!), it is natural to start adding activities to the scope.

The project's scope can also be too small: if you don't cover a full business process or a significant chunk of one, you'll be subject to all the problems associated with local optimization. The third common error is the grab bag, where an unrelated set of tasks is mislabeled as a process: throw in everything that's been causing you any trouble. These and other problems can usually be avoided using the techniques of process identification and framing that are the subject of this chapter. Three principles underlie these techniques:

+ It is easiest to identify processes in "bottom-up" fashion. Participants identify activities or milestones, and then apply guidelines for "stringing them together" and identifying the parts that constitute a process.

+ Scope is clearer if you also identify related processes that are outside your scope, and depict these graphically on an "overall process map." This technique also makes identifying processes easier in the first place.

+ Simply naming a process is inadequate for people to understand what's inside and what's outside of its boundaries. We employ a framework that includes a number of other items that help to clarify scope.

Framing the process: goals

Defining a true business process and articulating it in a way that virtually eliminates misunderstanding are "framing the process." It's really just another way of saying "document the scope of the process." The components of this scope statement or process frame are:

- Process name in verb-noun format;

- Event that triggers the business process;

- Result achieved by the process;

- Customer that receives the result;

- Other stakeholders and the result(s) they expect;

- About five to seven major activities or milestones within the process;

- Actors with a role in the process;

- Mechanisms (systems, forms, equipment, etc.) that support the process;

- Process timing and frequency;

- Related (but out-of-scope) processes depicted on an overall process map.

Two other components will be covered in the next chapter when we look at assessing a process and establishing its goals:

- Assessment of current process performance;

- Performance objectives for the new process.

If all of the above are specified, process scope is far better understood than if the scope statement was simply "our customer relationship management process." Framing can usually be done within a few hours, so it is among the highest value work of the entire project in benefit per hour. When defining scope, whether for a process improvement project or a home improvement project, an important principle is that it is just as important to clarify what's out as what's in. If you don't make it clear to all actual and potential stakeholders what you are excluding, you will inevitably face the wrath or disappointment of those who assumed you were going to help them. The overall process map is an important tool for avoiding this.

The overall process map

The overall process map is simply a depiction of a set of related processes, usually five to seven. By related, we mean that they deal with a similar topic (e.g., all involve maintaining a supply of spare parts) and there are significant flows between them. These flows are typically information, but could be goods or other items. Figure 5.1 shows an example.

The value of the overall process map is that it clarifies what is out of scope as well as what is in. In the process Procure Item, stakeholders might assume that paying the vendor, or establishing an ongoing supply contract for the item, is part of the process scope. In the example, Establish Supply Agreement and Pay Vendor are shown specifically out of scope. Alas, the need for an overall process map is clearest in hindsight, after suffering the delays and conflicts arising from unclear scope. More than once, we have been called on to assist a project that started without one. Often, they have done a fair bit of as-is modeling, and even some to-be models, before the problems start to mount up. Then, there is very strong agreement from everyone—from senior managers to junior analysts—that they need to go back and build a map putting their project in context. Typically, they also feel that they could have avoided slipping into other processes, and could have made their processes big enough to make a real impact.

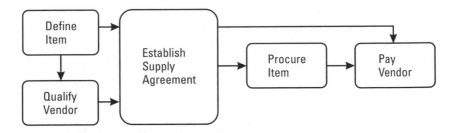

Figure 5.1 Overall process map for the Supply Management area.

These can be built at various levels of detail, from a map for the entire organization showing the highest level process areas, down to something much more specific. Ideally, an organization should have an overall process map, but most organizations do not. And of those that do, many do it wrong in the sense that the processes they show are actually their major functions—accounting, human resources, sales, manufacturing, logistics, marketing, and so on. Even if your project scope is less than a full process, you should use this technique. Just show other related process "chunks" of about the same size as your project, and you will at least have visually clarified what is out of scope (and possibly where some important flows or interfaces have to be accommodated).

Identifying your processes

Where to start?

Building the overall process map usually goes hand in hand with identifying your business processes. This can be done in top-down or bottom-up fashion, but identifying processes usually works best when done in a bottom-up fashion. That is, identify a whole bunch of individual activities or milestones that have to be achieved, and then string them together into a process. On the other hand, many authorities suggest a top-down approach: from the top (Operate Enterprise) you are told to identify the major processes by progressively decomposing. It sounds easy, but in practice, it is quite difficult. That is why experienced analysts have learned that even so-called top-down analysis usually has a significant bottom-up component: you gather more detail than you need, and then synthesize it into the higher level abstraction you were seeking. Other than just being easier, two advantages of this approach are (a) the clients always give you more detail than you want anyway, and (b) we analysts are actually better at capturing detail than anything else.

In practice, this is an iterative process, with the work from the process mapping changing the definition of the target process which changes the process map, and so on. Do a little of one, then a little of the other, with each activity refining and validating the other.

Let's look at a step-by-step, bottom-up approach for discovering business processes, and for organizing them into an overall process map.

Step by step

The steps in this section are given in a logical order, but you could do them in other orders—consider each situation case by case. Actually, it is an iterative process, in which a later step might alter the conclusions of an earlier step, so we provide a checklist at the end of the chapter. As long as all the steps are completed at the end, everything will turn out fine.

Brainstorming in general   The approach begins with brainstorming, which is an excellent technique for two reasons. Properly handled, it gives everyone a chance to participate, and gets them used to it. Second, it can generate a lot of raw material to work with in a short time. This turns out to be far more productive than agonizingly trying to get it right immediately. Here are the basics of brainstorming:

The first step is to open up. You need to break out of the box, limber up your mind, and even get a little silly. If you are able to do this in a group, a few brainteasers or games might help.[1]

Perhaps spend five minutes imagining that your company just found itself stuck with 10 trillion coat hangers and needs to think of unusual ways to use them. Have the group generate 25 suggestions as quickly as possible, being sure to get ideas from everyone—quantity, speed, and participation are the essence of a good brainstorming session. Next, in preparation for the *real* work, review the rules of brainstorming. The first rule is: no criticism or evaluation of any kind is allowed during the brainstorming session. You must not be critical in any way—even absurd and impossible ideas are encouraged. You are after quantity, not quality. It's okay to piggyback, or take another idea and modify or extend it. In fact, plagiarism is encouraged. At this stage, the sky's the limit, and everything is possible. The other rules are one idea per turn and say "pass" if you have nothing to say at your turn. Take turns, because if you go around the room in clockwise fashion (participants are seated in a semicircle or U shape), by giving everyone a turn, you'll encourage balanced participation when the team is forming. After you have listed as many ideas as you can, you might reward the person who contributed the most suggestions, and especially reward the person who suggested the most bizarre idea. Note that the best idea should not be singled out for praise.

---

1. See the *Games Trainers Play* series for ideas (e.g., Edward Scannell and John Newstrom, *Even More Games Trainers Play: Experiential Learning Exercises*, New York: McGraw-Hill, 1994).

Then it's time to work with all that raw material. Combine ideas, possibly by clustering similar suggestions, and remove the absurd, impossible (but make sure they really are!), and out of scope. Look critically to see if you have missed any ideas. Use a technique like multivoting to determine which ideas to pursue.

Brainstorm milestones   Even in an organization that is heavily functionally oriented, people have little difficulty identifying individual activities or milestones, which is what we will use. A milestone is any necessary result, whether it marks the end of a major process or is a step along the way:

- Product is reserved;

- Shipment is packed;

- Inventory is replenished;

- Order is accepted;

- Order is submitted.

Don't try to put the ideas in any particular sequence. More important, note that participants in a process identification session are more likely to come up with suggestions for milestones than they are to come up with the corresponding processes or steps. We are not sure why this is, but we have observed the phenomenon in many settings. It seems that milestones are like events, and it's easier for people to identify what has to happen (events) than to generalize that into processes. All we know is that it works. A sample is illustrated in Figure 5.2.

Link the milestones/steps together

Because it has to be done eventually, begin this step by renaming the milestones into steps by rephrasing the name in verb-noun format:

- Reserve Product;

- Pack Shipment;

- Replenish Inventory;

- Accept Order;

- Submit Order.

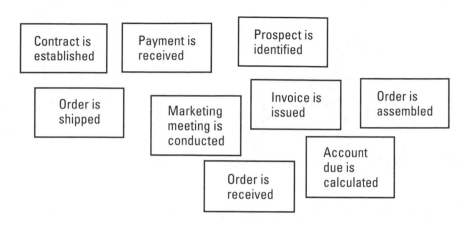

Figure 5.2 Partial results from a brainstorm for milestones.

Next, you will link these steps together by matching the output of one with the input of another. Simply ask the group to identify cases when a milestone is generally preceded or followed by another milestone. Stringing them together has another important advantage: it makes steps that were missed during the brainstorm more evident.

Next, we have to identify the ratio for each link: is it one to one (1:1), one to many (1:M), or many to one (M:1)? The example in Figure 5.3 includes each:

- Every time we have an instance of Identify Prospect, we expect to have one instance of Schedule Meeting, so we say they are linked 1:1. It may be that we don't schedule a meeting at all, but we are not worried about the zero cases.

- Every time we Establish Contract, we hope that eventually we will have many Receive Orders, so this is a 1:M link. We might receive no orders, but the minimum case is not what we care about.

- Finally, we may have many Ship Orders before we Calculate Account Due, as would be the case if we did billing on a monthly basis. This would give us an M:1 link. Note that if we invoiced on each shipment, this would be a 1:1.

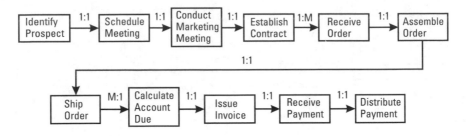

Figure 5.3 Analyzing the links between individual steps.

Assemble processes based on frequency and affinity

The trick in this approach is that a cluster of steps or milestones with 1:1 links generally constitute a well-formed process. This goes back to Eliyahu Goldratt and his work on constraints—if a work item (the object of a process) is intended to flow from one step into the next on a 1:1 basis, then we should try to synchronize or coordinate these steps within a process. On the other hand, 1:M and M:1 connections cannot generally be coordinated, because there are delays while the many build up. These types of links usually signify flows between processes that have quite different timing cycles. This technique doesn't work all the time, but it has a very high success rate compared to attempts to define processes top-down. An added bonus: this also gives you the major activities or milestones within a process, one of the key parts of framing it.

As shown in Figure 5.4, this approach gives three separate but related processes—Acquire Customer, Fulfill Order, and Collect Account Receivable—that could be depicted on an overall process map. Thus, if your scope was Fulfill Order, it would be clear that signing up new customers and collecting payment were not included.

Name the processes

Naming standards can make a real difference when identifying processes. They tighten up everyone's thinking, and focus attention on the essence of the process or step: the result it achieves. Business processes, *and the individual steps within them*, should be named in action verb/optional qualifier/noun format that clearly identifies the intended result. Usually the noun will be the grammatical object of the verb and describe an important business object or entity, for example, Pay Invoice, Receive Shipment, or

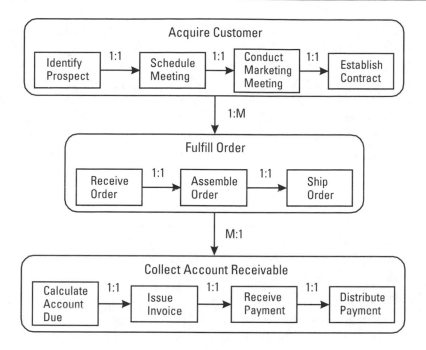

Figure 5.4 Forming processes from steps with 1:1 links.

Load Ship. Occasionally the noun will be an attribute of an entity, such as Record Customer Address. Note that when the process name is treated as a proper noun and capitalized to make it clear we are referring to a defined process.

The phrase must clearly identify the result of the process. For example, the result "order is taken" is achieved through the process step Take Order; "new product is developed" is achieved through the business process Develop New Product, and "distributor is acquired" is achieved through Acquire Distributor. Other examples include Pay Invoice, Hire Worker, Fire Worker, Settle Claim, or Receive Payment. In all cases, flipping the order of the action verb-noun pair indicates the result we expect from the process. That is, it does as long as you don't use mushy verbs.

Mushy verbs are easy to use, so they give the illusion that progress is being made, but they really don't tell us anything. For instance, what is actually achieved by the processes Monitor Shipment, Administer Application, and Track Project? Exactly what are single instances of "shipment is monitored," "application is administered," and "project is tracked"?

Determine Current Shipment Location, Accept Application, and Record Project Task Completion all use active instead of mushy verbs, and convey much more information.

Table 5.1 gives a list of verbs you should avoid in naming your business processes. Once, at this point during one of our educational workshops, a participant said, "Oh, no! All of my steps have mushy verbs!" We took a look, and sure enough, that was the case. And sure enough, the process map really did not tell us what was going on except in a very general way.

- Make sure that you don't confuse a business process with a function or department. You can count iterations of business processes, but not functions. "How many Legals did you do today?" and "How many Finances did you do today?" are nonsense. "How many lawsuits did you file today?" and "How many invoices did you pay today?" make sense.

- Often there will be a state change, where the status of the noun is different after the business process. After Pay Invoice, the invoice status is paid instead of due; after Receive Shipment, the status of the shipment is received instead of pending.

- In your overall process map, you may be interested in some of your target business process's neighbors at only a high level. In this case, you might name these business processes with a high-level name in noun-gerund form (e.g., Product Development, instead of Develop Product), but never generalize the business process you are directly working on.

- Include manual processes and steps as well as automated ones; there will often be some impact on your computer records even if the business process has no automation. If not, it will someday, and probably sooner than you expect.

Identify the triggering event

An organization's core business processes rely on stimuli from outside events as their reason for existing [3]. Supporting processes may be initiated by an internally generated event, although it might be traced back to external factors. You need to identify the event that initiates each business process to establish a boundary and as a starting point for developing your swimlane diagrams. The event is normally an action by an actor. For

Table 5.1
A few other tips to keep in mind:

VERB	BAD	GOOD
Act on	Act on application	Approve application
Analyze	Analyze incident	Determine incident root cause
Check	Check status	Approve credit
Handle	Handle forms	*Describe the action*
Maintain	Maintain customer data	Record change of address
Manage	Manage service request	*Describe the action*
Monitor	Monitor process	Identify process exception condition
Perform	Perform duties	*Describe the action*
Process	Process invoices	Pay invoice
Review	Review paperwork	Decide if application is complete
Track	Track shipment	Record shipment status change

example, an order is generated from outside your organization and stimulates your business to fulfill the order and invoice the customer. Payments are received and they stimulate you to cash the check and close the outstanding receivable. Some events are time triggered—action is initiated by the arrival of a predetermined date and time. For example, April 15 rolls around and you are stimulated to get your tax return filed, or it's time to run your biweekly payroll.

An interesting class of events are protocol events. These are events, other than the initiating one, by which we have the customer reinitiate the flow at various stages. They are only required because it is the process's protocol to require them. Often, they arise when the customer is "walking" the process's work item from one step to another. This is a major improvement opportunity: any protocol event you can eliminate will probably please the customer. This is also why you should involve selected customers in your process improvement sessions—often they are the only actors who know about *all* of these annoying protocol events.

Identify stakeholders and expected results

We have stressed results as a critical concept, but don't confuse results with objectives. This is easy given the similarity of the terms. An objective is a performance target, which may have been articulated in the process vision. A result is what you want the process to produce or accomplish. You can point to discrete, individual results, and we can count them. Here are some results:

- ◆ Order is taken;
- ◆ New product is developed;
- ◆ Distributor is acquired;
- ◆ Invoice is issued;
- ◆ Employee is hired.

Compare those results with some sample objectives:

- ◆ Reduce turnover to 4% per annum within 18 months;
- ◆ Increase circulation to 150,000 by 4Q;
- ◆ Increase advertising revenue by 10% this year;
- ◆ Decrease average cost of processing an invoice 5% by year end.

Another important idea is that the customer may not be the only stakeholder to receive a result. In addition to asking "What does the customer receive?" we need to consider "What other criteria must be met?" For example, the customer's order is satisfied (what the customer receives) and paid for (other criteria met). The results of a business process must satisfy the customer, but also satisfy you and the organization you work for. The customer's order must be filled, which no doubt makes the customer happy, but it must also be paid for, which makes your shareholders happy. For each process, ask "Who are the other stakeholders, and what result do they expect from this process?" One project was helped tremendously by this simple technique. They were providing catering services (running the lunchroom) on a contract basis at various manufacturing facilities. They had correctly identified the people buying meals as customers, but something was missing. Once they identified the other key stakeholder—the organization they were contracting to—they saw that they really had two customers, and both had to be satisfied.

There is often an artificial organizational barrier between operations and finance in corporations, often mirrored in the organization of the IT department. The operational people do a wonderful job fulfilling the company's operational mission, but a terrible job collecting the needed information to collect payment for the goods and services. Remember: "The job ain't done until it's paid for"—as long as it operates on the same timing cycle, you should consider the after-the-fact paperwork as an integral part of a complete business process.

Focusing on the result can often make process mapping easier. Stephen Covey [4] tells us we should start with the end in mind, and so it is with developing the swimlane diagram for a process. It is sometimes easier to work backwards from the end result than to work forward from the event. You will often, but not always, end up back at the same place—the customer who receives the result is often the same actor that triggered the process in the first place.

Identify the major steps

Your process scope will be much clearer if you identify the primary steps that represent the essence of the work the process involves. At this point, you don't care who does them or how—you simply want to list five or so significant steps within the overall business process. These steps could also be called subprocesses, components, activities, milestones, or tasks. What matters is that they represent the critical milestones, internal to the process, which must be reached in order for the process to operate. You probably have most of them identified already, from the steps that you assembled into processes in the last step. If not, you can use "decomposition" to identify the steps—just ask "What five to seven activities must be completed or milestones reached in order for this process to operate?"

Two versions of a Fulfill Order process are shown in Figure 5.5, one of which includes manufacturing and collections activities. If all there was to go on was the name Fulfill Order, observers would make different assumptions about what that meant, so this is a valuable tool for clarifying process scope.

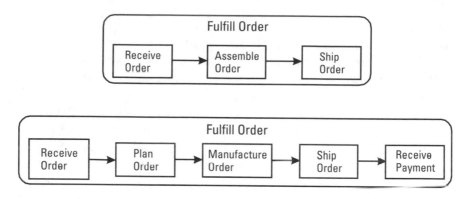

Figure 5.5 Two versions of the "Fulfill Order" process.

Identify roles

Finally, identify the roles, that is, the main organizations and job functions currently involved with your business process. The roles may include external organizations, such as Customers, Suppliers, or Regulators. There are cases where an information system can be treated as an actor, but this is not the norm. Actors in the Fulfill Order process may include:

- Customer;
- Outside Sales;
- Order Desk;
- Production Planner;
- Materials Expediter;
- Accounts Receivable.

This further clarifies scope of the target process. Along the same lines, you might also document the applications and data sources currently used by the process.

Develop glossary or preliminary data model

It is much easier to identify and work with your processes if you have agreement on the things your process needs information about; specifically, how each of the things is defined, and what information is needed about each. That is what a data model does—it depicts the things that a business needs to maintain records (data) about, and ensures that everyone is on the same wavelength about terminology and meaning before getting into the details of process and system design. As introduced in Chapter 3, the core of a data model is the entity-relationship diagram depicting the entities, relationships, and attributes that provide the structure of the record-keeping system. However, our main interest at this point is in the entity definitions— what exactly do we mean by a product, a customer, or an order? Different interpretations will have a significant impact on the scope of related processes such as Fulfill Order, and on the functionality that information systems must provide. Having a data model can also be an excellent aid to process identification. Each of the three entities just mentioned will have at least one significant corresponding business process—Acquire Customer, Introduce New Product, and Fulfill Order.

This is an excellent time to develop a basic data model, which includes a glossary or vocabulary. If you are not familiar with this technique, jump ahead to Chapter 15 for an introduction to the basics of developing a data model.

Choose your process

You would like to use an objective, analytic approach to defining your project, but in reality the road is fraught with politics, gut feelings, negotiation, and compromise. Usually we don't pick one, we pick some or all, and agree on a sequence. The process is chosen in one of two ways: by an analytical approach, or by what we call divine intervention. The latter is the most common, so let's start there.

Divine intervention

Process improvement and application development projects are often defined in response to a pressing business issue or need, a squeaky wheel, or someone with the checkbook, and so it does not meet the definition of a business process that we have recommended you use. Often your project will be scoped by divine intervention, as in: "Thou shalt fix business process X!" And X is not a business process in any sense of the word. In most companies, budget authority does not equate to business processes, and so the executive with the checkbook is unwilling to spend his or her budget to improve the tasks in another department. Remember, processes have been hidden by decades of organizations, reorganizations, and disorganizations. Business processes cross organizational boundaries—departments, budgets, and authority do not.

New technology drives a surprising proportion of projects. The CEO is on an airplane and meets a consultant, or reads an article in a magazine. We must have (choose one, or some combination) EDI, groupware, Web, imaging, intranet, extranet, e-commerce, and so forth. This tendency is not all bad—first telephones, then computers, then ATMs were that way. Probably no pressing business advantage could have been quantitatively shown, but successful implementations proceeded because there was just a gut feeling that this technology could change things for the better.

Some key issues for you are:

- Is this REALLY a business process?

- Is my executive team expecting cross-functional benefits from a project or process that is not cross-functional?

- Can I repackage this in an appealing way with the boundaries of a true business process?

Confirm your suspicions via the techniques discussed in this chapter. In most actual projects, the team receives some directive, and then iteratively manipulates it to better match a business process. This might not be possible, so if you can't get your project redefined, try to keep the whole picture in mind and remember to focus on the boundaries. That is where you can make gains for the overall process.

Analytic approach

Years ago, there was much more use of formalized strategic planning methodologies to direct an enterprise's improvements, but these have fallen by the wayside while divine intervention has become the norm. Just as well, they were often a once-a-year blitz that produced some weighty shelfware, after which the organization proceeded on whatever course it was already on. Besides, the truly great ideas, whether they spring from the executive or bubble up through the ranks, are just as likely to come from inspiration as from a formal methodology.

What would you do if you wanted to take a more rigorous approach? Goold and Campbell described a good approach several years ago in [5], and we have employed it successfully in a number of planning sessions for organizations that wanted a repeatable, more rigorous method. (We suspected they wanted the rigor to back up their hunches, but that's another story.)

The approach begins with identifying your organization's critical success factors (CSFs). A CSF is one of a small number of things that must go exceptionally well in order for your business to meet its objectives. "Completion of the XYZ project on time and on budget" might be an objective. A related CSF could be "Maintain an exceptionally high level of client involvement in requirements definition." See the difference? Rockart, author of the original article on CSFs [6], would say that you have about five CSFs, but most organizations identify between seven and fifteen. Second, identify your major processes. Again, there might be seven or so, or sometimes more. Note that depending on your interest and authority, you might be looking at the major process areas that comprise the enterprise, or smaller processes within a specific area. Third, build a matrix of processes versus CSFs, and for each cell determine the impact that the process has on the CSF. This could be done numerically from 1 (little impact) to 5 (high impact). Fourth, you will assess the "brokenness" of each process: 1 if it's in good shape, 5 if it's a mess. Finally, you determine where to focus your efforts by building a numerical ranking of each process. What you are looking for is a process that is highly broken and has a high impact on a number of CSFs. In the article they describe a less numerically intensive approach that involves some simple math: for each row (process) in the matrix, add up the number of highly impacted CSFs, and multiply by the brokenness. This will identify the process to work on first, but of course there are other issues:

- How difficult will process improvement be?

- Can the process be tied to the needs of customers?

- Is this large, complex, and "dug in," or is it fairly straightforward with some obvious "low-hanging fruit"?

- Are there political support and sponsorship for the process redesign?

- Is there a natural sequence or precedence? Does one process obviously have to be attended to first?

- Are there other issues driving selection of a particular process, such as regulatory concerns or competitive issues?

Although the approach on its own doesn't produce a definitive answer, it does provide some direction. We have seen it yield surprising outcomes, which leave participants slapping their foreheads saying, "Of course!" That's precisely when a rigorous approach such as this is most beneficial.

However you arrived at it, you now have the scope of your process unambiguously defined—named and framed. Now let's move on to assessment, so we can describe why your chosen process is getting all the attention.

References

[1]   Hammer, M., and S. A. Stanton, *The Reengineering Revolution*, New York: Harper Business, 1995, p. 19.

[2]   Koulopoulos, T., *The Workflow Imperative: Building Real World Business Solutions*, New York: Van Nostrand Reinhold, 1995, pp. 114–115.

[3]   Dickinson, B., *Risk Free Business Re-Engineering*, Kings Beach, CA: LCI Press, 1996, p. 96.

[4]   Covey, S., *The Seven Habits of Highly Effective People: Restoring the Character Ethic*, New York: Fireside, 1990.

[5]   Goold, M., and A. Campbell, "Many Best Ways to Make Strategy," *Harvard Business Review*, Nov.–Dec. 1987.

[6]   Rockart, J., "Chief Executives Define Their Own Data Needs," *Harvard Business Review*, Mar.–Apr. 1979.

6

Conducting the Initial Assessment

A case for action and a vision

Before you buy a used car, it is a good idea to take it to a good mechanic. Your mechanic won't just stand back and eyeball the car, but will systematically go through the major systems or components—the body and frame, the interior, the brakes, the engine, transmission, the rest of the drive train, the suspension, and so on. And so it is with a business process—you cannot just eyeball it and ask, "How is it?" That might be a good start, but only by systematically inspecting its components and sub-systems can you make a complete assessment. The same is true for establishing goals for the behavior of the new process—you must consider a variety of perspectives.

This chapter will describe frameworks to use when assessing a process so you can answer two questions:

- ◆ What's wrong with this process, anyway?
- ◆ What will be better about it when we're done?

The perspectives we will use are the stakeholders, the enablers, and some general metrics. The initial assessment will look at the process from the perspective of each stakeholder, to determine what, or even if, to change. This assessment will be based more on perceptions than on hard facts, because we will not yet have started a detailed study of the as-is process. That does not mean it won't be valuable—it will help us establish the improvement goals for the process, and identify specific issues that our as-is study (the next major step) must research and understand. We will also collect available information about process dynamics and metrics—"the numbers." After the as-is analysis is complete, we will perform a final assessment that will use the six enablers (workflow design, IT, motivation and measurement, and so forth) as a framework. We will describe it in this chapter, even though it might not be completed now so you'll know what kinds of things to look out for while studying the current process.

The assessment will be summarized in a framework called the case for action, and our improvement goals for the project will be summarized in a process vision. We will combine these with the information we learned during framing the process and produce a process summary poster. Publishing and publicizing this will help us explain the project and keep it on track. We must know the metrics that govern our business process, such as volumes, cycles, and costs, because you can't assess what you can't measure. Let's start there.

Metrics

Metrics, or key performance indicators (KPIs), will give us a feel for the dynamics of the process before diving into the assessment. Even fairly crude metrics will provide useful guidance to focus our efforts. One of us once got well into as-is analysis without having captured the numbers only to discover he had wasted time studying a case (a specific type of shipment) that was insignificant in every way—volume, resources consumed, and revenue. If you don't know how many and how much, do you really know if anything needs to change?

Another important reason to collect metrics is to evaluate success after you have finished—you will need a baseline against which to measure the performance of the new process. In some environments, this is crucial—without hard proof, there's no "good job!" and no support for your next initiative. But take care not to go after inappropriate measures, those that might encourage local optimization at the expense of overall improvement in the new process. Your organization might be awash in statistics, but most statistics probably relate to the performance of individual functions, not the process. Don't stake your assessment on those, or you won't get the results you intend.

For now, collect those metrics that you can, and refine them as you go—you won't be able to develop accurate metrics until after you have completed the as-is modeling. Often, someone such as a DBA[1] can provide statistics, such as volumes, by transaction type. If your organization has a data warehouse relevant to your process, all the better. You might be able to develop some queries that provide the measures you need. Those metrics will depend on the process and the issues that come up in the rest of the initial assessment. Use the lists below to stimulate your thinking about the measures you'll try to locate.

How many?

The essence of statistics is not standard deviations and Durbin-Watson coefficients, it's just counting. You must be able to at least count executions of your process at this point, because if you cannot count the process, either you don't understand it or it isn't a process.

The most basic counts involve volume, for example, 800 per week. Typically, you will want to determine measures such as:

- Total volume or frequency (e.g., new customer enrollments);

- Proportion of different triggers or cases (e.g., new versus reinstatement);

- Proportion of different paths (e.g., straight through versus credit or background check);

- Proportion of different results (e.g., accepted versus rejected).

Got the time?

How much time does it take to complete your workflow? There are three ways to measure its execution: cycle time; work time; and time worked.

---

1. Database administrators: a title commonly used by the people who are responsible for the design and tuning of your database. To tune, they need accurate counts of various record types, although often only at a high level.

Cycle time is the total elapsed time, end to end, from the time the cycle starts or is triggered until the cycle completes with all results accomplished. It is sometimes called calendar time, or wall-clock time for shorter cycles, because it is the time that would pass on the calendar or clock on the wall during the cycle. It is the time measure most obvious and relevant to the customer.

Work time is the time the process is actually being worked on. Most processes have at least some time during which processes are waiting and not being worked on; if all this nonproductive time could be eliminated, cycle time and work time would be the same. This is the goal of straight-through processing. In computers, work time is often called CPU time because this is the time during which the computer's central processing unit (CPU) is actually working on the problem.

Time worked counts the actual work hours of work expended on the process; sometimes more than one person (or other resource) is working on the process at a time: this measure would be the total hours paid for if workers are the resource being measured. If only one person at a time works on the process, work time and time worked are the same. Instead of people work time, you might need to measure work time with another resource, possibly time with a given machine or critical resource, especially if it is a bottleneck in your process. A computer with multiple processors would measure time worked as the CPU time of all the processors combined.

You might also need to measure peaks and valleys—your critical load. Throughout the calendar cycle (day, week, month, year), there are usually times that are busier than others. Statisticians usually call these seasonal variations, because the most obvious variations are those that change with the season of the year. You might want to identify these seasonal variations clearly, and compare the difference between the three execution times (cycle time, work time, and time worked) on the peak versus in the valley. Interesting patterns emerge—in a busy time, time worked can go down significantly because everyone is working so hard, yet cycle times can rise dramatically because of queuing.

These patterns will get even more interesting in terms of improvement opportunity when we track the opposite of execution time—wait time. There are four kinds of wait time: idle, transit, queue, and setup.

During *idle time*, the process is just waiting, perhaps because the work is not on a critical path, or because it has not been routed expeditiously, or just because the process is designed that way. It may be that an actor is working on an unrelated but more important task.

Transit time is the time spent in transit between steps. Strictly speaking, when the work is being moved, that is a step in itself, but no other value is being added other than transport.

Queue time is the time an item is lined up before a critical or bottleneck resource: the work item is ready to go on, but is waiting for the resources for the next step to get to it. In a manufacturing environment, partially finished goods will stack up before a bottleneck machine during queue time.

Setup time is time required for a resource to switch from one type of task to another. This is also most obvious in a manufacturing situation—the operator might need to mount a different bit on a milling machine before beginning work on a new lot of a different product type. It is the same in an office environment when an operator sets up for a new type of transaction, possibly by assembling reference material and supplies, and staying within a specific function on the PC.

After you have done some as-is modeling, you will want to analyze wait time in the different phases of the process, for instance, trigger to initiation (i.e., how long before you even get started on the process) versus the time lapse between steps, concentrating on known delays at first.

With all time measures, you will want to look at several measures: not just average or typical, but best and worst.

Who's involved?

The number of people, organizations, and places involved in your process is a vital concern: for each new involvement, another handoff is required. And each handoff is an opportunity for something to go awry. Some project estimating techniques recommend that you add some percentage, say 25%, to your estimate for your project for each new location involved. This reflects the additional complexity added by multiple locations. If applicable, consider the number of different languages (natural or computer) and possibly time zones involved. Other factors might be applicable to your process, such as labor unions, countries, and cultures.

You won't have precise information until after as-is modeling (it's amazing how many additional actors can be discovered!), but this will be a start. Try listing, and counting, the following for your process:

* People;

* Job classifications;

* Departments;

* Total number of handoffs;

* Labor unions;

* Locations;

* Languages;

* Countries and cultures;

* Whatever else is relevant.

Efficiency

No process is perfect. Typical measures of efficiency and effectiveness include:

* What is the percentage of scrap or rework?

* What is the percentage of errors?

* How many defects are produced, and where are they produced? The later in the cycle they occur, the more costly they are.

* How soon are defects discovered? Early detection is important as it leads to less waste, since all work done on an item that is going to be scrapped is wasted.

* How much iteration does it take to get it right? In the worst case, it is the customer who discovers it.

* How many customer contacts are there to complete the process? Are you contacting the customer to get information you could have collected (or even worse, did collect) before?

* How many compliments and complaints are received?

If appropriate, any of these can be further categorized by type, location, or other criteria.

To count defects and categories, a simple tally sheet is often enough to let you see the problems and opportunities for improvement. Just have the workers have a sheet of paper next to their workspace on which they mark a tally for each type of problem for a few days. Tally as many different ways as you can think of, for example, by type of defect, location, or method. You might be surprised how often the facts, as demonstrated by the tally sheets, were different from perceptions.

Cost

It's not just the bean counters that should be concerned with cost. Consider Goldratt's concept of true cost as expressed in his book, *The Goal* [1]. If a 5-cent gasket is keeping your most critical machine from running, the cost of that idleness could be millions of dollars, not pennies. Get at least a rough measure of the cost per execution, and the cost of defects, both in scrap and rework and in impact on the overall process. Also consider fixed versus variable cost. Fixed costs are those that you will pay even if you produce nothing: for example, rent and property tax. Variable costs are those that vary with output: materials costs, discretionary labor cost, and so forth.

Summary of metrics

So far, we have looked at the following as measurements you might choose to capture (Table 6.1). Avoid any urge to embark on a crusade for the numbers—the intent is to get an indication of process performance observed by the various stakeholders, and possibly where issues originate. Now that we have some objective measures, let's canvas those stakeholders for their assessment of the process.

Assessment by stakeholder

Everyone's a critic...

A stakeholder is any identifiable individual or group who has an interest in the business process. It is absolutely crucial that you assess the performance of the current process from the perspective of *each* group *individually*, and establish process goals for each. Some or most of the assessment will be subjective concerns and impressions, but if you can develop objective metrics, all the better.

Whatever type of process you are studying, there are three stakeholder communities that *must* be accounted for:

Table 6.1
Summary of Metrics

EXECUTING TIME	WAITING TIME	INVOLVEMENT	EFFICIENCY	COST
Cycle time	Idle	People	Scrap	Goldratt's True Cost
Work time	Transit	Departments	Rework	Cost per execution
Time worked	Queue	Handoffs	Defect by type	Cost of defects
	Setup	Job classifications	Errors	Fixed versus variable costs
		Labor unions	Iterations	
		Locations	Customer contacts	
		Languages	Complaints	
		Countries/ cultures	Compliments	
		Whatever else is relevant		

1. Customers (internal or external recipients of a result from the process);

2. Performers (typically employees or contractors);

3. Owners (including shareholders) and managers.

   It may also be appropriate to consider other stakeholder groups:

4. Suppliers;

5. Government or other regulatory agencies;

6. The general public or the community;

7. Industry bodies or trade associations.

Don't guess—ask!

Mentally walking a mile in their shoes would be a good start, but don't *assume* you know what each group wants—go further and *ask!* This is especially true for external customers. We tend to focus on the expectations of owners and performers, probably because we have such close contact. In fact, you'll usually hear plenty without even having to ask. Process customers, on the other hand...well, "we know what they want" is a commonly heard and commonly incorrect phrase. Consider the example of a financial services company that invested heavily in redesigning the process for sending transaction confirmation notices (e.g., for stock trades or asset transfers) to their customers, the account holders. They "knew" that the customer wasn't impressed with the three weeks it took for the notices to arrive, and set a goal of getting them in the mail within 24 hours of the transaction. After implementing the new process, it was found that most customers couldn't care less about turnaround time for these documents—in fact, they didn't want them at all, and were irritated by their arrival. If they thought there was any chance their transaction request hadn't been taken care of, they wouldn't have dealt with this company in the first place. Instead, what the customers had wanted all along was a single consolidated statement that reflected all of the activity for all of their accounts. The financial services company dutifully implemented this, but later (after the main competition) and at greater total expense than if they had checked with their customers in the first place.

The customer

The customer's perspective is of course of prime importance, but surprisingly, many projects never even explicitly consider the customer's perspective. The fact that most computer specifications are written from the viewpoint of the computer ("accept password") instead of the computer user ("enter password") is symptomatic of this problem.

Consider the process's effectiveness from the customer's point of view, but first ask if the actual product or service itself has the right characteristics. This might indicate that the main issues have nothing to do with the process. Then, check with process customers for their stories and impressions, keeping in mind some of the following questions.

How much effort is required of the customer? Does the process require too many interactions (protocol events)? Does the process require the customer to walk the transaction from one part of the organization to another, possibly reciting everything that has happened to date? Is the customer the only one monitoring the process?

CASE STUDY: THE LOUSY LAPTOP

One of us (Alec) recently ordered a replacement for a damaged laptop from one of the top direct-sales computer manufacturers. A trip was coming up which included a lot of time set aside for writing this book! The new laptop was beautiful, but unusable on delivery because of a minor problem. This quickly became serious because the manufacturer's problem resolution process was not supported by any mechanism for internal communication (e.g., between sales, customer service, accounting, and shipping), and had no provision for monitoring follow-up. Other than by the customer, that is. For instance, if the message wasn't received properly by shipping that they were supposed to ship a part, there was no reaction until Alec eventually called asking, "Where is it?" Or the replacement was held pending payment arrangements because accounting didn't know it was a no-charge replacement, and no one knew until—you guessed it—Alec called. A total of about a dozen problems like these arose while days stretched into weeks and months. Ultimately, weeks of time were lost, which had to be made up during the family vacation. This is not the kind of process that creates customer loyalty! Needless to say, when the other one of us needed a new laptop, he ordered from the manufacturer's competitor.

Do the rules and requirements seem reasonable? Could you explain them, with a straight face, to a customer? Do customer-contact staff appear to know what they're doing and have appropriate support? Is information about you and your transaction available to them? Consider your sensitivity to the customer, who asks: "Do these people appear to care about me?" or "Can they adjust service to suit my needs?"

The performers

Consider the viewpoint of the workers or the performers of the tasks that make up the process. A few years ago, we might have referred to this group as "the employees," but now they are just as likely a contracted organization, which can raise its own issues of information availability, process workflow, and measurement. In any case, you might ask "Is this how you'd do it if you had a choice?" or "Does this process help you meet your goals, or does it thwart you?" At one organization, the design of the process ensured, unnecessarily, that an accounting group predictably cycled between total overload and boredom. Customer service was then kept busy resolving errors that had been introduced because of the overload.

But remember, the workers are not the customers. If streamlining the work negatively impacts the customer, or improves a step at the expense of the process, it won't make sense to do it. There is always a tradeoff between the stakeholders' interests, but often on a project the workers are represented while the customers aren't. There is therefore a danger that we will design the best of all possible processes for the workers to no avail since customers desert us.

Managers and owners

Managers and owners (shareholders) must be considered—the process must be efficient and profitable. In a government or not-for-profit setting, the process must still be fiscally responsible. Does the process consume resources that would be better allocated elsewhere? Consider the opportunity cost as well as the actual cost. Opportunity cost is the gain not realized had you done something else with the resource. For instance, while the sales force is correcting errors, it is not selling. The lost sales are opportunity cost. Resources include people, time, money, equipment and facilities, and material and supplies. Does the process generate issues for management to deal with that distract from the important goals of the organization? Owners and managers need to ask: "Is this process contributing to my personal goals, my department's goals, and the enterprise's goals?"

Suppliers

A simple lunch involves products from two dozen or more countries, produced, transported, and processed by what amount to literally thousands of people. The degree of interconnectedness is amazing, and sometimes a small change in one process can bring unexpected changes elsewhere, like a butterfly in Brazil causing a cyclone in the Indian Ocean. Your organization's processes likewise exist in a web of interdependencies, and require the cooperation of suppliers, vendors, and subcontractors. You might ask a supplier questions like "How easy is it to do business with us compared to your other customers?" or "What errors or actions on our part cause difficulties for you?" Flexibility and responsiveness are prime in today's extended supply chain, so how quickly you and the supplier can establish an agreement is critical. You might even find yourself competing for the services of a supplier, as we saw in a Silicon Valley manufacturer recently— for them, supplier service became as important as customer service.

Other groups

The general public has many concerns: ethics, safety, privacy, and the environment. In the end, overlooking these viewpoints can be more costly than addressing them, if only because of public relations and legal considerations. The community may have issues with your involvement in local initiatives. Regulators may seek improvement in how swiftly and accurately your organization responds to information requests, or the number of complaints they handle. Consider the viewpoints of whatever other groups have a legitimate interest in the performance of your process, and above all—don't assume, *ask!*

Look at the process in terms of enablers

Next, we will consider the six enablers that collectively determine how our process behaves, or misbehaves, as the case may be. Generally, we don't look closely at the enablers until *after* modeling and analyzing the as-is process, but there's no harm in conducting a quick assessment beforehand. You need to be aware of the enablers so you know what to look out for during your study of the current process. Let's consider each of the six enablers in turn.

The workflow design

First, consider the current flow of the work. Look at the steps, precedence, flow, handoffs, and decision points to find any bottlenecks, losses, or inefficiencies. At this stage, you probably can't collect enough data to study the problem through complete and careful analysis, but you can ask those involved, "What is the one thing you would do to improve this process?" or "What aspect of this process causes you the most problems?"

Much of the book discusses workflows and gives examples of their use, so we won't look at any examples right now.

Information technology

Two watchwords for the twenty-first century—information and technology. Information technology is primarily manifested as systems, including the interface design, functionality, and information provided. In many cases, the interface includes embedded devices, remote sensing, smart cards, or other technologies unimagined a decade ago. The resulting systems have become critical to businesses at all levels: in many cases, the system *is* the business process.

You must consider the old and the new. What's old and doesn't work. What's new and might work, or has become a necessity. ATMs did not exist two decades ago, but they became a competitive advantage, and then essential—no retail bank would retain its customers without ATMs. The same is true of e-mail and voicemail—they went from nonexistent to essential in a few years. Computers are essential to many companies, and the Internet is not far behind. Cisco Systems processes three-quarters of all orders untouched by human hands. Charles Schwab's major competitor is not other traditional brokers like Smith Barney any more, it's Internet day trader companies.

And computer systems have no lack of downright dumb designs. Unintelligible error messages, confusing layouts, and navigational dead ends are distressingly common. A misplaced concern with machine efficiency has led to many of these: "the greatest programming sins have been committed in the name of computer efficiency."

CASE STUDY: NUMBERS EFFICIENTLY INEFFICIENT

In one case, numbers were substituted for mnemonic letters for the coding of ships in the computer system at a transportation company on the advice of a major accounting and consulting firm. This was in the mistaken belief that "computers are more efficient with numbers."[2] The ship President Kennedy that might have been coded JFK became the 311, and the President Roosevelt, that might be the FDR, became the 113. You can imagine the human and machine time lost to correct items from the Kennedy that were accidentally placed on the Roosevelt—errors that had never been seen when the letter codes were used. And of course Y2K [2], is the classic example of mistaken efficiencies. Although it is true there was once a good argument for storage savings, two-digit years continued to be used long after that argument held.

---

2.   In fact, both codes were stored as Cobol Picture X, which means they were characters to the computer and treated exactly the same in any event.

We not only need to do things right, we need to do the right thing. Many application development projects automate the root cause of a problem, for example, batching, a poorly designed workflow and its paper forms, or an unused report, thereby making it even harder to fix. As always, it's useful to look at a question from multiple perspectives. In this case, the bottom four tiers of our five-tier framework provide a useful guide. From the bottom:

1. Is the right data maintained in the record-keeping (data management) layer, and is the right information being captured from and presented to each step that receives automated support?

2. Are the right activities automated, or receiving automated support?

3. Are the user interfaces, including passive reports or queries, appropriate for the task and for the person using them?

4. Is the flow of work automated (and instantaneous) wherever possible and appropriate?

Motivation and measurement

This enabler includes how people are motivated to perform in a particular way, and how they are measured, which effectively become one and the same thing. C. R. Luigs, the former CEO of Global Marine Drilling, once said something to the effect that people don't pay much attention to what management says; they pay attention to what management measures. Measurement brings with it reward and punishment, which of course people respond to. Within the scope of this enabler, we also include how the process as a whole is measured, if it is at all.

We will spend a little more time on this one, because this is the most important enabler. As long as the other enablers are even barely adequate, this has the most impact on the performance of the process performers. In turn, if this impact is properly directed, it will have the most impact on process performance. We will look at a few examples of how the motivation and measurement schemes affected process performance:

1. At a major metropolitan radio station, sales representatives are measured and rewarded, via the commission check, for the number of ad orders they get. They are not measured (or "punished," via

decreased commissions) for errors in the order specs or pricing, nor are they measured on timely submission of ad orders for production. The consequences are predictable: late, incomplete orders. If there were measurements and rewards in place for landing new customers and for timely submission of ad orders, their behavior, and therefore the behavior of the whole process, would be different. As long as it is adequate, and doesn't distort behavior as it did in this example, nonmonetary measures are usually more important.

2. In one of our favorite examples, seen with minor variations at two different telecommunications corporations, an elaborate new customer service process was implemented, along with supporting information systems. The plan was that this would enable customer service representatives (CSRs) to better deal with the customer's issue, and more important, to "up sell," "cross sell," or even "down sell" other service packages or options. Unfortunately, the effort failed because the company didn't change two key motivation and measurement factors. They continued to penalize CSRs who spent more than 120 seconds on a call (guess how many calls were abruptly—sometimes in mid-sentence—terminated just before the magic 120-second mark). And they continued to pay the CSRs a clerical salary, even though they had to go through extensive sales training to meet their new responsibilities, and were under substantially higher pressure.

3. An internal Quality Control group was measured on the number of defects they discovered. Naturally, no matter how much the rest of the process improved, this group managed to find an ever-increasing number of defects, each of which introduced delay and expense in dealing with it. Copyeditors who are paid or rewarded based on the number of changes they make to an author's manuscript are also an example of this problem.

4. An IT executive once complained to one of us about the poor attitude of the company's Computer Services group, who were responsible for installing and tuning new database applications in a large, high-volume, transaction-processing environment. His complaint: These people seemed to be determined to prevent the

implementation of new applications that were essential to the business plans of the corporation. Their uncooperative attitude became a lot clearer when it was pointed out that these folks were measured on two, and only two, variables: system response time and system up time. Statistics were captured, charted, and distributed to the entire corporation on a daily, weekly, and monthly basis. And what's the surest way to negatively impact response time and up time? You guessed it—install a new application.

Obviously, the question for you is whether the measures of the performers support or impede process goals. This doesn't mean that the new process can simply replace individual measures with process measures—designing a new measurement scheme is subtler than this. Deming warned against mixing performance indicators for the process with evaluation measures for the workers. Just about any crude measure can be a good measure, and adequate to evaluate a process. The danger is when you start motivating individuals based on it. It skews numbers, and ruins the measure. Workers will perform to the measure, not the process, and may even cook the books. Worse, you will skew behavior adversely. Goldratt tells a story of a group that threw out some old machines because of "bad efficiencies" when they were still critically needed to keep production going. And we have all heard of the problems caused when there are incentives to pump up orders close to the end of a financial quarter—too many of them turn out not to be true orders, or orders stolen from coworkers.

Human resources

How do organizational structures, job definition, and skills impact the process? Organizational boundaries may introduce handoffs or segmentation that's undesirable, in the same way that excessively narrow job definitions can. Are people struggling to handle tasks for which they have no training, or worse yet, no natural aptitude?

Looking ahead, will the workforce need to change? Sometimes the only way to change people is to change people. Will new staff skills, training, and job responsibilities be required? Will selection and placement strategies need to change? Will the organizational structure and physical location of the new process be different from the old? Anything that impacts people's definition of themselves ("I am my job") or their network (peers, customers, suppliers, managers, direct reports) can be amazingly disruptive. If redeployment or layoffs might result from your new process, you might face severe morale and then productivity impacts throughout the organization, not just in the process you're working on. Make sure these concerns are addressed honestly and compassionately.

Don't forget the labor unions. In unionized companies, keeping the union involved can be critical. In some airlines and transport companies we've worked in, the work rules were positively Byzantine, impacting the ability to respond to short-term opportunities or temporary changes in conditions. These rules cannot usually be changed without union agreement. You'll need to take into consideration the effect of shifting work from one union to another, or changing the work of the individual workers, especially if it reduces total employment of a union's workers.

Policies and rules

Processes are usually guided by business rules and policies, many of which are now obsolete or for which the original rationale is long since forgotten. Some of these business rules are insidious because they are implemented in systems, while others are implemented in the workflow where they are more visible. "Bad" rules have an effect, because they need to be maintained, make jobs more complex, frustrate customers, and slow down the process. For some examples, just pick up any of Scott Adams' *Dilbert* strips.

These rules and polices don't exist in isolation—they reflect the bias of the organization, or at least they did at one time, and they impact process workflow, IT, and other enablers. For instance, a retail operation might have a bias towards customer service on one hand, or fraud prevention on the other. This will surely lead to different rules, and in turn different workflows. We'll examine this a little more when we look at the environment in the next chapter, but for now, consider a couple of cases.

In our example of the retail operation, there could be a policy that "refunds up to a certain amount can be handled by a sales associate on the retail floor, at their discretion, whether or not the customer has a receipt, and even in cases where we don't carry the product in question." This will have a very different effect than a policy that "all refund requests must be accompanied by a sales receipt and a completed refund reason form; they will be processed by the customer service and AP departments, and a check will be mailed."

Another example would be "requisitions over $1,000 must be approved by a department head, and requisitions over $5,000 must be approved by a department head and a vice president." Both rules manifest themselves in the workflow. These are typical examples of the kinds of rules that are in place. They degrade the process, because the system developers have to know all these, and system changes become a nightmare because the code is unbelievably complex. Customers are frustrated because they never get consistent answers, and so on. Imagine some of the rules in place at your government agencies for taxation, social welfare, and so forth, and imagine the impact on process workflow. In some government agencies we're familiar with, no amount of process redesign can improve customer service above a certain level because the rules established over the decades by successive governments are collectively incomprehensible, inconsistent, and incredibly difficult to implement and maintain.

Facilities

At last, workplace design and physical infrastructure (equipment, furniture, lighting, storage, ventilation, and so forth) is getting more attention. Many offices seem to be designed for anything but getting work done. In fact, for much of the activity in a contemporary organization, you could not design anything worse than a cubicle. There's too much noise and interruption for work requiring intense concentration. A one-on-one meeting or telephone conversation requiring privacy is equally hopeless; the cubicle gives the illusion of privacy, but no privacy—everyone can hear your conversation, but since you can't see them, you're worse off than if you were in the open. And in the age of highly collaborational group works, where discussions and meetings take up most of the day, the cubicle is useless. Meanwhile, the universal shortage of properly equipped meeting rooms continues to grow.

DeMarco and Lister talk about the "Furniture Police" and point out, "…for most organizations with productivity problems, there is no more fruitful area for improvement than the workplace. As long as workers are crowded into noisy, sterile disruptive space, it's not worth improving anything but the workplace." They talk of workers who come in early, stay late, or even call in sick in order to get work done [3]. Space, quiet, privacy, and the ability to avoid interruptions are key productivity enablers that are frequently ignored in modern office layouts.

From what we've seen, you can design and redesign workflows and information systems until the proverbial cows come home, but if you don't address the other four enablers—motivation and measurement, human resources, policies and rules, and facilities—it's all for naught.

Establishing rationale and direction

Everyone involved and affected needs to know what the project is planning to do, and why. That is really all we are going to do here—tell them. And, by making the reasons and goals of the project visible, we will tap into valuable feedback. The *process case for action* is a concise statement of why the current process cannot be left as-is, and the *process vision* articulates the goals for the to-be process. With minor variations, we follow the simple format first described by Hammer and Champy in [4]. Even though they are simple and short (both can fit on a single page), they are extremely useful in uniting people behind the goals of a process improvement project. Of course, at this time it's a good idea to assess whether the project is even feasible or desirable and make a go or no-go decision.

A case for action

Remember the question "Why are we looking at this process, anyway?" —the case for action gives the answer. It is essentially a problem statement, or rationale of what must change and why it must change. The larger and more entrenched the process is, the more essential this step. A good case for action will force an honest appraisal of the current situation—you're trying to sell the project to many people who'd rather not deal with the stress of change, or who honestly think things are fine the way they are. The case for action, as its name implies, encourages movement because it clarifies where you are, and why you can't stay there. It's persuasive, even gripping, but it must also be factual and unexaggerated. Otherwise, your audience will recognize that and discount the project accordingly.

The case must lay out each of the following five points—you can't skip any since the logic will be incomplete if you do. Fortunately, you did a lot of the work when you assessed by stakeholder.

1. *Business context.* What are the changes in the environment that make it necessary to change now? If you have gotten along the old way since the founding of the company, why must you change? Note that we're focusing attention externally, and asking what factors *beyond our control* necessitate change. This is crucial because the effect is that you avoid seeming to blame the current performers or managers. Remember, you must be careful how you describe shortcomings in the process—today's senior managers might have been the process designers! Besides, the process may have worked

just fine when it was implemented, but the environment has changed around it. Perhaps a new Internet-based competitor is gaining market share, or foreign competition is making your price unappealing, or employees are leaving for start-ups, or your business has grown tenfold, or you used to be a division of a conglomerate but now are a separate company.

2. *External problems.* Using the assessment you just completed, what are the problems perceived by the customers or other external stakeholders such as suppliers or regulators? What new requirements are you unable to meet?

3. *Internal problems.* In the same vein, what problems and unmet requirements are described by internal stakeholders, process performers, and owners/managers?

4. *Diagnostics.* What causes the problems you are facing today, and what can you change to eliminate them? Admittedly, this might require deeper investigation, and discovering root causes might become one of the goals of your project, but if you can make some inferences as to causes, you'll be ahead of the game.

5. *Consequences of inaction.* Perhaps most importantly, what will happen if no action is taken? What will happen if you don't do anything? As we've discussed earlier with respect to kaizen, in the competitive economy of today, companies that don't continually adapt and improve face the real possibility of extinction.

A vision

You need to articulate your vision of the new process for all to see. By its nature, the vision is a little fuzzier than the case for action. At this point, we can really only provide an image without detail, although we want to be as specific as possible. Some aspects of the vision are easy to produce, because they are simply the opposite of the assessment that was summarized in the case for action. That is, the vision will describe the perceptions of the stakeholders—the customers, performers, managers, suppliers, and so on—after the new process is in place. On the subjective side, it will also provide an image or feel for what you need to become—the kind of organization you'll be, how you'll operate, and how people will feel about being associated with it. As Hammer and Champy point out, a great vision will complete the phrase "won't it be great when…" Try to be quantitative as well as qualitative—for instance, how will you measure success, and what is the time frame for achieving it.

Another element that's extremely useful is the strategic differentiation of the process. What you're looking for is the answer to the question "Why choose us?" Assume that your process customers could select among several competing processes. You must be able to articulate what would make them select your alternative. Will your process be more flexible, more cost-effective, more convenient, more able to customize the product or service, or what? As it turns out, all processes need to have a style, and knowing this can have a profound effect on design choices later on. This is called "the improvement dimension," because it's the dimension or aspect of your process that will always take precedence when designing improvements. If you're interested, refer ahead to the section in the upcoming chapter.

And finally, don't promise (too much) more than you can deliver. Here's a sample from the "approve customer credit request" process we mentioned earlier:

Case for action

Our Credit Approval process has become a liability. We are now losing market share to our competitors because they can offer fast, hassle-free credit to new or growing customers. Our credit reps spend most of their time on applications from small customers, who generally pose no credit risk; and little time on large applications, where their expertise is really needed.

The specific failings of the current process are that approval takes far too long (up to seven elapsed days), we can't tell the customers where their application is in the process, we have to go back to the customers for additional information, and our most senior resources aren't used where they are needed most.

These deficiencies stem from a paper-based workflow that involves many departments and many stops and starts, policies that force all applications through the same process, and incomplete initial data capture.

Unless this process is improved, our market share will continue to decline until we are forced to withdraw from the market.

Vision

Small customers will receive instant credit approval, up to a predetermined limit, secured by a bank card. Further credit processing will take place after the customer has been set up to place orders. Applications involving higher credit limits will be handled within two days.

Automated support will be developed to provide improved communication with customers, track current applications, and provide supporting information.

Credit administration clerks will receive additional training to enable them to handle smaller applications in their entirety. Credit representatives will spend the majority of their time on applications from large customer and other high-value activities.

Staff will have more responsibility for and control over their work. All customers seeking initial or additional credit, whether large and small, will perceive us as the most responsive supplier, and the easiest to do business with.

One poster is worth a thousand words

Summarizing findings

Now that you know what you are going to do, and why, it is time to evangelize—to go on a road show to explain it to all concerned individuals. A useful tool is the process summary poster, which takes the main elements of framing the process, the case for action, and the vision, and puts them on a single piece of paper or image. The reasons to do so are threefold:

1. A certain percentage of people you need to reach are not going to read more than a one-pager anyway.

2. If you provide contact information, it can encourage valuable feedback.

3. If it's well done, it will be posted in cubicles, halls, notice boards, Web pages, and meeting rooms, where it will help to keep participants on track and in scope.

Prepare your poster in a professional manner, and then distribute it far and wide. Variations on the quadrant format in Figure 6.1 work well. Note that in the lower left, we've listed actors and mechanisms—the systems,

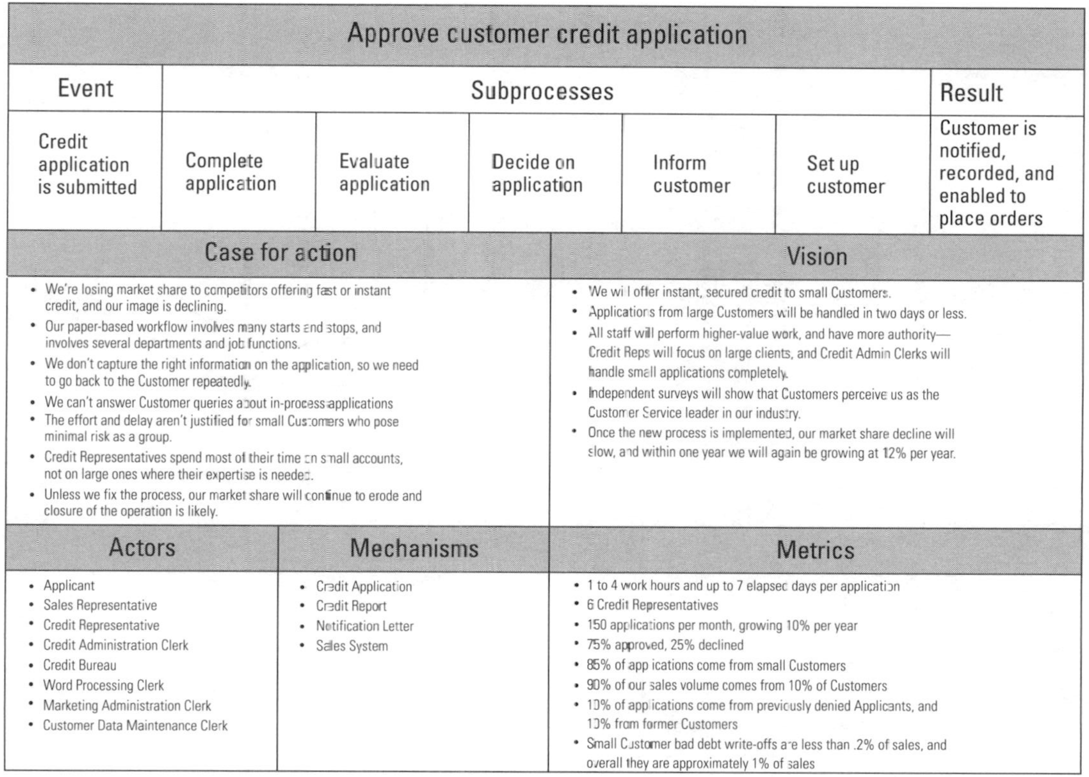

Approve customer credit application

Event	Subprocesses				Result
Credit application is submitted	Complete application	Evaluate application	Decide on application	Inform customer / Set up customer	Customer is notified, recorded, and enabled to place orders

Case for action

- We're losing market share to competitors offering fast or instant credit, and our image is declining.
- Our paper-based workflow involves many starts and stops, and involves several departments and job functions.
- We don't capture the right information on the application, so we need to go back to the Customer repeatedly.
- We can't answer Customer queries about in-process applications.
- The effort and delay aren't justified for small Customers who pose minimal risk as a group.
- Credit Representatives spend most of their time on small accounts, not on large ones where their expertise is needed.
- Unless we fix the process, our market share will continue to erode and closure of the operation is likely.

Vision

- We will offer instant, secured credit to small Customers.
- Applications from large Customers will be handled in two days or less.
- All staff will perform higher-value work, and have more authority— Credit Reps will focus on large clients, and Credit Admin Clerks will handle small applications completely.
- Independent surveys will show that Customers perceive us as the Customer Service leader in our industry.
- Once the new process is implemented, our market share decline will slow, and within one year we will again be growing at 12% per year.

Actors

- Applicant
- Sales Representative
- Credit Representative
- Credit Administration Clerk
- Credit Bureau
- Word Processing Clerk
- Marketing Administration Clerk
- Customer Data Maintenance Clerk

Mechanisms

- Credit Application
- Credit Report
- Notification Letter
- Sales System

Metrics

- 1 to 4 work hours and up to 7 elapsed days per application
- 6 Credit Representatives
- 150 applications per month, growing 10% per year
- 75% approved, 25% declined
- 85% of applications come from small Customers
- 90% of our sales volume comes from 10% of Customers
- 13% of applications come from previously denied Applicants, and 13% from former Customers
- Small Customer bad debt write-offs are less than .2% of sales, and overall they are approximately 1% of sales

Approve Customer Credit Application Poster, summarizing the results of "framing the process"

Figure 6.1 A "poster" summarizing the results of framing the process.

forms, reports, and equipment that support the process. Sometime, we have listed potential enablers (possible improvements) instead, to trigger discussion, but in many environments, it's a bad idea. It can stir up fear and uncertainty, and give people the idea that the outcome is decided, so there's no point in participating. On balance, we'd stick with actors and mechanisms, or whatever factors are relevant in the situation.

Where to now?

Now that we've framed the process, we could move on to studying the current process in detail so we have the understanding to improve it appropriately. That's the goal of Part III.

However, before we get to that, it would be wise to go through one more step, which could have gone just about anywhere up to this point. Just as we assessed the process, we will assess the environment within which the process operates. That way, we will know which factors are beyond the control of the process team—issues such as culture, beliefs, mission, and corporate strengths and weaknesses.

References

[1]   Goldratt, E., *The Goal: A Process of Ongoing Improvement*, Great Barrington, MA: North River Press, 1984.

[2]   McDermott, P., *Solving the Year 2000 Crisis*, Norwood, MA: Artech House, 1998.

[3]   DeMarco, T., and T. Lister, *Peopleware: Productive Projects and Teams*, New York: Dorset House Publishing Company, 1987, pp. 40–43.

[4]   Hammer, M., and J. Champy, *Reengineering the Corporation*, New York: Harper Business, 1993.

7

Considering the Environment

Everything is deeply intertwingled.
            —Ted Nelson, inventor of hypertext
Time for a front-end alignment.
            —Anonymous mechanic
Everything is connected to everything else.
            —The First Law of Ecology

Why bother?

We'll try to keep this short, because when the discussion turns to "squishy" topics like culture, mission statements, and corporate values, a few eyes are certain to glaze over. We notice this especially in our more technical or detail-oriented friends, the ones likely to fidget uncomfortably while the earnest HR executive proudly unveils "our latest statement of vision, values, and aspirations." To be sure, too much posterware, shelfware, and meetingware has been produced around topics like these, but the fact is, they *do* matter to the business of process improvement. A process that is designed without regard to the skills, attitudes, and behavioral norms of an organization will fail just as surely as one with a poorly designed workflow or information system. A few examples usually have even the hardest-headed technicians nodding in agreement—here is an obvious one that comes to mind:

An example

A consulting firm spearheaded the development of a new process for resolving disputes at a government licensing organization. The bright, young consultants working on the project were inexperienced in the ways of large government organizations, but were convinced, having just taken the course, that empowered work teams were the way to go. That became the basis for the new process, which was a complete failure. The process design looked just fine, but it was totally at odds with the culture of the agency. People were used to working alone, applying very prescriptive policies in narrowly defined jobs, under close supervision. There was nothing in their background that would prepare them for working collaboratively on creative solutions that do the right thing for all stakeholders. These were all intelligent people who wanted to do a good job, but you can't just sweep away the conditioning that comes with 10, 20, or even 40 years of working in a particular environment. Perhaps the Change Management course the consultants had been on did not make clear just how difficult issues of culture really are. Just as ineffective are processes that don't align with the strategy and goals of the enterprise, but we will skip further examples for now.

What we will cover

This chapter covers an array of topics, showing how to identify the basic issues of environment and culture that will affect a project. We will cover:

1. Mission and strategy, especially strategic differentiation;

2. Organizational culture;

3. Core competencies;

4. Miscellaneous questions for establishing business context and focus.

The thread that unites these topics is that they look outside of the process. They encourage a little soul searching and investigation so you understand the business environment, and how your project will help your organization achieve its goals. Having process goals is vital—to get where you want to go, you need to know where that is. But you also need to know what support and resistance you're likely to encounter along the way, the skills and attitudes of the people you are working with, and the grand scheme into which your process will fit.

These topics will be critical when you get to process redesign and implementation, but also in earlier stages. They provide a context for establishing process goals, and are essential for understanding the current process. For instance, a process design feature that would make no sense at all in one organization may prove to be the best choice at another.

Because there isn't a specific point in our methodology where you will "study environment," we had trouble placing this chapter. That reflects how you will use this material on your project—not at a single point, but as questions that you'll keep in mind throughout, recording information as it arises. In Chapter 3's overview, we suggest looking at the mission and strategy of the enterprise while *framing the process*, and then documenting culture, core competencies, and strategic discipline while *understanding the as-is process*. The information you gather will be critical when you are *characterizing the to-be process*, when improvement suggestions have to be evaluated in the context of skills, culture, goals, and so on. If you are familiar with the organization (e.g., you work there), you will be able to document the environment earlier in the project. If you are new to the organization (e.g., this is your first consulting assignment there), you will do this later after you have had more exposure to the environment.

And now, the disclaimers. Each topic could span volumes on its own, so our brief treatment will not be at the level you'd get in, say, an M.B.A. class on strategy or organizational development. And we're not pretending to be experts in these areas—we barely qualify as dilettantes. We can, however, say that the simple questions and frameworks provided here have helped immeasurably in guiding us on process improvement, application development, and other consulting assignments.

Mission, strategy, and goals

Business mission, strategy, goals

In general, what you need to know is why the business exists, what it hopes to achieve, and what it will do in order to hit those targets. This is a broad area, and many terms and concepts arise: mission, mandate, values, vision, goals and objectives, strategy and tactics, critical success factors, differentiation, stakeholder analysis, shareholder value, and so on. We will just provide an indication of the main questions that need to be considered, for two reasons:

1. The project team must share a clear understanding of the mission, strategy, and goals of the enterprise that the improved process must support.

2. Each individual process has its own mission, strategy, and goals, which also must be articulated, clearly understood, and aligned with those of the enterprise.

Now, let's get a little more specific with our terminology.

Mission

The mission articulates why the business exists in a more specific way than make money, fulfill legislative mandate, or promote special interests. In their Articles of Incorporation, corporations claim their purpose is "to engage in any lawful act or activity for which a corporation may be organized under the Law," but whether stated explicitly or not, every organization exists to do some things, and, just as importantly, not others. The essence of the enterprise's mission is a statement of "what we do, and who we do it for"—specifically, the products and services provided and the markets and customers served. There may also be an indication of the style in which the enterprise conducts business, or there might be a specific statement of style for each stakeholder group: customers, employees, owners, investors, communities, and so forth.

Strategy

Closely related to the mission is the way we define strategy, which is the specific competitive space the enterprise intends to occupy. Any enterprise should ask itself the following questions: Why would a customer choose us in the face of similar offerings? What strategic discipline do we use to differentiate our products and services? Is it low price, convenience, flexibility, innovative products, or what? Without knowing the answers, how can you focus your business processes? Surprisingly, we can also apply this concept in monopolies and government organizations where there doesn't appear to be a choice. We also use it in specifying the improvement dimension or philosophy for individual processes.

Goals

In order to focus its efforts and gauge its progress, an organization will establish goals (overriding performance targets) and objectives (intermediate targets). Try to make these as specific as possible, using the topic, target, time frame framework mentioned earlier.

Applying MSG to your project

Mission statements come in all styles and formats. Some follow the format we suggest, and others are very different. Here are a few examples that get their point across nicely, even if they don't follow the format we suggest:

> *Bill Gates: A computer on every desk running Microsoft software.*
>
> *Infantry: Seek out, close with, and destroy the enemy.*
>
> *Intel: Do a great job for our customers, employees, and stockholders by being the preeminent building block supplier to the worldwide Internet economy.*

Your organization may have a well-formulated mission statement, one that is too ambiguous to be useful, or none at all. The actual mission statement is not as important as knowing what your enterprise is all about, and what differentiates it from others. Using whatever resources are available, your team has to be able to answer the following questions:

1. "Which customers or markets do we—or should we—serve?"

2. "Which products or services do we—or should we—serve them with?"

3. "What differentiates us?" or, more clearly, "Why choose us over competitors or alternative providers?"

Given that there probably is not a lot of confusion over services and customers, our interest is primarily in the third question, "Why choose us?" which is the essence of strategy. Different strategies call for entirely different processes, with very different characteristics. The underlying information systems will also require different characteristics. Consider a couple of examples:

1. Two organizations were each in the business of providing corporate training, and many individuals have attended workshops and seminars from both. However, they were highly differentiated. One was a mass-marketer of $99-a-day seminars for administrative and support staff, while the other specialized in developing and delivering customized training for high-tech sales forces.

2. Two transportation companies were headquartered in the same West Coast city, and other than ostensibly being in the same industry, that was where the similarity ended. One specialized in cross-border trucking of agricultural products. The other specialized in "secure, discreet, worldwide" handling of small shipments—not necessarily fast, but secure from the prying eyes of competitors.

In both cases, the organizations were in the same industry but they certainly weren't in the same business. And of course, they had totally different business processes operating with totally different styles.

Strategic discipline

A particularly useful framework for looking at this issue was provided by Treacy and Wearsma in [1]. In studying the leading companies in a variety of industries, they discovered that the leaders had specifically chosen to excel in one of three disciplines. The "also-rans" had made no such choice, or tried to be great at all three. The choices are:

1. Operational excellence—Wal-Mart strives to provide the lowest cost product and convenient shopping experience through efficiency of operation.

2. Product leadership—Sharper Image provides a variety of leading-edge specialty and electronic products.

3. Customer intimacy—Nordstrom spends time with each customer to ensure they get what they need or want, and will tailor the shopping experience to individual customers.

Table 7.1 summarizes the three disciplines [2].

Market leaders choose one discipline to concentrate on, and build around it. Of course, organizations should be good at the other two as well, but it is important to understand it is not possible to be great in more than one discipline at a time, and certainly not all three.[1] By knowing which discipline they are focusing on, organizations have a wonderfully clear signpost for decision-making. This is another concept that applies to the enterprise but scales down nicely and applies to individual processes. Understanding the intended strategic discipline of a process makes design decisions far easier; otherwise, discussions can go back and forth endlessly. That's what had happened in the following example.

Table 7.1
Strategic Disciplines

| The Three Disciplines | | |
Operational Excellence	Product Leadership	Customer Intimacy
Core business processes that... Sharpen distribution systems and provide no-hassle service	Nurture ideas, translate them into products, and market them successfully	Provide solutions and help customers run their business
Structure that... Has strong, central authority and a finite level of empowerment	Acts in an ad-hoc, organic, loosely knit, and ever-changing way	Pushes empowerment close to the point of customer contact
Management systems that... Maintain standard operation procedures	Reward individuals' innovative capacity and new product successes	Measure the cost of providing service and of maintaining customer loyalty
Culture that... Acts predictably and believes "one size fits all"	Experiments and thinks "out of the box"	Is flexible and thinks "have it your way"

---

1. By the way, this isn't a "forever" decision—at least one of our clients had clearly mastered one of these disciplines, but in a maturing market has chosen to excel at another.

Strategic discipline in action

We had an experience with a large medical services organization where a major reengineering project had stalled.[2] We were called in to determine what caused the decided lack of progress on the project. The first day, suspecting conflicting goals were a factor, we took the project team through an explanation of the three disciplines, and then asked, "Which of the three disciplines has your organization historically concentrated on?" There was unanimous agreement—product leadership. There was also unanimous agreement the focus had to change as a result of market pressures and government regulatory involvement, and the new, core process they were working on had to stress the same discipline. However, exactly half the team felt the new concentration should be operational excellence—provide standard health care as consistently and cost-effectively as possible. The other half felt it should be customer intimacy—provide the most flexible, personalized health care for each individual patient. As they say in the consulting business, "Sometimes you earn your pay the first day." Without further prodding, it was obvious to everyone why the project was stalled—every proposed feature of the new process seemed to yield a discussion that went around in circles, back and forth, over and under, but never towards a decision. There had been such poor progress on the project because the goals were essentially at odds with themselves.

If your project team does not agree on the project's strategic goals, some or all of you will be disappointed in the results. If your differences are great enough, the entire project will likely fail as you tear it apart pulling in opposite directions.

If this topic interests you, you owe it to yourself to read [3]. It takes a long-term look (often spanning more than a century) at pairs of companies in the same business that were once in similar circumstances but where one is now far more successful. This book has been able to isolate a number of habits or behaviors of the great companies that are consistent across time, industry, and geography.

Faster, cheaper, better, or what?

This is a good place to address one of the most common mistakes we see, because it relates directly to the differentiator or style of a process. That

---

2. Actually, only one of us was involved, but we will use the royal "we" in this tale, and throughout the book.

mistake is assuming that the goal is simply to make the process faster and cheaper. However, like quality, that's almost a given. Don't assume that your goal is necessarily to lower costs, increase efficiency, and reduce cycle time. That *might be* the goal, and in some projects, it *is* the goal. But in many competitive environments, simply doing the same thing faster and cheaper will not make anything better. Even the most efficient blacksmith shops have been unable to thrive since the appearance of the automobile—don't buy a new bellows when you should get a gas pump! If your competitive environment has changed drastically, you might need to fundamentally rethink what you are doing, not just how you are doing it. A process that does the wrong things faster doesn't really help—we don't need rack-and-pinion steering and disk brakes on the horse buggy.

One of our colleagues has recently encountered two situations where the goal was to *increase* cycle times. Both were in similar areas—legal settlements and arbitration—and both had recently been the subjects of a process redesign that squeezed the cycle time down to the minimum. Unfortunately, the professionals involved also found out that the think time and cooling-off time had been squeezed out as well. As often as not, this escalated the dispute to the point that it actually took longer than it would have before the redesign, and participants were less satisfied with the outcomes! A classic example of haste makes waste.

Along with faster and cheaper, other process improvement goals that we have seen include:

- Flexible in meeting needs of individual customers;
- Easier for an entry-level workforce to adopt with relatively little training and support;
- Fewer customer interactions;
- Absolute auditability and adherence to applicable regulations;
- Accessible anytime, anywhere, via any medium;
- Easier to standardize and maintain at international locations;
- Less time and effort to integrate new suppliers or customers into the process;
- More suitable for support by commercial off-the-shelf (COTS) software.

So, you must set aside the notion that squeezing time, cost, and effort out of the process is automatically the goal, and identify the differentiator or strategic discipline for the process that best fits the enterprise's mission, strategy, and goals. Then ask, "What specific process characteristics will yield a significant advantage in achieving this differentiation?"

Think about a process you work with. Does it have a clear differentiator? If so, is it appropriate for current conditions, or should a new focus be established? And finally, what process characteristics (think in terms of the six enablers) would be most helpful?

Of course, once you have established the initial goals, you have to make success measurable by establishing relevant goals in topic, target, time frame format. For instance, for the goal of integrating new customers or suppliers, we would expect to see a goal that quantified how long it will take to integrate a new customer, and when that goal will be achieved.

Beliefs and culture

Another huge topic we'll reduce to a few paragraphs and a list of questions. Let's begin with a definition—French and Bell offer a good one: "By... culture...we mean prevailing patterns of values, attitudes, beliefs, assumptions, expectations, activities, interactions, norms, and sentiments (including feelings) and as embodied in artifacts. By including artifacts we include technology in our definition." [4] All organizations have a culture, whether it is explicitly stated or unconscious. You might regard it as negative or positive, as did one client who stated, "At our organization, culture is spelled with a K." In any case, you ignore it at your peril.

We have already given an example where a process didn't match the culture or skills of the organization, and therefore failed. But cultural misalignment can derail a project well before then. If the methods you employ in a project don't match the culture of the organization, any number of problems will arise. For instance, in one organization, it was a career-limiting move (CLM) to disagree publicly with anyone further up the hierarchy, even if everyone present knew that a statement was patently untrue or sheer fantasy. Clearly, the extensive use of facilitated sessions that we generally rely on was not going to work.

In a similar situation, one of us made a misstep that almost resulted in a project being canceled. A vice president of operations was in attendance, and everyone else seemed to be particularly docile. The vice president then made a statement that was so clearly wrong-headed, we thought he must have made it in order to stir up some discussion. We obliged by offering some alternative ideas. Whoops—wrong move. The vice president exploded in anger, and began walking out after noting, in colorful language, that the project ought to be canceled if we couldn't get our heads screwed on straight. Only a brave finance manager was able to calm him down. But in another organization, youthful and high-tech, with an almost opposite culture, we were initially startled by the constant challenge of ideas by everyone at a project initiation meeting, no matter whose idea it was. Again, that was just the culture in action—challenge, sometimes for its own sake, was considered the best way to develop the best ideas.

Clearly, culture has a huge impact, and—let's face it—it's not going to change without a huge effort championed by the most senior executives. So, you should take at least a few minutes to describe it. Not a big study—in some cases, a mere 30 minutes of work is all it takes to get real benefits. Sometimes, there's a bit of a chicken-and-egg situation—if you're an outsider, you need to know something about the culture before you can decide how to go about discovering it. If so, observe for a while or arrange a discussion with a few trusted insiders. Then, based on your findings, you might either arrange a session with your project team or conduct a series of private interviews. In either case, don't fall into the trap of believing, without verifying, official statements on the subject. We worked with an insurer that professed to have "an open, inclusive culture that embraced informed risk-taking and valued the ideas and contributions of all...." As it turned out, it was a risk-averse, exclusionary, command-and-control hierarchy that wanted everyone to keep quiet and do as told.

Everything stems from beliefs

Behavior at the aforementioned organization was motivated by a small number of central beliefs, including "management thinks, workers do." We find time and again that organizational behavior—what it does and how it does it—stems from a few basic beliefs, which we can also call assumptions or *paradigms*. Identifying these assumptions is so important that Chapter 1 of Peter Drucker's recent book [5] is "Management's New Paradigms." The first paragraph states: "BASIC ASSUMPTIONS ABOUT REALITY are the PARADIGMS of a social science, such as management. They are usually held subconsciously by the scholars, the writers, the teachers, the practitioners in the field. Yet those assumptions largely determine what the discipline—scholars, writers, teachers, practitioners—assumes to be reality." Drucker goes on to explain about paradigms: "They decide what in a given discipline is being paid attention to and what is neglected or ignored." And most important to our point here—"Yet, despite their importance, the assumptions are rarely analyzed, rarely studied, rarely challenged—indeed rarely even made explicit."

Drucker is dealing with the entire discipline of management, and outlines seven prevailing assumptions that need to be challenged. Our focus is a little narrower—make explicit whatever beliefs, guiding principles, or paradigms you can at the organization you are working within. This shouldn't be—it *can't* be—a major undertaking that distracts from the purpose at hand. But it will indicate areas of opportunity or constraint. If some of the beliefs are "there's always a better way," "we have a bias towards informed action," and "decision-making should be close to the action," then you are looking at an interesting project with many opportunities.

On the other hand, at one organization we ran an executive planning session, and the beliefs that emerged were "our clients are trying to cheat us, the public misunderstands us, and the media is out to get us." Unstated, but evident, was "and our employees couldn't care less." Whew! That certainly constrained the improvement options. At another session, the guiding principle was that above all, process and procedure (in the negative sense) had to be followed. That meant everyone could be engaged in the proverbial death march towards certain failure, and fully aware of it, but that was fine as long as protocol was obeyed.

Other cultural traits

After you have considered the issue of beliefs, you can ask a short list of questions to identify cultural traits that will impact both the methods you use on your project, and the characteristics of the new process.

1.   Are there stories or corporate legends that provide instructive examples? These might not be the stuff of Greek mythology—perhaps it's the tale of the killer product developed in the skunk works, but it just as well could be the story of Ernie working all weekend, writing checks by hand, to get the payroll out after a catastrophic system failure.

2. What factors continually get in the way? Examples that we have encountered include the slow pace of decision-making, political interference, the motivation and reward system, fear of change, a headlong rush to action, or the urge to study every point to death.

3. What factors are seen as expediting progress? This is often a shorter list than the preceding one, but might include being free to make the right decision to satisfy a customer, never focusing on the short term at the expense of the long term, or always being given adequate time, resources, and authority to complete a job.

4. How are decisions made? From the top, as in the classic hierarchy, or is there more empowerment? And is there a greater emphasis on intuition or facts?

5. Are all employees free to offer opinions or challenge decisions made by their managers?

6. Is the orientation towards the individual or the group? This can have a huge impact on the pace of decision-making—in some group-oriented organizations and cultures, progress can seem glacial because every decision requires soliciting everybody's input or calling a meeting. On the upside, rash decisions made without critical information can be avoided, and once a decision is made, it is implemented smoothly.

7. Whose opinion is valued? In one company we worked at, we were reminded daily that "We're a marketing organization," and those who were close to customers and markets were the opinion leaders. At a different, techno-centric organization, we were told, "The geeks shall inherit the earth."

8. Are there any identifiable behaviors that are rewarded or punished? Note that reward (like punishment) can be explicit: positive job evaluations, promotions, raises, awards; or implicit—praise, attention by management, input solicited for decisions, plum assignments.

9. Is there a high tolerance for ambiguity? If there is low tolerance, then activities must be tightly scheduled, jobs well defined, lots of facts assembled for decisions, and so on.

10. Does the organization favor results or following procedure?

11. Is the organization cautious or will it take risks? Collins and Porras note that one of the habits of visionary companies is that they set BHAGs—Big Hairy Audacious Goals.

12. Is the emphasis on relationships and social interactions, or on tasks and getting on with the job?

You do not need to answer all of these, and they are not the only questions. After you get a feel for an organization, use this list as a starting point to develop your own inquiries.

Core competencies

What are we really good at?

C. K. Prahalad and Gary Hamel introduced a new phrase core competencies—into the language of business in their landmark *Harvard Business Review* article [6]. In it, the authors demonstrated that world-class organizations had up to five or six core competencies that formed the platform on which their core products and services were based. Some of their observations parallel the advantages of process-orientation over functional-orientation:

- "Core competence is the collective learning in the organization, especially the capacity to coordinate diverse production skills and integrate streams of technologies. It is also a commitment to working across organizational boundaries." And...

- "Organizing around strategic business units is problematic because they under-invest in core competencies, imprison resources, and bind innovation."

A good example is 3M, with products like Scotch tape, Post-Its, diskettes, sandpaper, and many others that are thin and involve coatings. 3M's core competencies, as described by Hamel and Prahalad, are:

- Substrates;

- Coatings;

- Adhesives.

Canon's core products are based on core competencies in:

* Precision mechanics;

* Fine optics;

* Microelectronics.

Again, we will take a concept that applies at the enterprise level and scale it down to the level of processes or areas within the enterprise. The people, departments, functions, and jobs that will "work" the process have areas of strength—core competencies. We remember the CEO of a manufacturing company bemoaning, "I don't think we *have* any core competencies," but he was wrong. Even in widely criticized government organizations like the one cited at the beginning of this chapter, there are areas of strength. In that case, it was high-volume transaction processing, as long as the right transaction got to the right job function. They were also very good at internal administrative processes. That was not likely to change in our lifetime, so the only sensible path was to design processes that played to the strengths of the performers and minimized the impact of weaknesses.

As in the section on culture, we suggest developing an explicit list of strengths (and weaknesses, if you're feeling brave) for the areas your process will span.

Some questions to get started with

While we're on the topic of making lists...

As you can tell, we love frameworks and lists, especially at the outset of a project. They certainly aren't the only questions we ask, but they help to get the conversation started and to be sure we cover the bases. So, whether you are experienced or not, you might find some interesting ideas in two additional lists, both of which fit in here because they help to understand scope and context for your project.

Questions for establishing scope, objectives, and constraints

This next one is our default list of questions for getting started on a new development project. It started as seven questions to start a project—we analysts are always trying to get things into lists of seven—but it has grown over the years:

1. What is the primary business objective driving this project?

    • Business improvement, regulatory compliance?

    • How will benefits be measured? Using the topic, target, time frame method, for example, "throughput time will be reduced 25% within six months of implementation"?

2. What is the current situation?

    • Is there a particular problem or factor that motivated this project?

    • In general terms, how does the operation currently work?

    • Why is that not good enough anymore?

3. Is this essentially a business process improvement project? If so…

    • Which cross-functional business process(es) will or will not be supported?

    • What triggers the beginning of each business process, and what is the result (the completion criteria)?

    • How would stakeholder groups (especially customers, performers, and managers) each assess the current process for both strengths and weaknesses (specific areas to consider include cycle time, quality, employee satisfaction, flexibility, consistency, or whatever other variable may be important)?

    • Are there aspects of the current process that work especially well?

    • Are there areas that clearly need improvement, including job definition, tools and facilities, use of IT, information availability, performance measures, workflow design, training, or anything else?

    • What would be the main characteristics of the improved process, and what would differentiate it from a similar process at another organization?

    • How would success be measured? (Use the topic, target, time frame framework wherever possible.)

4. What is the technical or project objective?

    • Is a new application to be developed, existing ones enhanced or integrated, a commercial off-the-shelf (COTS) application selected and installed?

• THIS ONE IS CRITICAL—*Who* will use the application to do *what* (e.g., "Customers will use the system to check product stock levels")? This includes any use, from processing transactions to obtaining information via queries or reports.

5. Which business data will or will not be involved?

   • Business data areas (topics independent of current files or databases)?

   • Specific files or databases?

6. Organizationally, who will be impacted by this?

   • Which departments, job functions, or specific operating locations?

7. What areas outside of the process will be impacted, or will require interfaces?

   • Sources —where will data or work arrive from?

   • Sinks—where will data or work be passed to? Note—the earlier you can determine how much integration (interfacing) and conversion work will be needed, the better. Experience shows that these two areas often account for 70% to 80% (and even more!) of the development effort. If you don't budget for this work, you will end up in trouble!

8. Are there other initiatives we should be aware of?

   • Related projects?

   • Previous efforts (has this application been attempted previously? —if so, why didn't it succeed the first time, is there resistance to the initiative, and is there existing material we can utilize)?

9. What could go wrong?

   • How would we deal with it?

10. What could go right?

   • Would unexpected success or growth cause problems for us (e.g., inability to scale up the process, application, or platform)?

11. Have any significant issues or difficulties arisen?

      • Conflict, policy decision required, technical difficulty?

12. Are there any constraints we need to take into account?

      • Deadlines, regulations, strategy, security, audit, control?

      • Resources: staff, space, equipment, budgets?

      • Of the three main variables—scope, time frame, and resources—which are fixed, and which are elastic?

13. Have any important decisions already been made?

      • Approach, hardware or software platform, system integrator?

14. Have project structure and personnel been identified?

      • Project leader, analysts, business representatives, etc.?

      • Who is involved versus who should be involved?

15. Are you really the sponsor? (Be careful how you word this!)

      • Do you have the final say on scope, resources, acceptance?

      • What is the priority of this project—how important is it to you?

It matters!

We hope that this chapter has illustrated the importance of considering factors outside the strict scope of your business process—the environment. And further, we hope that although brief, it has given you some tools to clarify the environment you'll be working in, because *it really makes a difference!*

And now, at long last, let's get into the central topic of modeling the workflow of business processes.

References

[1] Treacy, M., and F. Wiersma, *The Discipline of Market Leaders*, Reading, MA: Addison-Wesley, 1995.

[2] Table adapted from *Fortune*, Feb. 6, 1995, p. 96.

[3] Collins, J. C., and J. I. Porras, *Built to Last: Successful Habits of Visionary Companies*, New York: HarperBusiness, 1994.

[4]   French, W. L., and C. H. Bell, Jr., *Organization Development: Behavioral Science Interventions for Organization Improvement,* Englewood Cliffs, NJ: Prentice-Hall, Inc., 1984.

[5]   Drucker, P. F., *Management Challenges for the 21ˢᵗ Century,* New York: HarperBusiness, 1999.

[6]   Prahalad, C. K., and G. Hamel, "The Core Competence of the Corporation," *Harvard Business Review*, May–June 1990, pp. 79–91.

Part III
Swimlane Diagrams—Nuts and Bolts

8

Workflow Process Modeling

Swimlane diagrams—what and why

This chapter covers the nuts and bolts—or the boxes and lines—of a workflow process model (WPM) or swimlane diagram. It provides the rules and guidelines for using the basic components—actors, steps, branching, and flow—and the next two chapters will preempt any difficulties by addressing the problems you will surely encounter. Chapter 9 illustrates techniques for managing detail, and Chapter 10 addresses the most common questions and difficulties. Throughout each of these three chapters, we encourage you to experiment with modeling parts of processes you are already familiar with—modeling from memory, as it were—to get a feel for the techniques. Chapter 11 will tell you how to build a workflow model with the participation of content experts. You can take a stab at mapping your own, complete business processes as you go through this chapter, or wait until you've read any of the chapters up to Chapter 11.

What is the attraction?

There are several formats for diagramming a business process, but like most people in the business, we opt for the swimlane diagram format. As described in Chapter 3, swimlane diagrams have become very popular because they highlight the relevant variables—who, what, and when—in a simple notation that requires little or no training to understand. Because they specifically show the actors who are involved in the process, a higher level of involvement and "buy-in" is likely.

Swimlane diagrams can show an entire business process from beginning to end and can be used both to understand the as-is workflow, and to design and depict the to-be workflow. It can show a process at any level, from a very high view down to one showing each individual task. These diagrams also ensure discussions are grounded in fact, because they depict what *really* happens for the as-is, or what is *actually* proposed for the to-be. This is crucial, because in practice virtually no one ever understands a complete business process, or even has a fully accurate understanding of their neighborhood in the process. All of this supports assessment—we can map, measure, and interpret, before or after implementation.

The basics

These diagrams, with slight variations, go by many names:

- Process map;

- Process responsibility diagram (PRD);

- Responsibility process matrix (RPM);

- Functional deployment chart;

- People-process chart;

- Line of visibility (LOV) chart;

- Activity diagram in Unified Modeling Language (UML).

In this book we stick with the terms swimlane diagram and workflow process model.

Swimlane diagrams show what is done, by whom, and in what sequence—"who does what, and when." Another way to look at it is, "Workflow can be defined as the flow of information and control in a business process." [1] Some authors describe a workflow model as depicting the three Rs: roles, rules, and routes [2], or routes, roles, and rules [1]. We prefer to think of the three Rs as roles, responsibilities, and routes:

- *Roles* are the actors or process performers who participate in the process.

- *Responsibilities* are the individual tasks that each actor is responsible for.

- *Routes* are the workflows and decisions that connect the tasks together, and therefore define the path that an individual work item will take through the process.

As Figure 8.1 shows, each actor in the process gets its own labeled swimlane, delineated by dotted lines. Each task is represented by a box placed in the swimlane of the actor that does it. Arrows indicate the sequence and flow of tasks.

At this point, you may be wondering, "If these diagrams are so simple and intuitive, why do we need an entire chapter, much less three chapters, to explain them?" The answer is that reading a properly done swimlane diagram is straightforward, but producing one is not—many situations arise that are not obvious how to depict. Let's look at an example that illustrates the common questions.

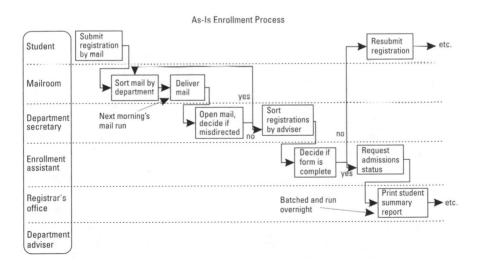

Figure 8.1 A swimlane diagram.

An example—the really big telephone company

At the Really Big Telephone Company (RB Tel), all sorts of people and departments are involved in customer contact activities. Analysts have determined the responsibilities of various departments, as described in the following paragraphs. You'll get more out of the coming chapters if you take 15 minutes now to develop a simple swimlane diagram from this information as an exercise.

Customer service...

...is primarily responsible for assisting customers who are having difficulty with an RB Tel service. When a customer calls RB Tel's main customer service number, they respond to prompts from an interactive voice response (IVR) unit, and service difficulties are routed to the next available Service Rep (other matters—billing, service, disconnect, employment—are routed to the appropriate department). The Service Rep identifies the customer and enters this information on a call log record (CLR) form. After the customer describes the problem, the call can be handled in a number of ways. If the customer simply doesn't know how to use a particular feature, such as call forwarding, the Service Rep will assist the customer, and record the details in the call log. (If the customer also asks about products or services, that is noted in the call log as well.) The CLR is then placed in the Rep's "completed" tray. If the Rep concludes that the problem is equipment related, or requires a software change at the Central Office switch, the call is transferred to Repair Services, and the CLR is placed in the "pending resolution" tray. If the customer needs phone service connected, disconnected, or changed, the call is routed to a New Service Specialist, also within Customer Service; CLRs are also placed in the "pending resolution" tray. Note that when New Service Specialists deal with a call that was transferred from a Service Rep, they complete a form describing how the call was resolved and so the Service Reps can close out their "pending resolution" CLRs.

The CLRs are picked up twice a day, and sent to Marketing Support, which is essentially a data entry department. They are entered into the service tracking system, and any that were pending resolution are printed and sent back to Customer Service, to await information from other departments that handled the call.

Repair service...

...is staffed by Inside Repair Technicians who handle trouble reports from customers who have either called directly or been transferred from another area such as Customer Service. In either case, the customer describes the problem, and the technician attempts to solve the problem using Xcheck, a sophisticated remote diagnostic system. Eighty percent of the time, they determine that the situation can be resolved by Central Office Technicians working on the switching software, so the diagnosis information is sent to them. The other 20% of the time, Outside Repair Services are brought on the line, and an appointment is made for an Outside Repair Technician to visit the customer's premises. In all cases when a call originated with Customer Service, any department that handled the call is expected to complete a form detailing their involvement and send it to Customer Service to record the resolution.

Service analysis...

...takes the call logs from Customer Service, and analyzes them, looking for opportunities to "up-sell" the customer. That is, they look for cases where the customer's inquiry indicates that they would benefit from subscribing to an additional service, such as a billing plan or call alert. Each prospect is written up on a "lead sheet." If Service Analysis feels more information is needed about the customer, they contact Market Database Research. The additional information provided by Market Database Research is added to the lead sheet if they still feel that the customer warrants an up-selling call. Otherwise, the lead sheet is discarded.

Telemarketing...

...takes the lead sheets produced by Service Analysis and contacts the prospects, trying to sign them up for a new service. They also generate their own lead sheets, using research from a number of sources. If a prospect commits to buying new service, the call is transferred to a New Service Specialist to finalize the details.

Market database research...

...handles a wide variety of queries from other departments who seek information about specific people or organizations (customers or prospects), the marketplace and industry in general, or on specific competitors.

They will examine the company's records to obtain further information on a customer, as when a customer has been targeted for up-selling, or when someone in the sales force needs additional information. They will often make use of external sources as well, such as government agencies, commercial information providers, or the Internet. A new line of business involves handling queries and research assignments from external customers.

RB Tel—questions raised

If you're like most people, you will encounter many stumbling blocks in trying to turn the preceding narrative into a workflow model. Of course, the first question should have been "What is the process we're looking at, and why are we looking at it?" but we didn't trick you, did we? You know that jumping into workflow modeling without having a clearly defined process is a surefire route to difficulties. Other than "What's the process here?" the questions raised by this scenario are:

"How do I show…"

+ Branching?

+ Optional steps?

+ The role played by systems or mechanisms such as the IVR:

  • When we hand off control to the system?

  • When the system is used to support an activity, but isn't given control?

+ Interaction with other processes?

+ The appropriate level of detail?

+ Activities such as a conversation that involve multiple actors (activities that span multiple swimlanes)?

+ Questions or comments?

+ Steps that do not happen in any particular order, but must all be completed before a subsequent step can begin?

+ Steps that interact continuously, or iterate?

+ Steps that are triggered by the clock ("temporal events")?

♦ Steps carried out by an actor who has a very small, one-time-only role in the workflow (i.e., do we show their step, and do they get their own swimlane)?

All of these, and others you may not have thought of, will be dealt with over the next few chapters.

Essential elements

Swimlane diagrams depict the actors involved, the steps they accomplish, and the flow of work between them as shown in Figure 8.2. The actors are listed down the left side of the diagram, and each is given a swimlane that extends left to right across the page. "Gravity-fed" diagrams can also be drawn, with the swimlanes extending vertically from top to bottom. These quickly get awkward, as a longer diagram will spill onto the floor rather than run across a wall. The steps, which are tasks or sets of tasks, are shown as boxes in the swimlane of the actor who performs them. Arrows show the flow of work from one step to the next. Actually, there is some subtlety here. Technically, the line indicates that the completion of the preceding step is a precondition for the initiation of the subsequent step. Eventually, we will get more precise and show not just which actor performs a given step, but also what previous steps must be completed before that step can begin. For now, let's keep it simple, and just say that the flow arrows indicate sequence. A flow from one actor to another, one that crosses the line between swimlanes, is called a handoff. A key point: A swimlane diagram traces the path of a single work item or transaction as it flows through the process—it doesn't try to depict multiple work items at a time.

In addition to showing what gets done, the diagram can show who—person, job function, company, and organization unit; how—paper forms, automation, and remote sensing; and when—event, sequence, and dependency.

Don't forget a title and date. When you are working furiously on your project, you might even need to show the time on the diagram—"Are you looking at the diagram as of 11:15 Monday morning, or the version of 3:15 Monday afternoon?"

The details

Actors and roles

Looking at Figures 8.2 and 8.3, actors are the swimmers actually doing the work shown in the swimlanes. There is no practical difference between an "actor" and a "role," so we use the terms interchangeably. Generally, an actor is any identifiable person or group that handles the work (whether or not it is a value-added contribution) between the initial event and the achievement of the process's result. An actor could be a role played by a person in an organization, such as an external customer or supplier, or it could be a job function normally assumed by a single person or a job title held by many. Sometimes, the actor is an organization unit such as a company, division, department, or work unit. In rare cases, it could even be another process. Information systems or other automated devices can definitely be actors.[1]

All of the work performed by an actor appears in that actor's swimlane. Some swimlanes will be much wider than others, because of complex branching or parallel tasks performed by that actor. Although we haven't

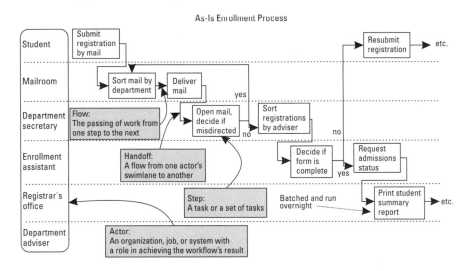

Figure 8.2 A swimlane diagram includes actors, tasks, flow, and handoffs.

---

1. But not every system that supports a process should appear in its own swimlane. We will provide specific guidelines later for handling these cases.

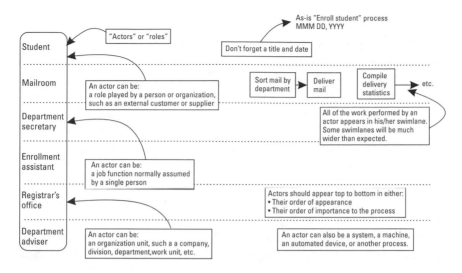

Figure 8.3 Guidelines for actors.

seen an automated tool that supports this, sometimes we have to "bulge" a swimlane to make room for a busy period. Actors can appear from top to bottom in their order of appearance, or the order of importance to the process, or even alphabetically. Many modelers always put the customer first, and systems last, with the others in some logical order.

It is not a common situation, but a single person can perform multiple roles in a process in which case each role should initially be given a separate swimlane. Place the swimlanes adjacent to one another, and provide some indication that the same person performs them all. If subsequent analysis reveals that the handoffs from one role to another occur seamlessly with no delays or other issues, then you can choose to collapse the swimlanes into one. However, if the handoffs prove to be a source of delay, error, or expense, then leave the swimlanes separate.

Process steps

A step is a task or set of tasks performed by an actor. We say set of tasks because in a high-level diagram, many individual tasks might be abstracted or simplified into a single box. They are also called responsibilities, activities, actions, or other names, but we'll use either "steps" or "tasks." Steps are shown on the swimlane diagram as a labeled box in the lane of the actor performing it. Steps can involve multiple actors; meetings and assists are situations in which two or more actors are required. In Figure 8.4, "accept order" is completed entirely by the Order Desk, whereas "develop production schedule" is completed in a meeting of some sort involving Production Planning and Delivery Logistics—the dotted lines over the Order Desk's swimlane indicates that they are not involved. "Resolve order discrepancy" involves all three actors.

Voluntary simplicity

Some modeling approaches distinguish among various types of steps. For instance, one classifies three types of steps: value adding, handoff, and control.[2] Another approach has different symbols for state change, transport, inspection, storage, or waiting steps. We keep it simple—a step is a step. This isn't to say ignore different types of steps, just you don't need to distinguish among them on the diagrams.[3] However, certain types of steps will always be named with the same verb, for instance, "decide."

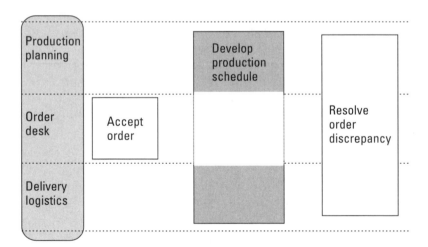

Figure 8.4 Illustrating process steps performed by multiple actors.

---

2. Quoted in James G. Kobielus, *Workflow Strategies*, Foster City, CA: IDG Books, 1997, p. 32.

3. However, when we later assess the as-is or design the to-be process, we will ask the questions implied by these categories—for each step, we will ask, "does this step make a contribution to the process, and if so, what type?"

Flowcharting templates offer a host of symbols as shown in Figure 8.5. This gives rise to a common question, "Why are these diagrams so simple? Couldn't they carry more information with a richer symbol set?" Our answer is, "No, the whole point is to make the key aspects of the process—who, what, and when—as obvious as possible." Our philosophy is to opt for simplicity, so the models are understandable to the *most* people with the *least* effort. In this simple symbolism, no training or interpretation is necessary. Additional symbols will record more data, but will convey less information for many audiences. Even in high-tech companies, some people won't even look at one of these charts if it contains something as simple as a decision diamond. We recognize this as a tradeoff—less rigor and detail, but better involvement and buy-in. For process work, that's a bargain we are happy to strike.

In the same vein, make liberal use of annotation on diagrams. A textual comment is better than a complex diagram or the use of arcane symbols. Occasionally, we will add an iconic symbol if it will help to convey a concept. A common example: showing a flow into a wire basket representing an inbox or an outbox.[4]

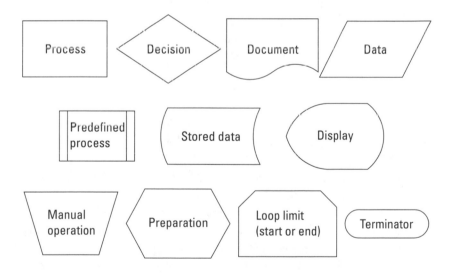

Figure 8.5 Flowcharting symbols.

---

4. Rummler and Brache add two symbols for specific types of annotations—goals or observed problems for a process step.

Which steps to include?

One of the difficulties you will encounter is deciding which steps to include in your workflow model. For instance, an actor will tell you about many activities, but most probably do not belong in the process being studied. (Remember, you are modeling a *specific process*, not all of the activity a person or department is responsible for.) Another example came up at an insurance company, where 5% of incoming claims were routed to an internal audit function and then returned to the normal claims flow. Whatever happened in the audit step never made any difference to the subsequent handling of the claims, so some analysts argued that it wasn't part of the process. In cases like these, a couple of simple guidelines always help.

First, remember that the process will usually trace a single work item or package of work items from trigger event through to result. That work item might be a service problem, an order, an engineering upgrade, a building permit request, an item being manufactured, a material requisition, a replacement part, or whatever it is the process deals with. The work item might appear to be transformed along the way, for instance, when the replacement part request is transformed into the actual replacement part. It might even split and follow different paths, as when the replacement part heads for the courier company, and the invoice or warranty details head off in another direction. Any activity that touches one of these work items, in any way, shape, or form, is almost certainly part of the process. To be more specific, we offer the mantra we chant we when making these decisions: "Show every step that adds value; moves the work along; or introduces delay."

Simply put, if it gets done, show it. The first guideline, "adds value," could be stated as "causes a state change in the direction of completion." Strictly speaking, it could also subtract value, or cause a state change in the opposite direction of completion. In either case, work is being performed on the work item, which includes inspection or validation activities. "Moves the work along" indicates that some steps may not change the work item in any way, except to transport it between other steps in the workflow. As we will see, many people mistakenly exclude these transport activities from their workflow models, for instance, by not showing internal or external delivery services that handle the work item. In those cases, factors that are important to process behavior are missed. Finally, "introduces delay" covers the third case—a step may not change the state of the work item, or move it along, but some subsequent step cannot proceed until the delay-introducing step completes. Our claim-handling example is a good illustration—subsequent steps in resolving the claim could not proceed until a claim returned from the audit step, even though the audit step didn't actually do anything *to* the claim.

Process steps—naming guidelines

Anyone who reads the diagram should be able to follow it, so we want to avoid cryptic step names like "MS-17" in Figure 8.6. To ensure this, follow the same guidelines for naming a process step as for naming a process (see Chapter 5). The step name is in verb-noun format, but often includes additional detail. In those cases, the text box for a step isn't just a name that tells us *what* is being done, it's a description that tells us *how*, if that is relevant. The components of the step name are:

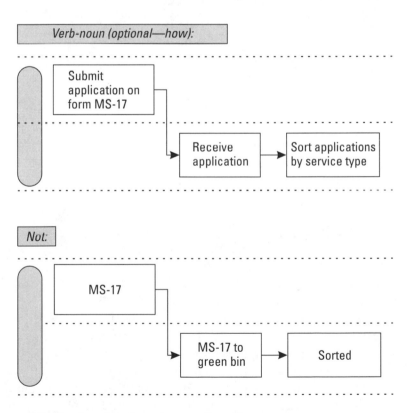

Figure 8.6 Naming steps in verb-noun format.

- Action verb (Assign, Validate, Sort, ...);

- Optional qualifier (Initial, Replacement, ...);

- Object(s) (Service Request, Payment, ...);

- Optionally, information on how (on Form MS-17, by fax, ...).

Another guideline to follow is that the step name should convey the result achieved by the step. To test this, flip the verb-noun step name into "noun is verbed" form, as in the following examples:

- Name—Receive PNO Application
  Result—PNO Application is Received;

- Name—Apply Parking Citation
  Result—Parking Citation Is Applied;

- Name—Issue Replacement License Plate
  Result—Replacement License Plate Is Issued.

As final reminder, the name is:

- Not an area or function such as "titling," "accounting," or "inventory";

- Not an event or result such as "claim arrives" or "claim is registered";

- Not based on "mushy" verbs (see Table 6.1) or jargon.

Go with the flow

Flow is the passing of work from one step to the next, shown as lines with arrowheads. In other methods, flow is known as routes, events, communications, or transitions. Sometimes, accomplishing the flow may actually be a step in itself, such as "Retrieve tray from mailroom." A handoff is a special kind of flow, one in which the work passes, or is handed off, from one actor to another. It's a flow from one swimlane to another. Handoffs are a focus for process analysis, because they are often a source of the "three deadly sins"—delay, errors, and expense.

The concept of flow is usually self-evident, but there are situations that cause trouble, so we'll go over some additional details. A flow line connecting two process steps means: "When the first step completes, the second step begins, or can begin." It may be a rule, as when the second step uses results from the first, or it might just be arbitrary. In either case, it represents precedence—"On completion of step A, step B can begin." An absolutely critical question to ask is, "Does the second step *actually* begin then, or is another step or event necessary *before* the second step begins?" All too often, modelers miss some of the flows or events that are necessary before a step can begin. We'll devote considerable attention to this in Chapter 10, but in the meantime try to keep in mind that there are often *multiple* flow lines into a step that all must occur before the step can begin—your job is to find them all!

A crucial point—draw your diagrams with the flow lines leaving the step from the right, and entering from the left. If the flow line means "B follows A," then the graphic should depict this—all too many diagrams visually convey the impression that steps are occurring in parallel when in fact they are sequential. An exception is that when returning or looping, the line may enter from the top or the bottom. See Figure 8.7.[5]

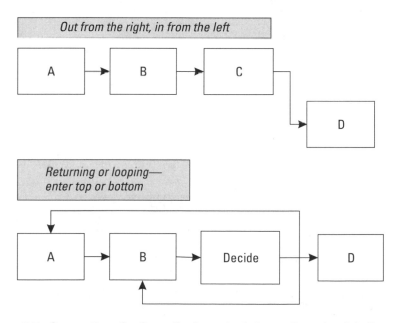

Figure 8.7 Conventions for flow—"in from the left, out from the right."

---

5. In this example, and several others in the section, we are not concerned about whether a single actor or multiple actors are involved, so we have not shown any swimlanes.

Avoid the forms in Figure 8.8—the flows may be accurate, but they don't convey timing and precedence. The objective is to graphically show sequence, dependency, time, and so forth. The objective is *not* to save paper.

If you have experience with an older form of process modeling, data flow diagramming, you might inadvertently confuse the concepts of workflow and data flow. The distinction is subtle, because whenever you have a workflow, it's virtually certain that data or information *is* the item that

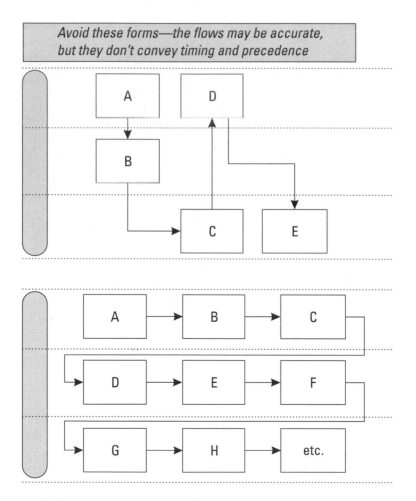

Figure 8.8 Flow lines—forms to avoid.

flows, or *accompanies* it. However, a data flow does not necessarily imply a workflow. Before we thoroughly confuse you, a definition is in order. On a data flow diagram (DFD), a data flow line between steps (called "processes" on a DFD) indicates that data produced by the originating step is used by the receiving step. For instance, a step "Negotiate discount" early in a process will produce data (the discount percentage) that is used by a later step "Determine invoice amount." On a DFD, these two steps might have a data flow between them, perhaps interrupted by a "data store" where the data "waits" until it is needed. A workflow model, on the other hand, might show a long sequence of steps before the process gets as far as "Determine invoice amount" because that is the flow of the *work*. The two cases are illustrated in Figure 8.9.

In most of our examples so far, the flow has been simple—one step followed by the next and so on. Of course, real processes exhibit more complex flows, which can be characterized as one of four types: sequential, parallel, concurrent, and conditional [1]. In a sequential flow, the simple case, work proceeds from one step to the next in order. In a parallel flow, two or more steps (or sequences of steps) proceed independently. In a concurrent flow, two or more steps must proceed at the same time. And in a

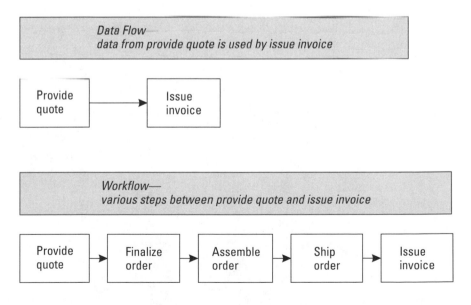

Figure 8.9   Data flow versus workflow.

conditional flow, a step (or sequence of steps) may or may not be accomplished at all, depending on the conditions. The nonsequential flows lead to various forms of branching.

Branching

The basic branch occurs with a conditional flow, when a decision is made which directs the workflow to *one* of two or more alternative flows. Many diagramming approaches use the diamond symbol to indicate a decision, but in the spirit of simplicity, use a box just like any other step. However, it is good practice to always use the term "decide" or "determine" when naming the step that decides which fork in the branch is taken. Figure 8.10 illustrates a simple decision between two branches. The key points to note are:

1. Be consistent in naming this type of step—we most often use "decide."

2. When showing a decision, there is exactly one flow line leaving the step, which then splits into two or more branches.

3. Each branch is labeled to indicate which decision outcome will follow that path, along with statistics if appropriate.

4. The branches are mutually exclusive—*exactly one* is followed. If parallel or concurrent flows are involved, a different representation is used.

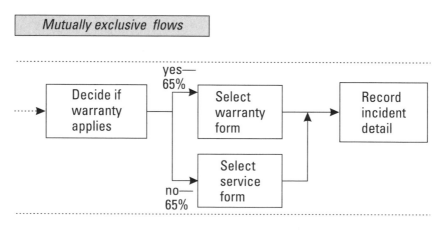

Figure 8.10 Illustrating a decision step.

5. Try to show the most common case as the top branch.

This structure can also be used to depict a single optional step. However, as shown in Figure 8.11, we would take the easy way out—simply annotate the optional step.

As noted, "decide" is a verb that should be reserved for specific situations. Use "decide" or "determine" when the process looks at data values (typically) to decide on which action to take next (e.g., Decide if Purchase Price = Manager Limit). "Sort" and "route" are similar reserved verbs, but are used when deciding where ("who to") a work item should go next.

Multiple flows

The last two illustrations showed mutually exclusive branches—there were two or more branches, but only one would be taken. In the case of parallel or concurrent flows, there are multiple flows, and therefore multiple flow lines, leaving a step.

A common situation is steps that do not happen in any fixed sequence, or may happen iteratively. For instance, in an insurance claim scenario,

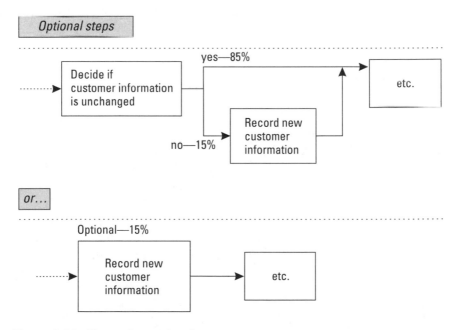

Figure 8.11 Illustrating optional steps.

customers who have an automobile accident call in to register a claim. The claims representative attempts to identify the customer who had called to determine coverage. However, some customers would immediately launch into a description of the accident, which the rep would dutifully record. Eventually, usually when the customer paused for breath, the rep would determine who the customer was, and possibly return to capturing more incident details. To illustrate all the permutations ("Decide if customer will let rep get a word in edgewise") would soon get ridiculously complex, so of course we opt for simpler representations that still get the point across, as shown in Figure 8.12. Both options show that Identify Customer and Record Incident can happen in any sequence, or even interleave, but *both* have to complete before Schedule Interview can happen. We prefer the option on the right, where the concurrent (or nonsequenced) steps are placed within a larger box. In the option on top, the fact that two flows enter Schedule Interview indicates that both must occur before that step will begin.

Also common is the situation when a step initiates multiple simultaneous flows. For instance, after booking an order, there might be a flow that begins fulfillment activities such as allocating inventory, and another, parallel flow that deals with setting up the receivable. Other flows may also begin that deal with other aspects of the order. Parallel flows are illustrated as shown in Figure 8.13 with multiple flow lines leaving a step, and the flows drawn one above another to visually convey that they happen in parallel, even if we can't precisely indicate the timing of particular steps.

A diagram style that you might encounter adds specific symbols to indicate different types of branches. In this style, illustrated on the right side of Figure 8.14, a fork can have one of three qualifiers, sometimes called an "AND branch," an "OR branch," or an "eXclusive OR branch." In the AND branch, all the forks will be followed, and their steps must be accomplished eventually. In an OR branch,[6] one or more forks (at least one, and possibly more) will be followed. In an exclusive OR (XOR for short) exactly one (one and only one) of the forks will be taken, which corresponds to our "decide." As you can probably guess, we don't use this style—it is precise, but not as simple, especially when the "X" or "V" symbols are employed.

---

6. This OR branch is sometimes called a *logical* OR to distinguish it from the exclusive OR.

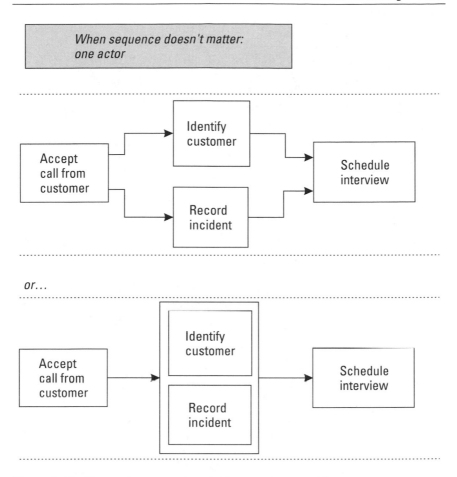

Figure 8.12 Illustrating steps that don't occur in a specific sequence.

What's next?

Armed with this review of the basic symbols and conventions for drawing swimlane diagrams, you could start to model a real business process. That is what we did when we first saw this diagramming style, and we quickly ran into the problem of managing detail—everyone does. It is not uncommon for progress on a workflow model to stall completely. Chapter 9 will provide some specific techniques for making sure you don't get hopelessly bogged down in details that prevent you from ever getting to the end of the process.

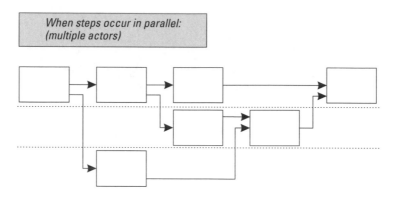

Figure 8.13 Illustrating parallel steps.

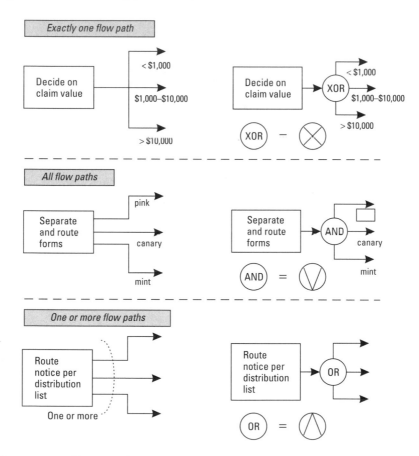

Figure 8.14 Alternate forms for decisions and parallel flows.

References

[1]   Kobielus, J. G., *Workflow Strategies*, Foster City, CA: IDG Books, 1997, pp. 4, 32.

[2]   Koulopoulos, T., *The Workflow Imperative: Building Real World Business Solutions,* New York: Van Nostrand Reinhold, 1995, p. 38.

9

Managing Detail

The curse of detail

When you set out to model the as-is process, your purpose is to understand it, not build the Winchester Mystery model. Sarah Winchester's famous home, the Winchester Mystery House, is located in San Jose, California. Sarah, the heir to the Winchester Arms fortune, became convinced she would live only as long as it would take to finish building her house. So she set out to build on her house forever. Some analysts seem to have a similar goal in modeling the current process—never finish! Unlike Sarah, who was sure she would meet her fate if she stopped building, you will surely meet a terrible fate if you don't stop modeling—your project will be canceled and you will never get to work on the to-be process! Once you understand the current system, you have completed the as-is modeling, and it is time to stop. In this chapter, we will look at techniques to help you achieve that understanding with a minimum of pain, so you can stop when it's time to stop, and move on to assessing the current process and designing a new one.

What's the problem?

Two reasons account for most of the problems encountered in managing detail. First, analysts jump right into a low level of detail instead of building layers of progressively more detailed swimlane diagrams. By getting to the details too quickly, process modelers almost guarantee they will immediately be thrust into unmanageable complexity. Imagine trying to develop blueprints for a house by starting with the details of the trim around the front door—you might eventually finish, but it won't be easy. The second source of difficulty arises when the modeler just keeps on adding more and more detail, seemingly unable to stop. In fact, they probably can't stop, because they are sliding down a slippery slope—each additional level of detail invariably raises more exceptions, each less significant than the exceptions dealt with in the previous level. Many analysts are compelled to deal with every one of these, but there is no end to it. For an analogy, consider that polishing metal is the introduction of progressively finer and finer scratches—you never eliminate the scratches, they just get smaller and more numerous until the polish is good enough. So it is with modeling a business process—eventually, it's good enough, even if there are countless tiny flaws.

Controlling the addition of detail

Three levels of workflow diagrams

Our main contribution to the problem of managing detail is that we have defined three levels of detail for swimlane diagrams. The first seems almost absurdly simplistic, but it allows you to get all the way through the process. The second adds specific kinds of detail, and the third even more. These three levels are referred to as:

- Level 1 or handoff level diagram;
- Level 2 or flow level diagram;
- Level 3 or logic or task level diagram.

This approach was developed the hard way—through trial and error—but it has proven itself on many projects for consulting clients and workshop participants. The most important concept is that by beginning with a very simple model, you can establish a framework within which it is easy to add progressive levels of detail. Most of the examples we will discuss are concerned with modeling the as-is process, but you can also use these same levels of detail when designing and assessing the to-be process.

The initial model, level 1, summarizes all the activity between receipt and handoff, showing one box for work done by an actor up to handoff or completion. Eventually, we could show every individual step or decision point, no matter how small, for each actor. We won't go that far unless it is necessary, and we never go so far as to show every single interaction with a system on a workflow diagram, because that kind of detail belongs in a use case scenario. Let's look at the details of these three levels of workflow model.

Level 1

Level 1 is the handoff level diagram, which is the one we will spend the most time discussing because it is arguably the most important—if you get it right, adding subsequent levels of detail is fairly straightforward. Since its purpose is to highlight handoffs, every handoff is shown, but detail about the steps is absolutely minimized—each time an actor is involved in a process, no matter how large or how small the contribution, it is shown as a single box. Thus, it has only one step (box) each time there is contiguous or uninterrupted work by an actor from receiving a handoff (starting a task or series of tasks on a work item) to initiating the final handoff for that work item (completing a task or series of tasks). An actor may have many steps in the handoff level diagram if each takes place at a different time in the process.

Figure 9.1 illustrates a handoff level workflow diagram. Note that a step like Review Credit Application will actually be many steps when detailed out in subsequent levels of detail. Each step summarizes the actor's involvement at a specific time in a process.

If this idea is hard to follow, attack it in reverse. Assume that an actor receives a work item, via a handoff, and begins to work on it. This work might involve many steps, including various decisions and handoffs, but proceeds without interruption either until the final handoff for that work item to some other actor, or until work ceases awaiting a future event or handoff. On a detailed swimlane diagram, we would see a whole series of tasks in one actor's swimlane, generally beginning with the receipt of a handoff, and ending with a handoff to another actor. All of the

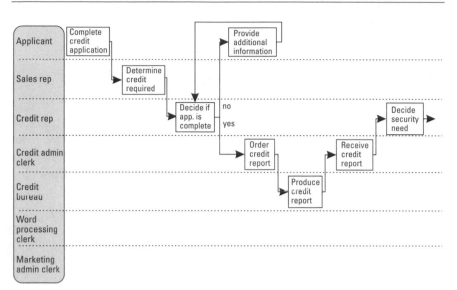

Figure 9.1a   A handoff level diagram for an as-is process.

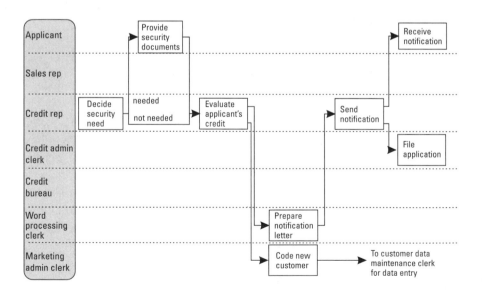

Figure 9.1b   A handoff level diagram for an as-is process.

uninterrupted work, even if it comprised 17 different steps, would be reduced to a single step on the handoff diagram. The exception would be if part way through these 17 tasks, the actor stopped working on that work item to wait for the arrival of another handoff or a predetermined time. In that case, the work would appear as two steps, each representing contiguous— uninterrupted—effort.

These diagrams are very simple to produce, although there could be minor difficulty when there are multiple handoffs along the way, or decisions that might cause a handoff. These will all have to be combined, in which case there would be multiple flows leaving the step, or one large decision fork that summarizes various intermediate decisions.

Issues and observations with the level 1 diagram

The handoff diagram is sometimes called an "involvement diagram," because it highlights each point in the process where an actor is involved. This leads to an important rule for these diagrams that at first appears counterintuitive. Even though we simplify the steps greatly, we don't simplify the actors at all—every single actor in the process is shown. The corollary is that as you progress through subsequent levels of detail, you'll add many more steps, but no more actors. A common objection to this rule is that if we are simplifying steps, we should also simplify the actors, perhaps by combining the different roles within a department and just showing the department as an actor. In extreme cases, you might choose to do this, but it eliminates one of the main benefits of the handoff diagram. Because each handoff is a potential source of delay, error, and expense, there can be tremendous benefit from a diagram that so clearly illustrates all of the handoffs. In fact, one of the fascinating things about handoff diagrams is that they can make process timing and dynamics visible. In one case, the handoff diagram made "yo-yoing" immediately evident—the workflow kept returning to the same control person over and over again, which over the course of the process introduced significant delay. In the detailed diagrams, which the project team had developed first, this wasn't obvious.

Each individual step may be simplified or abstracted so much from the actual steps being completed that a step effectively just says "this actor is involved at this point in the process." This can be a little distressing for the participants. One of the consequences of reducing an actor's involvement in a process to a single box is that trivial contributions and major contributions look exactly the same—just a single step is shown. Consider a real example. The manager of a retail store had many responsibilities at the end of the day, including balancing the day's receipts against the records in the system, and then preparing the bank deposit. This was a considerable amount of work, comprising many individual steps, and was often stressful as well. However, it showed up as just a single box on the handoff level swimlane diagram. Adjacent to it was a box of the same size that represented just a few moments of work for the sales assistant who signed a form witnessing that the deposit bag had been placed in the safe. Understandably, the store manager was a little miffed by this apparent trivializing of the contribution, so we had to explain (again) carefully that this part of the workflow model would soon be expanded, while the adjacent step would stay the same.

These diagrams also support understandable presentations by providing an overview, but the main benefit is that the job of modeling the as-is process is completed much faster. In practice, you will usually gather more detail than you need for any level of diagram, and then synthesize it to a simpler representation. However, because you are not allowed to include detail, these diagrams force you to finish. This avoids our natural tendency to "dive for detail" too soon and lose the forest in the trees.

Can we stop now?

Our guideline for when to stop modeling the as-is process is simple—as soon as you have done enough modeling to understand why the process behaves the way it does, you can stop. Occasionally, this will happen at the handoff level, when a timing issue or bottleneck is identified that is the root cause of the performance problems. Usually, we are not so lucky, and have to proceed to a level 2 diagram.

Level 2

Level 2 is the milestone level diagram, used to understand the key steps that determine flow or impact overall performance. It's also good for presentations at a more detailed level than the level 1 diagram. Building this one is easy if you have a good handoff diagram. Starting from the handoff level diagram, a flow level model adds steps to illustrate:

- Achievement of a milestone;
- Decisions that affect the flow in a significant way;

- The mechanics of any handoffs (both the "pass" and the "receive") that introduce delay, errors, or expense;

- Significant looping (e.g., "go back" or "repeat until").

Milestones are often significant events in the life of the work item. They usually entail a change in state or status, for example, "incident detail is recorded," "claim is registered," "appointment is scheduled," "license is issued," or "case is closed." It might take many steps to achieve the milestone, but don't show these at this time.

Examples of decisions that affect flow include "Decide if claim requires extended handling," if that caused a handoff to actors (e.g., the fraud investigations group) that wouldn't otherwise be involved. A minor decision within one actor's involvement wouldn't be shown, unless that led the actor achieving different milestones.

Cases where the mechanics of handoffs could introduce problems include "photocopy forms," "turn over to internal mail," "submit reimbursement request by mail," or "rekey data into ABC System." On the other hand, we don't need to show the details of an automated handoff that occurs instantly without errors.

As Figure 9.2 illustrates, a level 2 diagram is usually three to five times as large as the level 1 diagram. This provides a clue as to why you don't want to go to the level 3 diagram unless you have to—it might be three to five times as large as the level 2. Therefore, if you can understand your process at this level, that's great! Stop as-is modeling and proceed to assessment. We often find that it is unnecessary to go to a level 3 diagram.

Level 3

We call the level 3 diagram the task (or "logic") level model. Developers like the term "logic," and business folks prefer "task," but there are elements of both in this diagram. Previous levels show *what* happens, but not much detail on *how*. Level 3 makes the transition into describing the details of *how* the process is implemented. It contains individual steps leading up to a milestone, and details which characterize how the workflow is implemented such as "photocopy form," "fax estimate to shop," or "set up appointment using Adjuster Workbench System." It will also show the mechanics of any handoffs not shown in previous levels, or different cases (minor branching). In practice, if we go to a third level diagram, it's usually only for a part of the process.

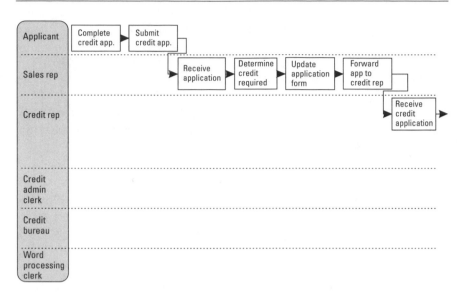

Figure 9.2a   A milestone level diagram for an as-is process.

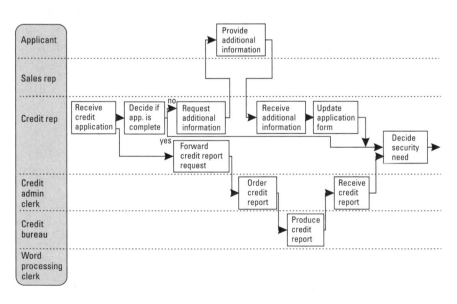

Figure 9.2b   A milestone level diagram for an as-is process.

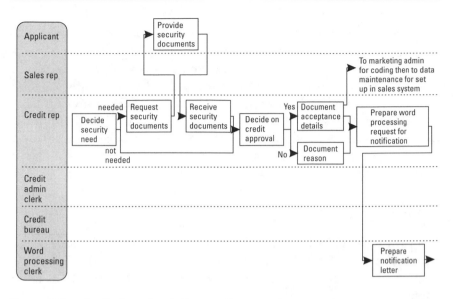

Figure 9.2c   A milestone level diagram for an as-is process.

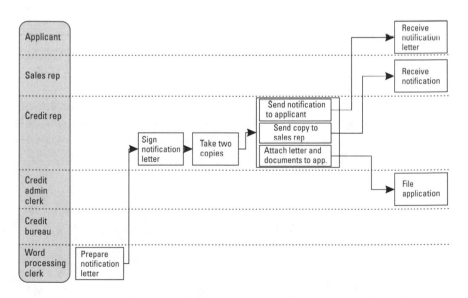

Figure 9.2d   A milestone level diagram for an as-is process.

How many levels to go to?

Remember—diagrams convey concepts, while narrative and other forms convey detail. If the diagram would be a complex maze of crisscrossed lines and decisions, *don't bother drawing it.* In general, if it's too complicated to draw, it's too complicated to generate an "aha!" Instead, record your findings, either in a structured narrative or using some other technique like decision tables. If you don't understand part of a workflow or uncover information that needs to be captured and conveyed, you might take it down to further detail than other parts.

Every time you gather a new level of detail, ask yourself if you actually learned anything new from it. If not, you have gone far enough, and do not need to depict the additional detail on a diagram. One of the frustrations in most forms of analysis is that you usually have to go too far to be sure you've gone far enough. That means leaving some detail "on the table" (well, maybe in an appendix) and resisting the normal urge to diagram it.

Restraint also has to be applied while developing these swimlane diagrams. Exceptions and errors will crop up regularly, which are tempting to follow up on, but stick with "sunny day" cases first. That means flagging branches that you aren't going to worry about just now so you can come back to them later. We will have lots more to say on this topic in Chapter 11 when we discuss techniques for developing swimlane diagrams, but in the meantime the essential guideline is to follow the mainstream case all the way through the process first, and then come back to the other variations later.

Managing detail is a big issue, but it is just one of the tricky problems you will encounter. In the next chapter, we will examine other questions and difficulties.

10

Questions and Difficulties

Introduction

Now that the basics have been covered, let's look at the weird stuff that will arise as soon as you get into a real case. In this chapter we will discuss common questions and difficulties often encountered while building a swim-lane diagram. Many of these situations were alluded to in the Really Big Telephone Company example in Chapter 8. There we looked at the basic tools, and in Chapter 9 we discussed a major difficulty, namely overwhelming detail. Here we want to preempt any difficulties by letting you know the solutions to the problems you will surely encounter. Through each of these three chapters, you can experiment with processes you are already familiar with: "modeling from memory," as it were.

We will be talking about the as-is model, but the techniques we will look at apply just as well to a to-be model. Many of these issues are about variations, both exceptions, and differences in procedure. For to-be, you can build one master version, and then adjust for local conditions and exceptions, while for the as-is you have to sort through the competing variations.

Avoiding paralysis by analysis

One of the great dangers of any analysis task is analysis paralysis. It is easy to become so involved with the minutiae of the problem that you spend too much time on it. Projects have been known to sink into a morass of analysis and never get out. You can get carried away with swimlaning, which may lead to analysis paralysis.

If you're struggling mightily with how to swimlane a situation, maybe you shouldn't bother, or you should adopt some other approach until you figure it out. It could be that swimlane diagrams are not the appropriate tool for the task. At some level of detail, words work better than pictures, and maybe a paragraph of explanation will be more enlightening than a swimlane. Especially for details, exceptions, and variations, an explanatory note can be easier to produce, and communicate better, than a complicated diagram.

If you are having trouble understanding or explaining a complicated situation, sometimes you will be better off to let the power of positive procrastination do its work: a difficult situation might resolve itself while you work in the areas you do understand. Even in the middle of a swimlane, a big cloud with a bunch of words that accurately describes what's happening is better than struggling with an inaccurate swimlane.

Sorry to say, the workflow analysis described in this book is not always the best approach to every problem. Collaborational tools like Lotus Notes have been called workflow tools, but in many cases they're a different kind of beast. They are suitable for executive processes and unstructured work like developing a strategy or a marketing campaign, they may be characterized by information exchange and milestones, but without fixed roles, responsibilities, or routes structure. These highly nonlinear processes do not translate well into workflow diagrams, and the most you should do is a rough, notional diagram.

Use cases don't belong in a swimlane diagram either—they are too detailed. You do not want to get down to the level of a tit-for-tat exchange between the system and the user. Swimlane diagrams are not the place to document detailed business rules or desk procedures.

So, swimlanes are a fabulous tool, but they are not the solution for every problem. Use a workflow process model (WPM) for what it's good for, and switch gears for what it's not. Don't let the tool get in the way. Our chant: "Don't bother, and don't get bogged down!"

Actors and other characters

Two recurring questions come up in regard to actors: what actors do I include in a swimlane, and are there actors that aren't people, for instance, systems or devices?

First and foremost, do you really have to show *all* actors? *Absolutely!* If they touch the work item in any way, shape, or form, they're an actor, and you must show them. The inclusion mantra: "Show every actor that holds the work, and every step that adds value, moves the work along, or introduces delay." A critically important corollary: Even in very high level diagrams, all of the actors must be depicted. You can summarize and simplify steps, but not actors, because it's so important to see all of the handoffs.

What about different roles in the same department? Can you just show the department as an actor (e.g., customer service), or do you have to depict the unique roles within the department (e.g., customer service rep and new service specialist)? Again, show all the distinct roles, as shown in Figure 10.1, because they do different tasks and there are handoffs. There is an exception: if there are different job titles, perhaps based on seniority, but

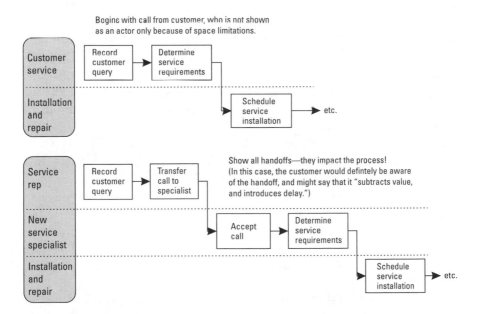

Figure 10.1   Illustrating all the distinct roles within a department.

they all perform the same tasks. In that case, there aren't actually different roles, just different job titles, and can be combined as one actor.

Well, what about the case where one person performs multiple roles—do I show just the one actor, or is there a swimlane for each role? Not surprisingly, there is a swimlane for each role, but only if the roles are all handled by one person because of resource constraints. If you hired another person, would two different people do the roles? If so, definitely show each role as a swimlane. If you would now have two people, each performing two roles, they are not really separate roles. Or, if an auditor would say, "Split this up," you should separate the steps.

If there aren't really handoffs, or the work flows seamlessly from one role to another (they don't do role A work in the morning and role B work in the afternoon), then you really don't have separate roles any more than separate steps denote separate roles. You might treat the person as if they were a department in your diagram to illustrate the situation.

Can a system or device be an actor? Some people think when mapping an as-is swimlane, there's no need to include systems, only people. WRONG! If a system assists in a significant way, mention it in the step description. If a system actually does the step, give it its own swimlane, if it is significant to the workflow. Remember our mantra: "Show every actor that holds work, and every step that adds value, moves the work along, or introduces delay." If it holds the work or adds value, moves the work, or introduces delay, it's part of the process. Would a diagram of the Amazon.com Fill Order process that did not show systems be a good depiction? Undoubtedly not, since so much of the process is done by the system, not humans. The system needs to be shown, although it might be simplified and abstracted. Another way to look at it is that if an actor "holds the work," show the relevant steps.

By definition, if they hold the work, they are either adding value, introducing delay, or moving the work along. However, people seem to find "actor holds the work" a useful guideline for deciding steps to include.

A batch system, such as overnight production of invoices, is another good example. It takes control of the work item, adds value, and introduces delay because subsequent steps can't proceed until it is done. Figure 10.2 illustrates this, as well as showing a case in which a system is mentioned in the step description.

Devices such as ATMs and IVR systems might be considered to be actors—they take control and add value. An ATM also holds work for

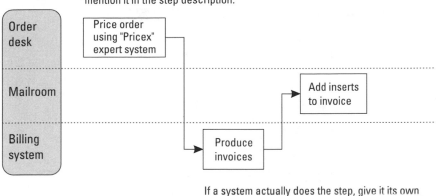

Figure 10.2   Illustrating systems as actors.

subsequent processing, so it can be said to introduce delay. Figure 10.3 illustrates the addition of an IVR system as an actor, and also illustrates steps in which multiple actors participate, a situation that is often handled incorrectly on swimlane diagrams.

On the other hand, an information system that assists a human in completing a step, such as an Internet-based order entry system, or a PeopleSoft human resources transaction, would not be treated as an actor. However, it could be mentioned in the step name: "Create order using Web site." Note, though, that if the system holds the work for later handling, we would again consider it to be an actor. This may seem a little arbitrary, but it is a workable way to manage the clutter of too many actors that don't impact the flow of work.

Likewise, an inanimate physical object like an inbox can be shown as an actor, generally completing the step "hold work." Without explicitly showing things like this, we might hide an important aspect of the process. Besides, these actors can hold the work independently of any other actor, and certainly introduce delay. One of the advantages of doing this is that it makes it more visually apparent when the process's work item is waiting. It also gives us the opportunity to ask how and when the work item gets to the inbox (or whatever), and how and when it leaves. As we'll see in the next

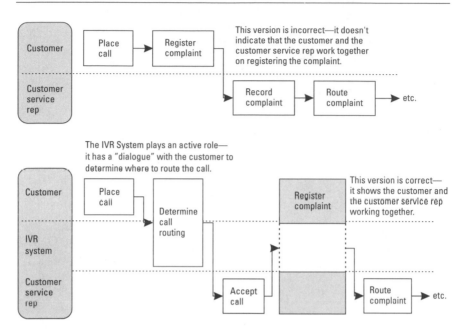

Figure 10.3 Illustrating steps involving systems and multiple actors.

chapter, when we review five key questions to ask when validating a swim-lane diagram, the question "How does it get there?" is one of the most useful—it often uncovers missing steps, actors, and rules.

Examples of inanimate objects that could be added to a diagram include:

* An inbox or outbox where items await attention or transport;

* A tub file where problem cases are left until time is allocated to resolve them;

* The order board (a corkboard with orders waiting for next step. Sometimes there are multiple boards, one for each stage.);

* The little metal carousel your order goes onto at a restaurant (hand-off from waiters to cooks).

In Figure 10.4, a pending orders board is added as an actor. An alternative if you don't want to add an actor, but still want to graphically show that work "waits" somewhere, is to add a step, but drawn with an in-basket icon

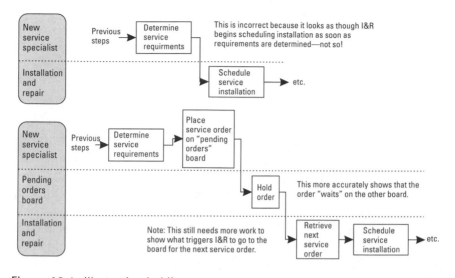

Figure 10.4 Illustrating holding areas as actors.

(or whatever) with work flowing in and out of it. There can be confusion about which actor's swimlane to put it in if it is a shared "work holder," so you are just as well off to add the swimlane. When there are many such work holders, we have sometimes added a single swimlane, labeled "work holder," into which we place a "hold work" step (e.g., the step would be "Pending order board: hold order"), labeled with the name of the appropriate work holder, whenever the work sits and waits. This makes it easy to see all the points in the process where work is waiting.

Note that we do not show things like the telephone network because it is more or less instantaneous (it doesn't really hold the work for any time, and doesn't introduce delay). Don't show the e-mail server, but you could show an e-mail inbox if it holds the work (actors do not check it instantly). Also, don't show something that holds the work but is under control of another actor (a truck, a delivery cart, a mailbag, and so forth).

Can another process be an actor? Yes, if it is a process we depend on, or a process we hand off to. It's not usual, but if we hand off work to a separate process, and wait for something to come back from it, the process itself is indeed an actor. You also need to have a swimlane for other processes that your process interacts with if the other process performs work that your process waits for (i.e., their performance affects yours). This is analogous to the batch system example. Note—be sure the other process is really an independent process, not activities that should be treated as part of the process being studied. You do not need a swimlane if your process does not expect a response.

Steps and types of steps

Do we need to indicate different types of steps? For instance, some steps move a work item, some enter or display data, some make decisions, and some add value by transforming the work item in some way. In the data processing world, the green IBM flowcharting template some of you have in the bottom of your desk drawer has a score of shapes for different types of steps: processing, decision, input, output, sort, merge. In this book, every step is a simple box. There's a reason for that. The simpler we keep the diagram, the greater the number of people who will be willing to look at it. We trade simplicity and participation for precision and detail.

Some diagramming styles show different types of steps. The style used by Ben Graham [1] employs five symbols: add value, transport, inspect, file or store, and wait. This adds power and precision, but there is a tradeoff—some people won't approach the diagram at all, and it will not be immediately obvious what the symbols mean. Some people like to add specific symbols for start and especially for stop, like a little round-cornered rectangle, and Rummler and Brache add two specific types of annotation: step goal, step problem. Use symbols like this sparingly, only if they are useful. Depicting the flow is enough to ask of any diagram without burdening it with too much detail.

We add some special symbols, but just a few. (Figure 10.5 illustrates these.) A labeled clock icon, indicating a time-based event (or trigger) can be useful without being distracting. We also find a lot of use for a cloud with a question mark in it, indicating "we know something's going on here, but we don't know yet what it is—we will get back to it." Or, the cloud can contain narrative explaining that whatever is going on is too complicated to depict with a swimlane diagram, but needs to be captured. Note that we liberally sprinkle annotations into our diagrams.

Finally, we have no qualms about inventing symbols or icons if there is a need in a specific situation, as with our suggestion to add an inbox icon. The rule is if it helps understanding, feel free to use it, but don't try to

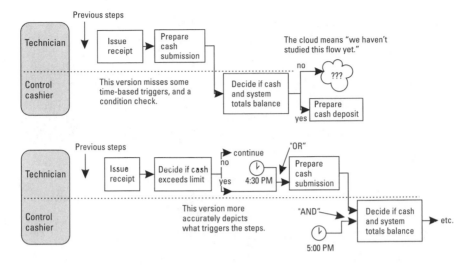

Figure 10.5 Additional symbols, including time-based (temporal) events.

highlight too many different things all at once. Some tools make heavy use of icons—every single step is an icon, but we want to emphasize flow, not steps or technology.

What do you do with a step that has no output? It just dangles. Sometimes that's okay, other times it's not. The question to ask is: "Has this actor completed the responsibility at this stage of the process?" If so, and there is no follow-on activity or handoff to another actor, then this dangling activity is fine. A good example: the File Clerk does "File Original," and that's it, he has no further work with the process's work item. If not, then clearly we must discover the subsequent activities or the handoff.

What makes it go? (inputs and outputs)

A great benefit of swimlane diagrams is that they are intuitive. Everyone immediately understands that the flow line indicates that tasks happen in a particular sequence, or that work (or control) flows from one task to the next. But we can be more precise. What the flow line really means is *precedence* and *dependence*—the step at the arrowhead can't go until the step at the other end has been completed. One of the most important aspects of a workflow diagram, often *the* most important, is accurately showing what "input flows" are necessary for a step to begin. Some particular concerns are:

- Does the diagram correctly show multiple inputs (or outputs) to a step? Two different lines going into a step means something very different ("AND"—both must occur for the step to begin) from two lines joining and then going into the step ("OR"—one or the other must occur before the step can begin). The same is true on output. Figures 8.10 through 8.14 demonstrate these conditions.

- How do you show steps that are done according to a schedule? They begin in response to a temporal event, which we show as a little clock icon, usually in addition to some other flow.

- How do you show the use of batching, counters, or limits? Easy—it's a decision. The question is, who makes the decision?

- How do you show "just because I got around to it"? We would show this as an untriggered decision by the actor to reach into a "tub file" (like the proverbial "job jar"). By "untriggered," we mean there is no input flow from either another step or a temporal event.

These are illustrated in Figure 10.5, except the untriggered decision, which is rare in practice. In the "five key questions" section of the next chapter, further examples are presented.

Variety is the spice of life

Sometimes you will have to build different models of the same process. There are many reasons to do this in both as-is and to-be models. A judgment call is often involved. For instance, as-is modeling might reveal variances in how different locations carry out a process, but that doesn't mean they all need to be illustrated. Don't bother documenting variations that don't matter—that is, they don't contribute to a significant difference in process behavior. Let's look at the main cases:

There are significantly different versions of the same process, and they must be understood so you can discover if differences are important and must be preserved, do gap analysis (i.e., compare them to a new "master" process), perform implementation planning, or discover best practices.

- *By location.* Pay Employee is different in the United States and Korea because of legal or cultural differences; it will be different in the to-be as well. In Korea the expectation is that payment will be in cash, whereas this would be almost unheard of in the United States. We frequently encounter situations where legal constraints vary across an organization's operating locations, and this must absolutely be understood in order to meet legal requirements.

- *By organization.* The Packaged Goods division does Receive Shipment differently than the Health and Beauty Division. This could be important to discover best practices, or because of conventions among an industry's trading partners that will require some differences to be maintained in the to-be.

There are significantly different cases of the same process. For example, different versions of Receive Shipment process for:

- Receive Gas or Consumable;

- Receive Repair or Service Item;

- Receive Direct Inventory Item (raw material or component).

There are significantly different stages within the same overall process. Fulfill Order may have three different front ends, depending on whether the order is received over the counter, by mail, or via the Internet. If each stage is just a few steps, they can probably all go on the same diagram. However, if each stage is more complex, involves multiple actors, and those actors participate in the other stages as well, it might be too complex to show on a single diagram. Each would then be diagrammed separately, with each flowing into a connector at an "OR" on the diagram for the rest of the process. Similarly, there can be multiple variations within a process (Notify Customer via e-mail, phone, or mail) or multiple endings.

A cautionary note: Sometimes a decision is made at the front end—"decide what case this is"—and the process flows into one of, say, three separate parallel streams. This should generally be drawn as three separate diagrams. Sometimes this is mistakenly shown on one diagram, with a lot of decisions along the way, when in fact the performers aren't making decisions; they know what "case" they are working on. The moral: Don't try to put too much on a single swimlane diagram, multiple understandable diagrams are better than one complex one. Or, don't use decisions to illustrate different cases (or versions or…) when there aren't actually decisions being made.

Note that there can be different versions in both the as-is and to-be processes. For example, the as-is may have different versions by location or the to-be may have different versions by case. For to-be, we generally build one master version, and then adjust it for local conditions: legal, cultural, pragmatic/operational (e.g., different skills or resources), and so forth.

Closing arguments

We could talk about theory and obscure cases, but now let us put this into practice and look at techniques for developing a real workflow process model with a group of subject matter experts. Chapter 11 tells you how to actually go about building a workflow model with the participation of the content experts, and the key questions to ask when validating it.

Reference

[1]   www.worksimp.com

Part IV
Understanding the As-Is Process

11

Techniques for Modeling the As-Is Process

Introduction

Now that we understand the theory (rules and conventions), we can move into the practice—how to actually build an as-is workflow model. You need techniques to get started (which is often the hardest part), to maintain progress (avoiding inappropriate detail and distractions), and to validate the model. It's not as simple as just grabbing a pen and starting a diagram. We will progress through:

1. Building the team;

2. Organizing and initiating the modeling session;

3. Getting started by building the handoff (level 1) model;

4. Adding detail with a flow (level 2) model;

5. As necessary, developing a task (level 3) model, and even doing some task analysis if the situation warrants it.

There is no one right way to proceed—every situation is different, and each analyst has different strengths. We will provide solid frameworks, but you will need to augment and adjust to suit the situation. The right technique is the one that works—produces the necessary model without having to quell a rebellion.

Difficulties can and will arise—these will be dealt with in the next chapter. Two bear mentioning now, because they come up so often, and they are so important to our philosophy and approach.

Issues at the extremes

Many teams encounter at least one of two issues, the extremes of time spent on as-is modeling—too much, or too little (or even none).

First and foremost is getting the as-is workflow model done within your (and the project's) lifetime. We could tell a horror story here— the 167-foot-long as-is model that consumed all of a project's time and resources, resulting in the cancellation of a promising project. Many projects fail because the team gets bogged down in detail and runs out of time and the project dies on the vine, or the participants (subject matter experts) get bored and/or frustrated and stop participating effectively. The problem—each additional level of detail begets more detail which begets detail. A key concept—we are seeking to understand the as-is, not document it in excruciating detail! We address this by providing techniques that make use of the different levels of detail we introduced in Chapter 9. You will want to quickly build a first level (handoff level) workflow model, and then add controlled amounts of detail, one level at a time, but only if a gating checkpoint is passed that confirms the need for additional detail.

Second, at the other extreme, is getting started at all. There may be pressure to skip as-is modeling altogether, as suggested by some of the early books on BPR (later ones recognized that this step is essential). Experienced project leaders and analysts usually do not object. Resistance typically comes from the extremes: senior managers or detail-oriented technicians. Fortunately, this happens less often now. People who have skipped the as-is step have been burned, and now recognize that it is essential, even if they're not thrilled about it. The two most common reasons: They think, "Hey, we all know how this works," or "Why waste time mapping a process that we're going to replace?"

The point is: we're seeking to *understand* the as-is, not *document it in excruciating detail*, and if the as-is *really is* well understood, this step will go quickly. Skipping this step is a false economy—experience shows you'll pay later because:

• You must understand the as-is in order to identify specifically why it behaves the way it does (the good aspects to preserve and the bad aspects to eliminate, improve, or replace).

• It will ensure focus on fact, not opinion, and demonstrate that improvement is possible.

• You will need to establish a performance baseline in order to show improvement and justify the project.

• You need to know who (job titles or actors, and organization) will be affected to get their input.

• You need to know who will be affected to prepare for training, and so forth. This is critical—you must understand current tasks to know if they must be carried out in the new process, and besides, people's jobs are changing.

• You will also need to thoroughly understand the current process in order to maintain interfaces to other systems and commitments to other processes. This is also critical—there are ALWAYS important interconnections and dependencies that will be disrupted if they are not identified. Similarly, some are useless and might be re-implemented if they aren't understood.

There are a couple of strategies if there is opposition to as-is modeling. Both rely on the supposition that if you can demonstrate that the current process isn't well understood, the participants will see the value. As noted, if the current process actually is well understood, this will go quickly.

One strategy is the "please, humor me" approach. Say, "Let's just spend enough time to see if we're essentially on the same wavelength." Get permission to run one session (approximately three hours) to produce a hand-off level model, using the cloud diagram approach described subsequently. This session often demonstrates that everyone is not on the same wavelength about who is involved and what the critical handoffs are. You then have agreement to proceed.

The other strategy is to try to capture important information without formally doing as-is modeling. First, review information from the process frame (you will have to do this anyway). Do we all agree on the event and result that frame the process? Do we agree on the main milestones between the event and the result? Have we accurately listed all the actors (the people, organizations, systems, and so forth) that have a role in achieving those milestones? Does anyone else contribute or have a stake? When everyone is on board, ask a few key questions:

- Would it be possible to list the main tasks or responsibilities of each of these parties? Let's try.

- Will anyone else be impacted (i.e., their work will change in some way that must be planned)? How will it change?

- Do we know all the interactions or connections with other processes (inbound or outbound)? Let's build a quick list.

If the answers to these questions came readily and with agreement, then you probably have enough information that you don't have to do as-is modeling and you're not going to convince anyone it's necessary. Usually, though, these questions raise differences of opinion and there is agreement to do at least a little as-is.

Assembling the team

Give some thought to team diversity. A mix of perspectives is crucial to accuracy and progress. Otherwise, results will be skewed, crucial activities will be missed, and you will keep hitting a wall when you don't have the right person to answer a question. The participants must be able to work together in a group session. This will take much longer if you try to do it as a series of one-on-one interviews.

Participants must include representatives from all relevant organizational units or areas, which might be defined by organizational structure or functional area, by geography, by product line, by customer or market, and so forth. "Relevant" means they play a role in the as-is process, or directly depend on it in a significant way. In the simple case, you will have representation from each organizational unit that participates in the process, and won't have to worry about factoring in geography, product line, and market segment. Good luck!

Participants should include management or supervisory personnel and front line workers or individual contributors. A common reaction: "Oh, no! Not all at once, they can't work together!" Well, they do in other successful organizations, and besides, they have to, or process improvement will fail. Both perspectives are essential, and in our experience, each group always learns from the other. Individual workers learn from each other what other areas do, what the interdependencies are, and they learn from management about the organization's issues and direction. Management learns what really happens at the front lines now (as opposed to 5, 10, or 15 years ago) and what issues or obstacles their people face. It may initially be uncomfortable, but the facilitator (which is you if no one else fills the role) and the structure imposed by building a model help everyone to participate. Working on an as-is model has proven so successful at improving communication, developing a broader understanding, and team building that we have recommended it even when the process doesn't apparently need improvement.

Participants should include customers and suppliers. A common reaction: "Oh, no! We can't let them see how bad the process is!" They probably already know, and besides, they almost surely know some things about the process that you don't. Sometimes the customer did substantial work that the internal process performers were not aware of. The customer might ride herd on the process or act as the tickler file to ensure that things keep happening. Other times, the customer carries out handoff and transport activities. A personal example: I contacted the dealership when a major home appliance failed, and they provided me with paperwork for the authorized service organization, which in turn provided me with paperwork for the local repair agency. I can attest this was an opportunity for delay, error, and frustration. Customers and suppliers may be internal to the organization, or external to it. There is the most reluctance to including external customers, suppliers, or other trading partners, but in the age of e-business and e-commerce, where business processes cross the firewall (i.e., organizational boundaries), it is becoming a fact of life.

In general, everyone who touches the work must be involved. This might involve, for example, IT staff. Computer systems, especially batch processing, may play a critical role (add value, move the work along, or introduce delay). IS or IT representatives should therefore participate, although with the caveat to stay out of eye-glazing detail. (A long, complex batch job stream should be mapped out in a separate session—IS only.) Major process improvements have been accomplished using modern enterprise application integration (EAI) tools by linking batch (and other) steps in real time. There are even cases where IT staff performed significant, daily "babysitting" of systems, such as watching for exceptions, revising or correcting data, or routing work. As before, they should participate in the sessions, with the same caveats: no eye-glazing detail. We discuss these in more detail in Chapter 12.

Preparation

We don't want to turn this into a book on facilitation or project management, but here are a few miscellaneous points and guidelines.

Team organization

The sponsor, or the sponsor's chosen representative, is critical. One key role for the sponsor is to help to identify and secure participants. You probably won't have the pull on your own to obtain the necessary release time. Generally, a project is organized into the core team, full time, responsible for all aspects of running the sessions including preparation, facilitation, and documentation. You will need a project leader plus one or two people acting as process analyst, and one or two people with broad subject matter expertise. You'll also need participants representing various areas, whose participation level will vary with area or level of detail.

Scheduling

How long will it take? The short answer is: "Longer than you think." A process with 10 or 15 actors, and scores or hundreds of steps, will not be mapped in one 3-hour session, more like three to five half-day sessions. Full-time availability of the participants (content experts) is ideal, but unlikely. Everyone is busy these days, and full time may be more than you can use anyway. Realistically, two to three sessions per week, each lasting half a day (the morning is preferable), are a realistic goal.

Facilities

This item can make a big difference. A dedicated room is hugely beneficial—you can leave materials up, have core team meetings on site, avoid distractions, and so forth. Cramped rooms produce cramped results. Ideally you will have a room that allows participant seating in a wide U or semicircle. Allow no energy holes—you will want participants as close together as comfortably possible, with no empty chairs. You need large whiteboards at the front (the open side of the wide U). Walls of whiteboards are the best. You'll need good air circulation and climate control, and plain side and back walls (no pillars, windows, artwork, and so forth) to allow posting of material. If there are windows, they should be at the back. Interruptions are a problem, so you will need a way to control e-mail and voicemail time.

Supplies

In addition to a PC for documenting results, you will need:

- Flipchart pads;

- Pens (whiteboard and permanent);

- Butcher paper or other wide roll of paper;

- Big Post-Its ("yellow stickies").

Starting the modeling process with a facilitated session is the most workable approach—it's hard to abstract behavior into a model while observing it. However, always finish by confirming your conclusions through direct observation. The usual cycle is:

1. Plan.

2. Hold a team session.

3. Do field work (interview and observe).

4. Back to step 1, and repeat as necessary.

The kickoff

How you start makes a difference. Start on time, give a pep talk to establish scope and direction, and provide an overview of what's to come. Then get on with it! Don't bore them—do it fast, and put them to work as quickly as possible, ideally within 15 or 20 minutes.

During the introduction to the first session, the more that can be done by the sponsor (or other big shot) the better. Have them summarize key points from the charter and process frame: event, result, key actors, milestones, relevance to mission, strategy, goals. Describe the problem, business imperative, and goals. Material from the Case For Action and Vision can help. Stress why participation is so important.

The facilitator or the lead process modeler will then introduce workflow models, and the method of the session will follow. If the group hasn't seen one before, show a sample workflow process model, although not from their area. A flow (second level) model can be used to explain the four components: actors, steps, flow, and handoff. Explain that this can get bogged down in detail, so we start with a handoff level model. Show the handoff level model corresponding to the flow model you just showed them, and then explain the concept. Tell them that it might be frustrating at times when important details are omitted, but this will provide a framework for gathering that detail.

To avoid bogging down in detail, we will follow four principles that also may be frustrating, but are proven to help maintain progress, especially at the outset. They all relate to the idea that we constantly strive to get all the way through the process, and then come back to fill in the details. These guidelines should be summarized on a flipchart and posted during the session.

- Starting with the "mainstream" (normal, most common, "sunny day") case, model one case (variation) at a time.

- At a decision point, follow one branch, and mark the other with a cloud or "???". You'll come back to it later.

- *Do* focus on "what's next." In the handoff model, keep asking, "Who gets the work next?" and in other models keep asking, "What happens next?"

- *Don't* dive for detail, especially detail that doesn't belong at that level.

Building the handoff level diagram

It's usually easier to gather content or build a rough framework than it is to build even as simple a diagram as a handoff level model. Accepting this, we will look at two alternatives for gathering information (all the while avoiding unnecessary precision) and then turning that information into a handoff diagram.

The first approach is to build a cloud diagram. The idea here is to trace the involvement of the actors without worrying (yet!) about what they actually do at the points they're involved. We also refer to this as an "involvement diagram." It captures "dynamics without details." By hiding details of individual steps, it actually does a better job of showing the structure of the process. Not much preparation is needed—you just want a long whiteboard (probably multiple adjacent whiteboards) or some convenient drawing surface. The method:

1. Draw a swimlane for each process actor you identified during framing. Leave some room, because you'll probably find additional actors.

2. Start with the initiating event.

   If it's a timer, put the clock on the diagram.

   If it's an actor doing something (including deciding if a counter or threshold has been met), put a cloud in that actor's swimlane. Why a cloud? To show that we are intentionally keeping it vague right now. It correctly implies it's nebulous and imprecise.

3. Ask the all important question: "Who gets the work next?" Ignore all the details of the work performed by the actor who has the work right now.

4. If it always goes to the same actor at this point, draw a cloud in that actor's swimlane and return to step 2. If it varies (that is, there is a decision), draw a fork on the right edge of the cloud, choose the mainstream path, connect it to a new cloud in the next actor's swimlane, and return to step 3. (The other branch/branches of the fork just go to a big "?" to indicate that we need to return.) Figure 11.1 shows what one of these can look like.

5. When you hit an endpoint of the process, go back to the earliest incomplete branch (fork) and pick it up from there, following the same method.

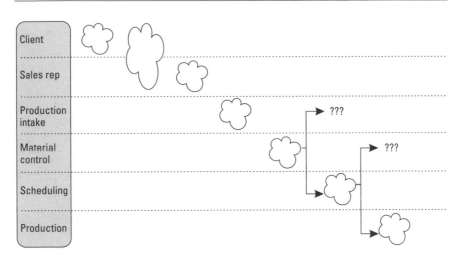

Figure 11.1 Using "clouds" to illustrate the pattern of involvement.

6. Perform an initial validation by walking through a few scenarios and revising the diagram as necessary. A more thorough validation will be described in the next section, "The Five Key Questions."

The second approach is collecting tasks and assembling a workflow diagram. The first approach focused on involvement: "Who is involved at what points in the process?" This second approach is more bottom-up. The idea here is to more or less randomly identify individual tasks (who does what) through brainstorming without regard for sequence and flow, and then organize and cluster the tasks to produce a handoff level. Then verify the structure, and proceed with gathering additional detail. Note that this is similar to the bottom-up technique used successfully for project planning and the one that we used for discovering processes.

In preparation, create some large (4 × 6 or 5 × 8) Post-Its (big yellow stickies)—depending on facilities and number of participants, between one-fourth and one-half of an 8½ × 11 inch sheet of paper—divided by a horizontal line about one-fourth of the way down. We'll explain why in just a moment. On the longest plain wall surface you have, tape up as long a sheet of butcher paper (or plotter paper or whatever kind of rolled paper you're using) as you think you might need. Leave room to add another strip below, in case you need it to accommodate additional actors. The method:

1.   Brainstorm for significant steps or tasks, recording each suggestion on one of the large Post-Its. The name of the actor responsible for the step goes above the line, and the step description goes below it. This can also work very well with individuals or breakout groups separately identifying tasks—this avoids herd mentality. Then combine individual results, and see if synergy results in additional ideas. If people can't put each step in verb-noun format, don't worry—anything that captures the idea is good enough for now. Don't interrupt the flow, just get something down you can refine later.

2.   Lay out the steps in approximate sequence on the paper—now you'll see why Post-Its are so useful—they are easy to manipulate (cluster, move, and so forth). Try to keep the steps for the actors approximately in their swimlane, even though swimlanes may not be drawn yet, and certainly won't be labeled. Absolutely don't worry about precision at this point; you won't know the precise sequence and flow of steps. You just want to show roughly where steps are happening in sequence or in parallel.

3.   Now, have the group look things over and ask, "Did we miss any important steps?" This is where the power of this approach becomes apparent; by laying out the approximate structure of the process, missing steps become more obvious. They can be added while it is still relatively easy to do so (i.e., swimlanes and flow lines are not yet specific, so it's easier to slide the Post-Its around).

4.   Add swimlanes, labeled by actor, to the paper and place the steps in the right swimlane. (Order here will vary.)

5.   Wherever an actor has a contiguous set of steps (from receiving a handoff to initiating a handoff), reduce them to a single step as per the central principle of the handoff diagram. Don't throw out the details you have captured; you'll want them for subsequent diagrams. A good technique is to stack the steps being reduced, and add a new Post-It on top with the summarized step name. Naming the step in the handoff diagram may be awkward. If you have to use "and" and "or," or otherwise get wordy, don't worry about it.

6. Add flow lines between the steps, being careful to account for decisions and multiple flows. These will stack up at the left and right edges of the step box. The step in the handoff box may summarize several steps, with flow lines coming in or out of these steps along the way. These will all be placed at the left and right edges of the step.

7. Try to improve step names to reflect the totality of what happens while that actor has the work. It is likely that a few step names will still require "and" and "or."

8. Perform an initial validation by walking through a few scenarios and revising the diagram as necessary. A more thorough validation will be described in the next section.

The five key questions

Any time substantial progress has been made on your swimlane (completing a whole level of detail, or at least a major phase), you must stop and validate the model. An excellent method is to review each step in the swimlane diagram, one by one, and ask each of five specific questions about it. The questions work through a step from left to right, beginning with the inputs (the flow lines coming in from the left), the actual work of the step, and the outputs (the flow lines going out from the right). Asking these questions almost always leads to the discovery of additional actors, steps, triggers, and flows. This rigorous procedure prevents glossing over ambiguities and missed details. After we review the questions, we will provide a real example of a swimlane diagram that was significantly altered (and improved!) by asking these questions. The five questions, in sequence, are:

1. "What makes it go?" This is one of the two most important questions, because it uncovers missing trigger conditions for a step, which is a fundamental aspect of workflow. Often a diagram will show a single flow line entering a step, but the question is: "Is the flow line (or lines) shown *really* all that it takes to trigger the beginning of the step?" Often, it turns out that a flow line from a step performed by some other actor is required. Even more common is the case reviewed back in Figure 10.5—a temporal event (e.g.,

"close of business") and/or a condition (e.g., "total receipts = cash drawer limit") is also required before a step can begin. The example we will review includes many steps that are triggered by a schedule.

2. "Is anyone else involved?" This question often uncovers one of two common errors.

    A step is shown being performed by a single actor when there are actually two or more participants (a meeting,) or there is a handoff to another actor as shown in Figure 10.1.

    Sequential steps, performed by different actors, are drawn when actually there is one step (a meeting) simultaneously involving multiple actors, as shown in Figure 10.3—clearly, the complainant (the customer) and complaint taker (the customer service rep) are both involved at the same time.

3. "Does the name of the step accurately convey the result?" The purpose of this question is to ensure that there really is a legitimate step, the participants agree on what the outcome of that step is, and that the name conveys the result. Practically, this most often means ensuring that a mushy verb hasn't been used unless there is absolutely no other choice. Remember the table of "Verboten Verbs" from Chapter 5?—use it! The most common ones we encounter are "process" or "handle," which say nothing, and "monitor" or "review," which are usually hiding decisions. If we see a mushy verb, we usually ask this question first, so we can clean it up before investing any more work in it.

4. "Are all outcomes shown?" As in question 1, sometimes a diagram will show a single flow line leaving a step. The most common error (often masked by a mushy verb) is to neglect to show that there are two or more possible outcomes—in other words, a decision is being made. We specifically ask, "Is a decision being made here, and if so, what are all the possible outcomes?" The other common error is to miss a parallel flow line. In the case of Figure 10.3, it wouldn't be unusual to discover that the step "route complaint" had a flow to the appropriate specialized service rep, but missed a notification (flow) to the customer's assigned sales rep. We ask, "Does this step initiate work or a notification for any other actors?"

5. If there is a handoff, "How does it get there?" This is the other most important question, because it uncovers missed actors (intermediaries or transport mechanisms). When we ask "How is the work transported from actor A to actor B?" we sometimes discover that additional actors who perform a delivery service are involved—our upcoming example is full of such cases. In some cases the handoff is accomplished by an information system running in batch. In both cases, the additional actors might introduce delay, error, or expense.

Figure 11.2 shows a swimlane diagram that was presented to us for review. The process had been modeled because it took excessive time between the time an applicant submitted his application for a cross-jurisdictional business license and the time he received his assessment, pro-rated across the different jurisdictions. This initial version failed to show where the delay was occurring, but after asking the five questions and revising the model accordingly, it was clear where the delay was being introduced. Figure 11.3 illustrates the revised version, but only the first third or so—after the rating technicians completed their assessment, we discovered a parallel flow to the program manager, who monitored every application, which resulted in an extensive review! What was really interesting about this example was how much improvement was possible from simply rescheduling some of the delivery and pickup activities. (Eliminating them was not a possibility, because of the collective agreement.)

We emphasize that these questions must be asked, for each step, at each new level of detail: after the initial handoff model, after the flow model, and so forth. However, they are most important at the handoff

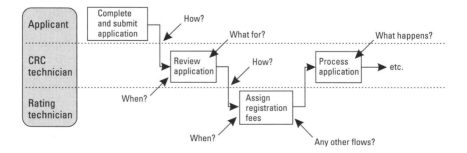

Figure 11.2 Initial version, before the "five questions" review.

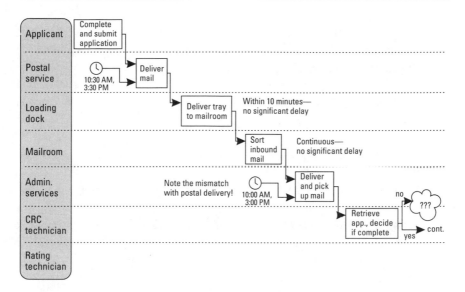

Figure 11.3a Revised version, after the "five questions" review.

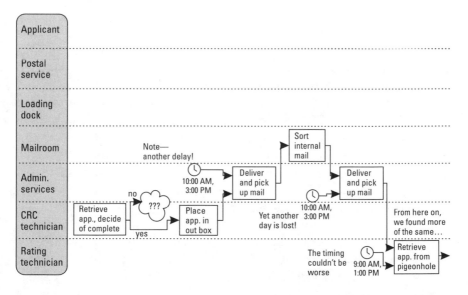

Figure 11.3b Revised version, after the "five questions" review.

level, where they almost always uncover missing actors and steps. The rest of the work proceeds far more smoothly, without continual redrawing, if all of the actors and their "contribution points" have been identified.

One more question: "can we stop now?"

There are stories of workflow process models stretching to 50 feet, 100 feet, or more. Generally speaking, that much detail in one diagram is useless. It can actually be harmful, since the finer the level of detail, the more variation there will be. Even if it is irrelevant, there will be a temptation to show it, creating a vicious cycle. The finer the level of detail, the more words it takes to describe the diagram, so the people working on the chart will be working hard, but actually accomplishing little of value.

Thus, it is important to stop before you slip into modeling useless detail. After completing a level of detail (for instance, developing the initial model, testing it with a few scenarios and the five questions, and making necessary revisions), one more question must be asked: "Do we really need to add more detail?" In general, stop when you understand why the process behaves the way it does.

You only need to add more detail if you are not confident that you understand the workflow. If you do not yet understand how the overall flow and dynamics of the as-is workflow impact its performance, or are not confident that you have identified the main activities that currently must be completed, handoffs within the process, and handoffs (or interfaces) to other processes, you need more detail.

On rare occasions, you will be able to stop after the high-level handoff model is completed. We described a case in Chapter 9 when the handoff model illustrated the central problem with a process' workflow (continually returning to a control point), so it might have been possible to stop as-is modeling at that point. Generally, though, this level will mask important steps, decision points, and milestones that contribute to the performance of the process, and you will have to proceed to the flow level.

The second level flow diagram shows the significant milestones and decisions while an actor has the work, but not any of the details of how the actor accomplishes them. Most of the time, we find that this level of detail is adequate to understand the as-is situation. Some parts of the process may need additional detail.

Subsequent levels of detail

Getting the handoff level diagram completed is the critical starting point— if you have done this properly, the remaining steps will go smoothly. From this point on, we just add controlled amounts of detail until it is time to stop. That is the reason for the paradox—we had a lot to say in the previous section on producing the simplest diagram, but now that the diagrams will get more complex, we have less to say. There really isn't a lot to say; we are just applying the guidelines that we explored in Chapter 9. Here are a few key principles:

- When collecting additional detail, it's generally easier to capture it in list or point form rather than trying to swimlane it immediately. When building a list, it's easy for people to spot missing or incorrect steps and rectify. With diagramming, there can be a tendency to resist changes, even essential ones, because they are so much work.

- In general, unwanted detail can be tricky for a facilitator to handle. If you just say, "That's too detailed for now," the participant may get frustrated and clam up. Usually, we say "Hmmm, sounds like we'd better capture that" and then put it on a "parking lot" (stuff for later) list. Or ask the participant to summarize.

- Follow the principle of "expand by three to five times." Each step in a handoff model should typically ("typically"—there are always exceptions) expand to no more than five in the next level.

- In most cases, and this is important, you usually have to go too far before you know you've gone far enough. You will gather some information, but essentially abandon it without turning it into a diagram. That is, you will list some points about the next level, and then say "Hey, there's no 'aha' in here." When that happens, save your notes but don't take the time to develop a swimlane diagram! Some analysts find this very difficult—"I've gathered the information, I must format it!"

Some specific guidelines for the milestone (level 2) model:

- First, remember what Chapter 9 said—this level adds steps that depict:

Achievement of a milestone;

Decisions that affect the flow in a significant way;

The mechanics of any handoffs (both the "pass" and the "receive") that introduce delay, errors, or expense;

Significant looping (e.g., "go back" or "repeat until").

- Therefore, for each step in the handoff model, start by brainstorming the significant milestones and decisions. Try to keep it under five. Remind participants that a milestone is just that—an important state or point has been reached. It is different than a simple task. Some steps in a handoff will not break down any further—they represent a single milestone or task.

- If there is a mandatory sequence, put steps in that order and ask: "What have we missed?"

- If there isn't a mandatory sequence, the steps can be placed in a dotted box when you draw the diagram.

- Ask how the "handoff in" and "handoff out" are implemented, and if there are any problems. If so, add steps to depict those.

- After you have done this for a few (three to five) steps from the high-level handoff, draw the corresponding part of the milestone level diagram, but only if the new information is worth drawing, as discussed earlier. People like to see the diagram starting to evolve, rather than capturing lists for the entire handoff diagram before starting the new milestone diagram. While drawing, you might find there are important loops that have to be added.

- Walk through a few scenarios to ensure that all steps, decisions, loops, and handoffs are shown.

- Ask the five key questions.

Some guidelines for the task (level 3) model:

- Chapter 9 noted that "Level 3 makes the transition into describing the details of how the process is implemented. It contains individual tasks or steps leading up to a milestone, and the details which characterize how the workflow is implemented such as 'photocopy form' or 'fax estimate to shop.' It will also show the mechanics of any handoffs not shown in previous levels, or different cases (minor branching)."

- In practice, if we go to a third-level diagram, it is usually only for a part of the process that is confusing or problematic.

- The essential technique is the same as it was for building the previous level. Take each step from the flow model and ask, "What are the individual tasks or steps that make up this step, or lead to this milestone?" Remember: you are looking for tasks and mechanics.

- It is often useful to have an actor (one of the participants) describe actually doing it, while the facilitator tries to capture it. Then ask, "Did I get this right?"

- Once enough facts are gathered, shift to drawing the diagram, but only if the new information is worth drawing, as discussed earlier.

- Walk through a few scenarios to ensure that all steps, decisions, loops, and handoffs are shown.

- Ask the five key questions.

Conclusion

Remember the modeler's motto: "Good enough for now!" In his book *Rise & Resurrection of the American Programmer*, Ed Yourdon discusses the concept of "good enough software." [1] He attributes this concept to some of Microsoft's paradoxical success—they ship software with thousands of known bugs, yet are extremely successful where it counts, in the marketplace. The only logical conclusion is that the ultimate judge of quality, the consumer, has decided absence of bugs, the computer scientist's definition of quality, is not the measure (or at least not the full measure) of quality.

In our modeling projects, we will need to keep this concept of "good enough" in mind. Ask, "What is the underlying purpose of this model, and will further effort further the goal?" If not, it's good enough.

Reference

[1]   Yourdon, E., "Good-Enough Software," in *Rise & Resurrection of the American Programmer*, Upper Saddle River, NJ: Yourdon Press, 1996, pp. 157–181.

12

Difficulties with As-Is Modeling

As-is modeling: tips, tricks, and traps

Unfortunately, modeling the as-is process doesn't always sail along smoothly. While preparing for the process modeling session, or even worse, during the session, certain problems just keep coming up. You will encounter them, since clients, associates, and students report the same experiences and concerns. This chapter will arm you with some defense strategies—it is a bit of a grab bag of issues and approaches arranged under five broad topics:

1. Securing or coordinating participation, and dealing with "mystery areas";

2. Applying a process orientation when it is not appropriate, and vice versa;

3. Facilitation or modeling issues arising during the session;

4. The role of systems in a process model;

5. Disagreements and multiple process versions.

Before we look at specific problems, there are two things to remember. First, there are many other things that could go wrong, but they can be avoided by framing the process well and securing effective sponsorship. Even some of the issues covered in this chapter might be headed off during framing, so do not skip that phase or you'll waste time, frustrate the participants, and probably embarrass yourself.

Second, some issues, especially those of the "How do I model XYZ situation" variety were covered in previous chapters, so review them, especially Chapter 10, which covered problems with the swimlane diagramming technique, before your modeling session. In the heat of the moment, you might forget certain guidelines that we have covered already, especially those that deal with multiple versions (cases) of a process, and handling (or, more precisely, not handling) detail and complexity.

Missing participants and mystery areas

A common lament: "We can't get all the right people together to look at the process." There are two main variations: you can't arrange involvement of all the areas that should be involved—they are too busy, or just not interested; OR you have arranged the involvement of the right areas, but you can't get all the people together at the same time and place for working sessions.

This is not what you want to hear, but let's face it—if you can't secure the commitment and participation of the people you need, your project is off to a bad start and implementation isn't going to go smoothly. This is true in any kind of project, and probably more so in process improvement. There is no miracle cure, just a dose of reality and some options to consider—you will have to soldier on just as you would on any other kind of project. There are a couple of strategies, but no magic. Let's consider each case.

Case #1—you can't secure involvement

If you can't get an important internal area to participate, what does that say about the project's chances of success? Participation is critical for buy-in, and buy-in is critical for a smooth implementation, so insufficient participation is a good predictor of trouble ahead. This is an issue for the sponsor. First, go back to your sponsor (you do have an executive sponsor with sufficient span of authority, don't you?) and get assistance in getting the necessary groups involved. Along with setting scope and objectives, this is the sponsor's main responsibility. If that doesn't work, and you cannot get the scope changed (or transfer to another project), there is an approach you can try, although it's a little underhanded. Build a swimlane that either shows the missing area as a big cloud labeled "unable to determine" or "couldn't arrange interviews." Send it to the nonparticipating group for their review and ask innocently if they can provide the sort of detail the other areas have provided before the model goes to top management. In the few cases where we have used this approach, it gained cooperation immediately. Of course, this only helps you understand what they do. You will still have a problem on your hands when it's time to change their procedures. Or try this variation. Instead of the cloud, fill in what you can, and say, "This is our best guess, could you please correct any errors?" The message is "Speak now or forever hold your peace—we have to go forward with something, and this is it."

If the missing participant is internal, perhaps you can find someone who used to work in the area who will represent the nonparticipant as best they can—to "wear a hat" and represent that point of view. If the missing participant is external, try to find someone who has (or has had) direct contact. For instance, if you need the customer's perspective, can someone from customer service or sales fill in? Or, if you need a supplier's perspective, can someone from engineering or purchasing fill in? Sometimes an external consultant can fill in effectively. Remember, though, that these are generally poor substitutes; current knowledge from the specific perspective you're seeking cannot be replaced.

Case #2—you can't arrange meetings

This never used to be a problem, but nowadays there is generally more work being done by fewer people, so scheduling problems are common. Also, as organizations and their people become more geographically distributed, distance and travel are more common issues. This is arguably better than the first situation—at least the groups want to participate, but they are too busy or distance is too much of an obstacle. Don't get too upbeat, though—a cynic would argue that they still don't care enough to take the time or trouble to attend working sessions. As in the previous case, maybe they can attend a limited set of sessions—kickoff and review. If the problem is distance, maybe a virtual (electronic) meeting is possible. Some facilitators are using NetMeeting with a simple drawing tool like Visio, or videoconferencing tools. New Web-based collaboration tools are appearing all the time. Your organization's training or corporate services department may be able to help.

Applying and misapplying process view

There are cases when the approach in this book and the problem area don't match. You must use the right tool, and no tool applies to all situations. Imagine you find yourself running a session and you get the uncomfortable feeling that this isn't "workflow" as you understand it. Framing goes well, but now you find that there actually isn't any defined flow of tasks and actors. You constantly hear "Well, it depends…" You find there are:

- ◆ Collaborations (defined information transfers);

- ◆ Lots of shared data;

- ◆ Milestones or gating points.

You have stumbled into the "other workflow." Many tools, notably Lotus Notes, are referred to as "workflow" but they could be called "information flow" or "information exchange." Their niche is knowledge management, *collaborative* processes. This book's techniques are designed for *transactional* processes. If we encounter one of these situations, we run. But seriously, we actually focus on clarifying the structure, content, and meaning of the information[1] and on defining the milestones. Then we run, and find someone with experience in this area to take over.

In another case someone (maybe you, maybe the client) has decided to follow a process workflow-based approach on a project, but it turns out that "process" isn't really the problem. Here is a case study.

A client retained us to look at a particular business process, so we developed a process-based agenda. The session went okay, but it was clear that the process workflow was fine—the right people did the right things at the right time. The problem was information access—in this, and other processes the participants worked in, access to complete, accurate information was the limiting factor. Note that a situation like this usually bears

---

1. A less structured form of data modeling.

more than a passing resemblance to the previous case—the "other" work-flow. We still managed to use a process-based agenda, but careful as-is modeling and to-be redesign weren't part of it. What did we do?

First, we asked, "Whaddaya need?" but in a more sophisticated way. This gave us the lay of the land in terms of information terminology and definitions. Then we brainstormed the events that drove a need for information (e.g., "complaint is received," "license renewal is due," etc.). We strung the events together into a semblance of a process, which also made missing events stand out, so they were added. This is done for completeness; otherwise, people might zero in on one area. Finally, we walked through the events (essentially, the steps) that made up the process and for each asked, "What information is needed?" The process-based agenda ensured that we covered the field rather than zeroing in on one area. Also, we ended up initiating minor process changes, especially where support staff was involved in retrieving information.

And now, here is a case we are seeing all the time, which is the inverse of the preceding case. Imagine you need to determine requirements for a new application. But you soon recognize that the overall process is being ignored and only a piece of it is under consideration. Participants don't even see it as a complete process. The current classic example is "Webifying" a transaction or "e-ing" (as in e-business or e-commerce) an area; in other words, putting up a Web front end without an integrated business process. This will typically raise customer expectations so they can fall even further.

How you handle this depends on your comfort level and credibility with the sponsor. You have an obligation to point out that if the complete process isn't integrated, the results are almost certain to be negative. You can determine/demonstrate what needs to be included by "nibbling at the edges." For instance, in an on-line ordering e-commerce initiative, ask, "What has to happen to get current customer, account, and product information to the site, along with the customer's previous order activity? What has to happen to complete the interaction that the customer has initiated? When is it fully completed, and what else can happen along the way (e.g., out of stock situation, order changes)?" This is usually enough to get the scope reconsidered. If not, do what you can to expedite inputs and outputs, and then run.

A similar situation: You're stuck in a silo, dealing with less than a complete process. The scope of your project is a particular function or department, but you have been asked to develop workflow models. Actually, you have probably been asked to "improve our department's processes," even though, by definition, you are not dealing with a complete process. Try to identify the pieces of the various processes the department deals with. Otherwise, you'll go crazy trying to fit it all on a single swimlane diagram. Identify arrival events, departure events, and the paths that connect them. Clean up the really goofy steps, and then really concentrate on the boundaries—getting work in and getting it out.

How do I depict or emphasize? I'm overwhelmed

"I can't model this! I don't know how to show this!" Don't let the swimlane diagram technique get in the way. Never let your inability to model something prevent you from capturing it. Some techniques:

- Describe it in quasi–use-case format or narrative format (that is, "actor does action" form or just a point-form description).

- Use traditional tools such as "structured English" or pseudocode (e.g., If Then Else), decision trees, or truth tables.

- Simply add an annotation to the diagram (we do this all the time).

- Add a big dotted box with some narrative in it.

- Add a cloud.

And, if you discover something important, and don't know how to depict it, feel free to invent a symbol:

- For instance, if tasks by a certain actor are continually interrupted, show lots of jagged arrows labeled "interruptions" coming in to the area. Draw flow lines with zigzag lines as well. Also show the same process step drawn multiple times with zigzag connections between them to illustrate interruption.

- Another example: you might sometimes add an icon for an inbox (see the discussion in Chapter 10). This is an example of inventing a symbol to get a point across. Various modeling tools or graphics tools (e.g., Visio) have icons for all sorts of things. You should use them when they help, *but sparingly*! Remember why we use a simple "everything is a box" diagramming style—because it provides maximum clarity and accessibility to the maximum number of people. Diagrams with literally dozens of different icons are cute, but they confuse more than they inform.

- Don't be afraid to use some other kind of diagram, especially of something physical that people can relate to, like an office floor plan or a shop floor layout.

Over the course of a project, you might need to highlight different aspects, such as:

- Wait time;

- The role of systems;

- Total cost;

- Duplicated effort;

- Unnecessary constraints.

But don't try to show them all at once—if you highlight everything, you highlight nothing. That is one reason you shouldn't use a lot of special symbols. You might draw one diagram that highlights the time a work item spends in actual or virtual in-baskets (e.g., by time-scaling the diagram and "flat-lining" the periods when an item is waiting), and you might draw another diagram that emphasizes something entirely different, like duplicated effort. When the special diagram has served its purpose, go back to the plain-vanilla model before highlighting another aspect.

Facilitation (and interaction)

The subtext here is "read books and take courses on facilitation skills, and presentation skills too." All the modeling skills in the world will not help if you can't focus a group on the task at hand, obtain balanced participation, and keep the session moving. Here are some miscellaneous issues that relate to facilitating groups or dealing with people.

- Dealing with off-topic, out-of-scope, late, or ahead-of-time points; ideas out of the blue; or total non sequiturs.

First, you need the framing material and your session plan posted so you can use it when asking how the point fits. Without it, you are lost.

Second, just because you don't understand how a comment or point fits, don't assume the participant is off topic. Do the Lt. Columbo routine: "I'm not clear on how this fits in." When we apply "constructive ignorance" (asking "dumb" questions), we often uncover important facts or ideas, and discover the "off-the-wall" comment was right on the money.

If, however, it cannot be related to the topic at hand, use the parking lot, bin list, or whatever you call it. Record the point. This acknowledges or validates whoever contributed. It gets the point out of mind so everyone can concentrate on the topic at hand. Often, items on the bin list resolve themselves.

♦ Jargon is fun to use, because it makes you feel like you're one of them, but be careful. Things always seem to make sense at the time, so be sure you record what is actually happening so you will remember later. Someone from another area should be able to follow the model. *Always* use the terms that you agreed to in the glossary/data model, and stick with verb-noun format for step names.

Bad: "Complete Form CS-39";

Good: "Request Transcript Using CS-39."

♦ Another pitfall is confusing the "as is" with what "should be." Model reality, not policy, and discourage criticism from the "rule happy" folks. You know, internal audit, training, or some other group that "knows" how it ought to be done, and insists on attacking participants—"That's not how it's supposed to be done!" This stifles participation. You may have to take them aside and explain that if they don't stop jumping on participants, the facts won't emerge at all, which won't help anyone.

♦ Similarly, stay focused on "as is," not "could be." Note any improvement or redesign ideas or "low-hanging fruit" on an ideas flipchart and move on. Above all, control the urge to leap into the design of something like a Microsoft Access application.

- After the modeling session, you may find that the client really likes version 1—"So that's how it works!" But don't stop unless you have confirmed the model by reviewing it with others (who weren't in the session) and by direct observation.

  Be sure the project is discussed with staff before interviews and observation and they know who you are and why you're there. Major problems develop when people assume the worst (you are the downsizing police).

  And accept that sometimes the situation is too sensitive for walk-arounds—leave it to one of the managers or supervisors people are used to seeing.

- If during the session, people are a little reserved, it may be perfectly natural. People define themselves in terms of the job they do, and if you're interfering with that, you are interfering with their identity. Be sensitive, not like the one analyst who still makes us cringe. In a process modeling session he looked at what one group did, an evident nonvalue-added activity, and happily exclaimed, "Hey, these people don't actually do anything!" Participation fell off rapidly.

Systems and whether to show them

There is usually much more systems involvement than participants are aware, but you will sometimes encounter resistance to including this in your workflow modeling session. One line of reasoning is that what happens inside the machine is just "techie stuff" and is not part of the real process. Wrong! Remember the "holds the work, adds value, moves the work along, introduces delay" test? Another line of reasoning is that the discussion shouldn't stray into IT issues because once the systems people get started, things rapidly spiral downward into excruciating detail. Unfortunately, too often right! This must be managed using the levels of detail approach. There are a few common cases:

- "Babysitting" by IS/IT staff. IT personnel might monitor jobs, check report output, "diddle the data," and so forth. This must absolutely be shown—the IS person definitely has a role in the process. The difficulty might be in deciding how much of the batch process to show leading up to the IT person's involvement.

◆ There are process steps that are substantially less automated than many people are aware. A recent, but classic, case—the e-commerce site where orders were captured on the Web, printed, and manually entered into the order entry system! No discussion here—these "human glue" steps must be shown.

◆ This is the toughest one—there are extensive, complex batch processes that are part of the process—vital links in the chain between event and results. These systems deserve a fuller discussion, which is provided in the next section.

Batch systems

In an example from our experience, a government agency had literally weeks of batch jobs. The process was not understood at all by business people, and poorly understood by IT—individuals understood their piece of the job stream, but not the whole thing. It had a major impact on client satisfaction because clients had to wait over two weeks for a license. There was resistance to depicting it in workflow model: "That's technical stuff that has nothing to do with the business process!" It was obvious, though, that unless this was addressed, the customers would still be dissatisfied, no matter how much front-end process redesign was done. The real challenge is to depict what actually happens in the batch job stream without getting into the complexity of every sort, merge, copy, and processing step. To gain understanding of a process like this, you must abstract the detail into understandable business terms, using the swimlane format that the rest of the process will be described in, but there is no way around it— it's hard!

It is often difficult to find IT resources who have the technical skills to trace through the batch processes, and who can also explain in everyday language what is being accomplished. In some cases—and this is frightening—no one knows anymore what some of the programs are doing. Fortunately, during Y2K remediation, many organizations opened up these old programs, figured out what they were doing, and documented them. Better yet, sometimes they actually restructured them or threw them out!

We have tried various approaches, not all of which worked. For instance, try creating swimlane diagrams on which each subsystem had its own swimlane. It works well when the subsystems are clearly delineated; often, though, it was not clear what constituted a subsystem and its boundaries. Also, to split work across subsystems often drives you to too low a level of detail. In other words, no one could build the diagram, and no one could understand it. Time to try something else.

One option that worked: we added one swimlane to the workflow model for *each* day in the cycle that a typical transaction would work its way through, and created a step for each significant milestone on that day (e.g., Day 4: "Transmit contract record to national clearinghouse," Day 5 and 6: "No activity," Day 7: "Receive activity report from national, merge with Secretary of State activity reports, print summary reports"). Showing each day as a separate actor was unusual, but it did a good job of highlighting the delays and serial nature of the process. As usual, it was hard to synthesize out the main milestones. The actual job steps were so arcane that only skilled, experienced professionals could tell us what was actually happening.[2]

The other option that worked was similar except that there was only one swimlane for "Batch Systems." In those cases, we added vertical markers to indicate "day boundaries"—each time the process went through an overnight batch job cycle.

And of course, there has been the odd case where we could not interest the business people in seeing a model of the batch processes, so we just had to tell them the conclusion: "It takes eight days to accomplish what should happen almost instantly. If you're interested in improving this, we can prepare estimates."

Disagreement

This is the one that seems to terrify people new to running sessions— "What if I'm up there running a session to build a swimlane diagram, and everyone's arguing about how the process actually works?" Sounds bad,

---

2. This is similar to a business process in which each actor's tasks are so small and specialized that it's almost impossible to discern the overall process. In batch jobs streams, technically similar tasks (e.g., edits) might be combined into one program, so that complete business steps or activities are spread across many programs.

but if you take a deep breath and step back, you can handle it. Some general principles:

- Usually there is some difference in perspective for the disagreeing parties. The key is to discover what it is:

  Geographic location is the most common ("Akron handles receiving differently than Sydney");

  Organizational location ("Sales awards bonuses differently than Tech Support");

  As-is versus should-be ("What is actually happening is different than what the operating procedures state");

  In minor cases, the difference is that individuals perform the same step differently ("Juan and Alice conduct follow-up inspections differently").

- Before diving into detail, try to list or describe (narrative) the key differences. Then try to ask, "Are these significant differences?" and "How important is it to resolve them?"

- If the differences are not important, perhaps you can model a typical approach with a few narrative annotations. Or develop the typical or mainstream flow first and then add variations.

- If the differences are substantial (more than just one piece of the process) and they matter, then the best approach is to do a separate model for each variant. You will eventually have to understand each location's as-is process anyway, to plan implementation, and you can sometimes identify best practices from various sites. Always agree to model *one case at a time*—this avoids the endless circling that will happen if you try to model them all at once.

- A second alternative, almost as good, is to have representatives from the most typical site (if there is such a thing) participate in drawing their form of the process. Then review with other groups, and they can usually highlight the differences easily.

Conclusion

This chapter should have brought you to the point where you are ready to make a thorough assessment of your current process. The next chapter will cover that in detail.

13

Completing the As-Is Assessment

What's going on here?!—Everyone, or so it seemed when you were a kid.

Introduction

So, what have we accomplished so far? We have completed phase 1, frame the process, during which we established the target process and its boundaries and performed initial assessment (stakeholder-based) and goal setting, and we are well into phase 2, understand the as-is process. We have completed as-is workflow process modeling to whatever detail was useful and learned a lot more about the process along the way. It is time to transition into reengineering—to consolidate our understanding of the factors impacting current process performance. Resist the urge to leap into design of the to-be process (that is phase 3), and instead take a short time to conduct a broad-based assessment of the as-is process.

You might feel sure you know the root causes of the problems in the current process after completing process workflow modeling. But not so fast! If you perform an assessment as described in this chapter, you might find the root cause of an issue is completely different than your initial impression. For instance, your initial assessment for a permit application is that the cycle time is far too long. After as-is modeling, your team might feel that an IT solution based on a workflow tool will address the problem by expediting the movement of the permit through the process. However, an enabler-based assessment might determine that the real problems are inappropriate staff performance metrics (rewarded for finding fault, no matter how inconsequential) and narrow job definition (too many people each looking at too small a piece of the puzzle). The IT solution will have virtually no impact if these other factors are not addressed. We have seen it more times than we care to count. Take a moment to think about it. Have you seen cases where new processes or IT really didn't make the desired improvement? Why not?

You want to perform an assessment that will help your project address the issues that really matter—let's see how, starting with a recap of the goals of this step. The goal of *assessing the as-is process* is to determine the root cause of unsatisfactory performance in the process, specifically addressing stakeholder issues determined during initial assessment and unsatisfactory performance with respect to goals established in *framing the process*. A secondary goal is to suggest process characteristics for consideration during the next phase, *characterizing and designing the to-be process*. These suggestions (and that's all they are right now—suggestions) will include process changes and aspects of the current process to retain. We will also confirm whether or not we need to proceed with process change at all.

As illustrated in Figure 13.1, assessment is part understanding the as-is, and part designing the to-be—they're inseparable. It's natural that you cannot point to a fault in the as-is process without imagining improvements for the to-be. Instead, capture ideas about how the process can be improved. And don't just dwell on what is wrong. It is essential that we also identify the good aspects of the process that should be preserved.

Ideas about the new process—whether current features to retain, or new process designs—will not be decided upon until the next step, so, in a way, this is like brainstorming—capture ideas, and then let them gel a bit before assessing them and making decisions. The approach follows a step-by-step method that has evolved over a number of consulting assignments. The intent is to ensure you don't jump into solutions until you properly understand the problem.

The approach is step-by-step, but it isn't Industrial Engineering 101—it is less formal, and perhaps more subjective—but it seems to strike

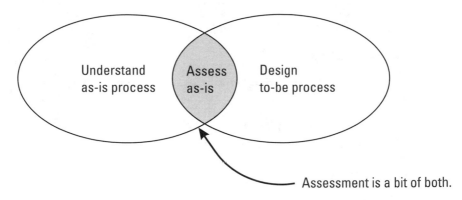

Assessment is a bit of both.

Figure 13.1   Assessment is part as-is, part to-be.

a good balance, and it works in practice. It will not always be easy—like redesign, it's part technique, part inspiration. But this chapter will provide a framework to help inspiration come. It utilizes a framework, in this case, an assessment based on the six enablers introduced in Chapter 3 (workflow design, application of IT, motivation and measurement, and so forth) to ensure that a broad view is taken. Otherwise, it's too easy to drill down in one area while ignoring others. It often yields surprising discoveries—people focus on workflow design and IT (naturally), but the solution might lie in motivation and measurement or in job definition. To prevent diving into the wrong details, we identify the process's leverage points. In the best Stephen Covey tradition, this forces attention on the "big rocks first." The key steps are:

1. Confirm initial stakeholder assessment and process goals from framing.

2. Capture first impressions of process strengths and weaknesses.

3. Make the initial decision on what to do with the process—leave it as is, abandon it, improve it, and so forth.

4. Identify leverage points.

5. Assess by each enabler in turn (workflow design, IT, and so forth).

6.   Optionally, assess individual steps.

7.   Consolidate process suggestions.

8.   Make the final decision on what to do with the process.

A caveat: Do not skip this step. It might look overwhelming, but it should only take a couple of days. It will be well worth it.

Getting ready

In addition to the core team, this step will ideally involve the people (process analysts *and* content experts) who participated in the as-is mapping. Along the way, they have built up a lot of knowledge and impressions, probably much of it undocumented, and you want to capture it in the form of an assessment ASAP. Even if only the core team (process analysts only) can actively participate, this should never be a back-room activity involving only the consultants, analysts, or process improvement experts. That has been tried, and often when a supposed fault was found in the process, there was a good reason for it to be that way. More importantly, the process team and the folks back at the ranch will never buy into an external assessment—they must participate.

As per our usual default, this is best done in a facilitated session. You may have individuals or small teams to do detail work, but the norm is that it all happens in session. If your group isn't familiar with the business of process improvement and the kinds of things that other organizations are doing, prepare a brief (15- to 30-minute) presentation on the principles and practices (with examples) of process improvement. The notes (symptom/modern alternative) in the "Assess by Enabler" section of this chapter can provide raw material for the presentation.

Confirm initial assessment and goals

Capture any new information that has come out while mapping the as-is process. Look at your summary poster from Framing the Process (Part II) and ask:

- Would the process case for action (especially the stakeholder assessment) be any different now based on what you learned while doing the mapping? Be sure to ask the question for *each* stakeholder.

- Would the process vision be any different now based on what you learned while doing the mapping?

Capture first impressions

We don't want our formal steps to get in the way of recording the obvious. At this point, participants will probably have some strong ideas about the process. Open up the floor and brainstorm for significant first impressions, including problems, features to keep, and possible improvements. These ideas will eventually come out anyway, but you are better off to do it now—let participants get the ideas off their chest so they can focus on our step-by-step assessment. Otherwise, they will be distracted while they look for an opportunity to make their point. In fact, this technique is useful in most facilitated sessions. Call it venting. It gets gripes and worries off participants' minds so they can concentrate on the task at hand. But a caution! You must strictly control this, or it will spiral into unfocused details. You really do only want first impressions. Try using a timebox—allow only 20 minutes of session time. Or, you can limit content—give each participant three slips of paper, one for each of their top three concerns. Toss the slips in a box, and review one at a time for quick comments and recording on flipcharts.

Decide on approach

Before going any further, take some time to decide if you need to. Go further, that is. The future of the process is not necessarily that it will be redesigned. There are five possible courses of action:

- *Drop/abandon:* This process is not necessary, or the benefit will never justify the cost. It is rare, but we had a case where a software license validation process cost several hundred thousand dollars per year and consumed skilled resources, but delivered no benefit (never uncovered problems). The company decided to abandon the process rather than reengineer it. (Technically, this is the ultimate in reengineering.)

* *Outsource*: It would be a more effective use of resources to have a supplier carry out the process. Traditionally, this has been the choice for generic, infrastructure activities such as cleaning and catering. Companies are increasingly doing this in areas such as billing, receivables, help desk, network operations, PC support, and so forth.

* *Leave as is*: The process is fine; the issues were elsewhere (e.g., no one follows the process, or training is needed). Apply the 10% rule: if the new process will not be at least 10%, better leave it alone.

* *Improve*: The basic structure of the process is okay, but specific improvements are possible.

* *Redesign*: The process should be fully redesigned.

We are increasingly skeptical of the distinction between improve and redesign. We use the terms because they have been an intrinsic part of the literature. In practice, though, it's a continuum, and within a process, some aspects may be improved, while other phases are totally new, designed from the ground up. Either way, the intent of this step is to provide a moment of reflection before carrying on. And you will revisit it after you complete the assessment.

Identify leverage points

What is really important in the process? Looking for leverage points can help you find out. A leverage point is a step, stage, or aspect of the process that has a disproportionate impact on overall performance. It is likely to be the root cause of the most significant problems. In other words, if you could fix the problems at the leverage points, you would significantly improve process performance, possibly with surprisingly little redesign. Note that you might discover leverage in either of two areas within the process itself—for instance, at a particular step, or the absence of a needed enabler, or within the cases or variations the process must handle—for instance, it could be that "issue building permit" works well except for a single type of new construction within a particular zoning area. Let's look at some examples of leverage points.

An order fulfillment process based on a "build to order" model had unacceptable fulfillment time and defect rates. Finished goods were currently shipped to a separate quality control facility (a holdover from an acquisition) for inspection and calibration, and then shipped back to the production site for consolidation and shipping to the customer. As well as the obvious delay, the shipping introduced more defects than if the goods had stayed at the production site, so the leverage point was to "eliminate shipping of finished goods to a separate quality control facility." Presumably, this would be accomplished by moving quality control to the production area, but that is an idea for assessment (see Chapter 14).

Another advertising order fulfillment process, very similar to a radio advertising example mentioned in Chapter 6, generated unacceptable error rates and stress levels in the production department of a monthly magazine, which led to customer complaints and lost revenue. A mobile sales force took orders for advertising that required custom production work back at the magazine's offices. The assumption was that something was wrong with the internal order booking and production activities, but when pressed for the leverage points ("What single change would make the most difference?"), a different story emerged. Because they were expected to "sell, sell, sell," the sales reps stayed in the field selling and didn't submit orders until the last minute. If they could somehow "get the order back to the production department in real-enough time" (the leverage point), then the major problems would disappear with no other process changes. Possible remedies appeared in workflow design, the use of IT, the motivation and measurement scheme, and so on, but finding solutions isn't the immediate concern. If ideas arise now, fine, capture them, but you don't have to do this until the design stage.

If they aren't forced to consider leverage points, people will initially start looking at comparatively minor aspects of the process, or symptoms. Perhaps it's just easier for people to focus on the 80% cited in the famous 80/20 rule. This is also known as the Pareto Principle, after V. Pareto, an Italian economist. He noted that in distributions (in particular, income distributions), 80% of the distribution usually goes to 20% of the observations. For example, 80% of the wealth is held by the richest 20% of households, 80% of the workers are employed by the largest 20% of companies, and so forth. By this reckoning, we would expect that 80% of your problem could be caused by 20% of your process steps or cases. In some circumstances, and your process might be one of them, the 80/20 rule becomes the 90/10 rule: 90% of the problems are caused by 10% of the process. You must concentrate on the vital few defects that cause the majority of loss, not the trivial many [1].

But how to identify the leverage points? They may be obvious, or they may require a more structured search. Here are two approaches:

1. If there are different cases that your process must accommodate (these should have been listed during framing), then list them visibly to the group.

2. Walk through the process, following one case at a time.

During each approach, ask:

• Is one of the cases the source of a disproportionate share of problems?

• If so, why? What has to change about the case or the process to remedy this?

Once the leverage point is identified, capture any improvement suggestions on an ideas flipchart for use during the characterize and design step.

Assessment by enablers

The concept of process enablers introduced in Chapter 3 is familiar by now, but here is a quick recap. An enabler is one of the aspects of a process that "enables" it to perform properly. More to the point—if an enabler is absent or inappropriate, it becomes a "dis-abler." Finding both cases is important. The six enablers are:

1. Process workflow design
   (actors, steps, and flow);

2. Application of information technology
   (applications, databases, computers and other devices, networks, and communications);

3. Motivation and measurement
   ("reward and punishment" schemes);

4. Human resources
   (organizational structure, job definitions, selection and placement strategy, skills, and training);

5. Policies and rules
   (self-imposed or external constraints and guidelines);

6. Facilities design
   (workplace layout and equipment, or some other categories appropriate to your situation).

Figure 13.2 expands on Figure 3.1 and puts this in context. It shows the process, with the organization's mission, strategy, goals, and objectives, the process' goals, objectives, and differentiator, and organizational environment above, with the six enablers below.

- A process supports the organization's mission, strategy, goals, and objectives.

- It aims to achieve its own goals and objectives according to the chosen differentiator.

- It is constrained by organizational environment (culture).

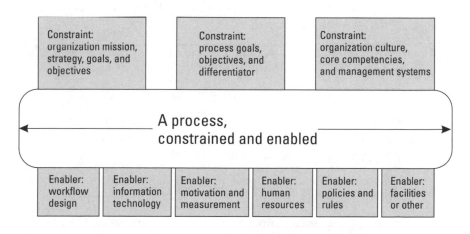

Figure 13.2 The process in context with goals, constraints, and enablers.

Look at each enabler in turn, and canvass the group for suggestions on how that enabler manifests itself in the process, whether positively or negatively. Record these assessments, and when improvement ideas emerge (they will!), also record them on an ideas sheet. Keep all of these suggestions, even if they appear dubious at first. If you want to be a little more structured, capture assessments and ideas in a matrix with four columns: enabler (e.g., IT), issue (the problem), alternative (a potential improvement), and notes.

Participants often struggle with this, because they can't always say a problem is specifically one enabler or the other—"I don't know whether this problem belongs in human resources or in workflow design." For example, if a process has too many handoffs, is that workflow design, or a human resources environment that has defined excessively small jobs? It is probably both, but it doesn't really matter. The idea of following this framework is not to force an issue into one category or another; it's to force us to consider alternatives that might otherwise have been missed. Now let's look at some of the things we will be looking for when we consider each enabler.

Assess by enabler: workflow design

Workflow design is not necessarily the most important enabler, but it is central to this book, so we will provide a little more information here. There is no end to the possibilities, but here are the usual suspects when looking for workflow design flaws:

- Are there too many actors (e.g., three people doing minor tasks that could easily be handled by one of them)?

- Are there too many handoffs (see previous question)?

- Are there nonvalue-added steps (e.g., rekeying information, reconciling different sources)? A good test—would a reasonable customer pay to have this step completed?

- Are there noncritical steps holding up the main flow? Does the work item wait while recording, filing, or whatever is completed?

- Is there excess serialization? Are steps happening in a sequential fashion when they could occur in parallel? This often happens with processes that were originally paper-based, and the source document (like a claim or credit application) could only be on one desk at a time.

- Is there an obvious bottleneck? That is, is there an under-resourced step that all work items must pass through, whether it's value-added or not? Note that a bottleneck isn't automatically bad—sometimes it can serve to regulate the flow of work through the process, or through parallel paths in the process, and actually prevent worse problems (collisions and backups) later on.[1]

- Does the process yo-yo, continually returning to the same control point?

- Do exceptions or tough stuff get in the way of the other 80% or 90%? Do problem customers get the attention, while the easy ones wait?

- Conversely, is there a mechanism to ensure that tough stuff eventually gets dealt with instead of languishing in a tub file?

- Is the process "one size fits all" wherein there is one complex process with lots of decisions, exceptions or complexity to cover all situations (small dollars versus major exposure, long-term customer versus unknown), for example, a purchasing process costing $150 in administrative costs to order $5 worth of office supplies?

- Are escalating approval or information loops built in? That is, does each layer in the corporate hierarchy decide if the dollar amount of a requisition requires a higher authority? This can look like yo-yoing.

- Is there a role that coordinates other roles or tasks? This is often a symptom of a bad process in which actors are working in isolation, lack information or authority, and so forth.

- Is the process undocumented, leading to each individual or area doing it their own way?

- Are individual tasks or desk procedures undocumented, again leading to inconsistency?

- Are roles undefined, leading to confusion about who is responsible for what?

---

1.   We will expand on this point. See the restaurant example coming up shortly.

- Are cause and effect separated in some way, or more commonly, are work and inspection separated? This introduces delay and rework of intermediate steps, and the doers don't learn what they are doing wrong.

- Is there poor collaboration across organizational boundaries, as in: "We're working at cross purposes"? This typically results from local or internal measures as opposed to process-oriented or customer-focused measures that focus on outcomes, not tasks.

As a separate category, we'll look at what we've come to call a "Goldratt assessment"—looking for workflow designs, or policies and rules, that impose constraints on inputs or outputs to the overall process, or to steps within the process. The prime examples are unnecessary (policy-driven) delays or batching. Lately, we've found it useful to think in terms of straight-through processing (STP). STP occurs when a process that for merly had many delays built into it now takes place virtually instantaneously, without human intervention, perhaps because the automated facilities of some enterprise application integration (EAI) technology is shepherding the transaction through various system. The EAI tool automates human interventions and performs the necessary translations along the way, and invokes each system in real time rather than waiting for batches or limits. Imagine that every transaction or work item could sail through the process with no delay or human intervention. Then look at every obstacle to that. This includes:

- Batching by time (hourly, daily, etc.);

- Batching by numerical limits (wait for 50 orders);

- Batching by dollar limits (wait for $1,000 worth of orders);

- Slow transport or delivery;

- Approval steps;

- Data rekeying or reformatting.

These are all variations on not doing something as soon as possible.

Please note that these symptoms are not always problems. For instance, having separate inspectors and coordinators may use the abilities of experienced individuals to leverage the effectiveness of entry-level workers. An example:

My teenage son got a part-time job in the kitchen at a well-known casual, high-energy, high-quality restaurant. In no time, he was cooking appetizers, and then supervising. I expressed amazement: "Son, I know you can grill a mean sandwich, but how in the world do you cook all those appetizers, and start them at the right time, and get them to the right spot all at the same time? It's amazing!" He said: "Dad, it's the process!" I couldn't believe my ears. "The process?" "Yep, the process. The procedure for making each appetizer is precisely defined, so anyone can do it. Also, they know how long it will take, within seconds. So a line coach tells each worker when to start what, so that a table's order of appies will be ready all at the same time." He also explained the role of an inspector at the other end of the line, expediters, servers (as opposed to waiters), and so forth. By designing a repeatable process and putting skilled people in the right QC or coordination roles, the restaurant could achieve excellent results with junior kitchen staff. Note, however, that coordination and inspection didn't take place invisibly—it was instant and right there.

Assess by enabler: information technology

This is a big topic too, but we'll restrict our discussion to a few key questions. Are any of the following characteristics evident?

- Unavailable information, or a lack of shared data?
- Rekeying (duplicate entry) of data?
- Data structures that have inconsistent formats, structures, or semantics?[2]
- Reconciling different information sources?
- Missing functionality; or manual activities that could be automated?
- Awkward interfaces?
- Lack of support for workflow?
- Existing automation that blindly replicates an earlier paper-based process ("paving the cowpaths")?

---

2.   See Chapter 15 on data models for further explanation.

Wherever possible, is IT being used to:

* Automate activities (free up human labor for higher value-added work)?

* Support self-service, or eliminate intermediaries?

* Resequence or parallelize steps that otherwise would happen in some strict sequence?

* Duplicate scarce expertise?

* Eliminate barriers of space (geography) or time the way the Internet has in many processes?

Are modern alternatives being used wherever beneficial?

* Mobile computing (pen-based, wireless, PDA, GPS, etc.)?

* Things that know what they are: self-identifying tags, smartcards, Jini?

* Biometric interfaces devices: voice recognition, face recognition, hand geometry readers, retinal scan, and so forth?

* The device that hasn't been invented yet?

Do IT architectures include:

* Use of middleware to integrate applications across disparate platforms?

* Use of EAI technology to integrate applications into business processes or to integrate different data sources into a single "canonical" view?

* Inventory of shared data and transactions?

* Evolutionary or disposable applications?

Assess by enabler: motivation and measurement

Motivation and measurement is the enabler that surprises less experienced analysts with its importance, but experienced people almost invariably know that it's the most important of the enablers. The bottom line is captured in the C. R. Luigs idea mentioned earlier: People don't pay much attention to what management says; they pay attention to what management measures. And experience has confirmed this time and time again —no matter what management says about what they want a process to achieve, it's what management measures (and rewards or punishes) that dictates how people and processes behave.

Here are a couple of case studies. Motivation and measurement as an enabler first crystallized for me in the mid-1980s. I had been studying the slow rate of behavioral change in an IS department where I was consulting. Management strongly wanted certain changes to take place, but it just didn't happen. Presentations, pep talks, and bulletins from management did not change anyone's behavior, no matter how passionate the delivery was. It dawned on me that this organization revered adherence to project budgets and schedules. Project leaders were dinged if they came in more than 10% over estimates, or (unbelievably) if they were more than 10% under estimates, and were showered with praise and promotion if they consistently came in on target. Management wanted to improve client satisfaction, and encourage good analysis that would lead to application stability, flexibility, and extensibility, but there were no measures for these variables, and consequently no change.

That's when I learned about Luigs's idea, and shortly thereafter had a chance to put the idea that measures drive behavior into action. This case was introduced in Chapter 6. The vice president of IS had stated his extreme dissatisfaction with a computer services department that was in charge of a high-volume, production transaction-processing environment with thousands of users expecting subsecond response time. Along with maintaining and tuning this environment, the computer services group migrated new applications into production. The vice president's complaint was: "Our application developers have to jump through flaming hoops to get a new system into production. It seems as though the CS people feel their entire function is to keep anything new out of *their* production environment. I've told them I want to see some responsiveness and flexibility, but nothing has changed, and I'm ready to outsource the entire function!"

I suggested we take a minute and look at how this group was measured, and sure enough, that explained everything. First, there were absolutely no measures in place relating to getting new apps in quickly. All that was measured was up time and response time, and statistics on these were summarized hourly, daily, weekly, and monthly. They were analyzed, trended, charted, and distributed to every operational manager in the organization.

They were also conspicuously posted in public areas. So, it was no mystery to CS what they were measured on. And what's the surest way to negatively impact up time and response time? You guessed it—migrate a new system into production. Case closed, or at least explained.

Another classic example: After the fall of the Iron Curtain, a team of Western manufacturing experts visited a tractor factory in the former Soviet Union. One of them spotted a lab-coated individual walking among the newly built tractors. Every so often, he would scratch a fender, break a headlight, or pull out a wire. More amazing, this individual worked in a quality control function. Can you guess the motivation? QC was measured on the defects they found. When quality improved, there weren't enough defects anymore, so QC had to artificially introduce them in order to justify their existence. This may be an apocryphal story, but we've seen exactly the same phenomenon in office environment, and so have you:

- If the project control office is rewarded for finding faults in a project plan, then, no matter what, they'll find faults.

- If a copyeditor is measured on the number of changes he or she makes, then expect lots of arbitrary changes.

- Think of examples from your own experience—they're surely there.

A key point: Distortions in behavior are often caused by local measures or piecework measures, rather than measures that include all relevant customer outcomes or process results. A second key point: As we pointed out in Chapter 7,[3] implicit measures are every bit as important as explicit, statistical measures. Implicit measures include "Way to go!" from management, or the approval that comes from adhering to cultural norms. We remember the systems manager who was always thrilled to see a prototype, so she always got one whether it was appropriate or not.

Now, after that preamble, it turns out that there aren't really very many questions to ask. It's just important that they be asked in a structured way. Start at the outside of the process, with the process's customer, and work inwards.

---

3. Speaking of Chapter 7, Considering the Environment, many of the ideas in this section hearken back to that topic. If you skipped it, or can't remember it, this would be a good time for a review.

From the customer's perspective:

* What are the desired outcomes? (This is reflected in the process result, and in the process differentiator.)

* What measures would emphasize the desired customer outcome?

* Is that how the customer currently measures the process? (You might have to negotiate some attitude adjustments with the customer.)

Note that there may be other external stakeholders to consider, such as regulatory agencies or trade/industry associations.

From the organization's, or the process owner's, perspective:

* How is the process currently measured?

* Is that appropriate? Is there appropriate focus on customer outcomes, or inappropriate attention to internal convenience or efficiencies?

From the perspective of the departments or functions involved in the process:

* How is their contribution to the process measured?

* Is that appropriate? Is the process considered at all, or do the measures stress task completion, convenience, or efficiency within the function?

From the perspective of the process's individual actors:

* How is their contribution to the process measured?

* Is that appropriate? Are the measures based on task completion, or on quality or contribution to process (or process phase) outcomes?

* Are there measures that reward new abilities?

What you're looking for in all cases is a misalignment between how the customer would measure the process, and how the organization measures the process and its participants. And it's not that internal efficiencies shouldn't be measured at all, just that there should be balance with measures important to the customer. And we certainly want to eliminate measures based on tasks that simply shouldn't happen. For example, "transcriptions per hour of Field Inspection Report to Head Office format"—don't measure it, eliminate the transcription. A reasonable customer wouldn't pay for reformatting and transcribing, which is a classic nonvalue-added activity. Another example is "settlement corrections handled per clerk per hour"—eliminate the errors instead of measuring the correction activity.

Assess by enabler: human resources

"Human resources," encompassing organization structure, job definition, skills, and training, is a complex and sensitive topic. Entire books and master's degree programs are based on single aspects of human resources, so we can't do it justice in a page or two. But that doesn't mean we'll ignore it—we will just keep it simple by listing a few simple questions to consider.

We haven't included any questions that address organizational structure. That's because the design of the organization (divisions, departments, sections, teams, etc.) in the absence of other factors doesn't make much difference. What really seems to matter is how people, organizations, and processes are measured, and how individuals, jobs, and tasks are aligned.

Let's see if you agree—collectively, we authors have almost 50 years of experience in private and public organizations, and neither of us can recall a case where the dreaded "re-org" in the absence of other significant changes made much difference. How about you? On the other hand, there are lots of examples of organizations remaining intact, but new job definitions and measurement schemes having a huge impact. This is highly relevant to process improvement, because so much has been made about the problems of functionally based organizations, and the superiority of team-based organizations (especially the self-directed, empowered, cross-functional, process-based, customer-focused variety). But whatever their faults, functionally based organizations are generally easier to manage than the alternatives—you have similar people, with similar backgrounds, performing similar work. They're also easier to staff, a pool of expertise develops, and all the other advantages that made specialization attractive in the first place appear.

On the other hand, there are cross-functional teams, which unfortunately were thought to be a panacea in the mid-1990s, just as reengineering was a few years before. Teams have fallen out of favor in many environments because they can be very difficult to manage—you have different sorts of people, with different backgrounds, making different contributions to some overall goal. When teams work, they can be incredibly effective, but they require a degree of management skill, and attention to motivation and measurement (and training and…) that isn't easy to come by. A good case in point: How do you motivate, reward, and retain a star performer in an environment where measures and rewards are team-based, and competition for stars is intense? Currently, we're seeing good results with a combination of:

- Functionally based (traditional) organizations;

- Appropriately "rich" job definitions;

- Well-designed processes and measures that encourage the flow of work towards the desired process outcome.

So don't give organization design more attention than it deserves. There are a couple of other points to consider. In some organizations, especially in small startups, the notion of job definition is foreign—a nonissue, in fact. Everyone is expected to be highly skilled and motivated, and to do whatever needs doing. Generally, it's only with size and complexity that this becomes an issue. And, as noted earlier, it's often hard to separate process design issues from job definition issues—if the workflow has too many handoffs, then it's likely that on the human resources side the jobs are too narrowly defined. What you're investigating is alignment among:

- Skills, knowledge, and experience of the actors (or candidates);

- The boundaries of their responsibilities, as constrained by job or role definitions;

- The requirements of the process tasks.

Let's look at some of the questions. This will not be an exhaustive list, so just remember the key point: "Are the right people, with the right skills, in the right jobs, performing the right tasks?"

Are the skills, knowledge, and experience of the actors well matched with the tasks they perform? This can go both ways. Highly skilled or scarce resources might spend too much of their time doing lower skill or administrative tasks that are not a good use of their time. In one (failed) reengineering project, doctors had been provided with word processing software so they could update their own records rather than having stenographers do it from dictation or handwritten notes. It was a disaster—the doctors resented it, most were inept typists at best, and it took far too much of a scarce, expensive resource's time. The stenos weren't very happy with their jobs eliminated. In another case, an outside sales force was burdened with a lot of administrative activities that could have been handled much more effectively by sales assistants.

The reverse can happen. In one case, all customer service reps, from the newest hire to the most experienced individuals, had to handle any type of issue from any type of customer, even though there was a call screening and routing function. Experienced staff didn't spend their time dealing with cases that required their skills and experience, and junior staff made many errors in handling calls that were beyond their ability. The reasoning, by the way, was that a sink-or-swim environment ensured that only the best candidates stayed around; we were unconvinced. Ironically, reengineering projects have led to many mismatches, such as the case where technical specialists were suddenly expected to participate in customer service and sales activities without any training, or, frankly, without even the temperament for client contact. Assembly-line workers have been burned out by enriched job responsibilities that were beyond their natural abilities, even with training. Sometimes long-term workers are perfectly happy with their supposedly dead-end jobs because they can talk or daydream while doing mindless routine.

Look for skill dilution from excessive specialization and fragmentation. This is a common problem after 200 years of specialization. In addition to getting less from human resources than is possible, boredom and lack of ownership lead to more errors, not fewer. Some clues: What is logically a single task requires multiple participants; individual contributions are almost mechanical; people frequently say, "That's not my job!"; jobs aren't "vertically loaded"—workers don't use the information they create, or detect and correct errors that they have introduced. Has a job been created to coordinate fragmented work—a tracking clerk, traffic manager, expediter, lot coordinator, and so forth? This isn't automatically a problem, but it can indicate that other jobs are excessively limited or operating without the information they need.

Has recruiting become an issue because either the jobs are so complex that no entry-level candidate is suitable, or the jobs are so simplistic that no one wants them?

Assess by enabler: policies and rules

This is fairly straightforward, and will probably have been caught when you inspected the workflow and saw some decision points and checks that left you asking "Why?" Those were probably "policies and rules" that have gone unchallenged but are ripe for rethinking.

- Why *do* we hold special book orders until the total value for a publisher exceeds $1,000?

- Why *do* we require the applicant to provide three years of income tax returns when a valid credit card would handle any conceivable risk?

- Why do we require at least three bids on any service requisition with an estimated value of less than $5,000, especially when we know that it will cost more than that to solicit, review, and select from the bids?

- Why *do* we refuse to allow credit card payment for international orders, including Canada-U.S. transactions?

- Why *do* we insist that vendors emboss a contract with their corporate seal?

You get the idea. What you're looking for is any constraint or requirement that the business imposes that impacts the conduct of a business process. Many of these are easy to spot, because they show up as a decision point in the workflow, but others may be subtler. Just ask if every validation or decision is truly necessary. If you don't catch these now, the *challenge process* that we introduce in the next chapter will almost surely highlight them.

Assess by enabler: facilities

With facilities, you're looking for cases where the workplace and equipment interfere with the process. The local library was a good example until a recent redesign. There used to be separate counter areas; one for checkout, and the other for paying fines or fees, picking up holds, and so forth. Each area required a person to staff it, because they were "contained" and there was no easy way to move from one to another. This meant that even in slow periods, two people had to be on counter duty. Customer satisfaction suffered as well—if customers were checking out books and found that a fine was due or that a reserved book was available, they'd have to leave the checkout line, stand in line at the other counter, complete their business there, and then return to the checkout line to complete their transactions. Also, there were two separate checkout lines, and one always seemed to move more slowly than the other (the one I was in).

The solution was obvious. A single, large counter area serves both functions, with a single checkout line up being handled by one or two staff members who can also accept payment, retrieve reserves, and more. In busy times, a third person handles a line just for fines, registrations, and so forth, and in slow periods only one person needs to be at the counter.

A few questions to ask:

* Does distance between people whose tasks are linked introduce transport or communication delays?

* If work is collaborative in nature, are there suitable facilities (i.e., meeting spaces)?

* Does the physical environment make the job more difficult or unpleasant than it would be otherwise (ventilation, glare, noise, interruption, lack of privacy, etc.)?

Assess individual steps

Assessing the individual steps in detail is optional—it can be overwhelming. So you should do this only for critical or complicated processes. The other assessments will probably catch any problems that this very detailed assessment would, and we have a step in the next phase (the challenge process) that will probably catch anything that's been missed.

There's a book on writing called *Bird by Bird* [2]. The origin of the title is advice the author's father gave to her brother when the lad had to write a term project about ornithology and felt overwhelmed by the work ahead. The advice: "Just take it bird by bird." So, if you need to do a detailed assessment, but feel overwhelmed, our advice is to "just take it step by step." For each step, ask:

- Is this step necessary?

- Does it yield a useful result?

- Would a reasonable customer pay?

- Does the most appropriate performer handle it?

- Do handoffs among steps introduce error, expense, or delay?

- Is the step triggered in the most appropriate way?

- Is this the step occurring at the best point in the sequence?

- Is this the step implemented or supported in the best way?

Another way to look at assessment of individual steps is this: "A process can be seen as a value chain. By its contribution to the creation or delivery of a product or service, each step in a process should add value to the preceding steps." [3] Ultimately, what is most important about each step is whether it is adding value, or is not adding value.

Consolidate ideas

In addition to documenting the assessment, you will want to organize the list of process improvement ideas that were generated alongside of the assessment. They'll be needed in the next phase, when we will assess, select, and consolidate (characterize). Actually, two things will be listed: ideas for improving the process and process characteristics to preserve.

This may also be a good time for the team to highlight quick wins, also known as "low-hanging fruit." What is critical is that a quick win really is:

- Quick and cheap (cost-effective);

- A win: a significant improvement that doesn't have an opportunity cost (distract team from more important long-term stuff) and doesn't impair things in the long run.

But be careful. All too often, so-called quick wins become projects with a life of their own, detracting from important project goals, and leaving a dead-end solution as their legacy. We hate to pick on Microsoft Access applications as an example, but in large corporations we are seeing substantial investments in redeveloping Access applications that were originally seen as quick wins but didn't have the architecture to scale up past a few desktops. You've been warned.

Confirm approach

Take one final look: looking at what's right and wrong, are you still comfortable with the decision to redesign? Could the quick wins conceivably be good enough, especially with respect to other opportunities? Remember, just walking away is sometimes a highly cost-effective approach.

We have done a lot of work without actually getting into redesign yet, but we'll see that all of our effort so far will make redesign much easier and more effective than it would have been.

References

[1]   Kume, H., *Statistical Methods for Quality Improvement*, Tokyo: The Association for Overseas Scholarship, 1985, p.18.

[2]   Lamott, A., *Bird by Bird: Some Instructions on Writing and Life*, New York: Doubleday, 1994.

[3]   Rummler, G. A., and A. Brache, *Improving Performance: How to Manage the White Space on the Organization Chart*, New York: Jossey-Bass, 1995.

Part V
The To-Be Process and Transition to System Requirements

14

Characterizing and Designing the To-Be Process

If at first the idea is not absurd, then there is no hope for it.
—Albert Einstein

Look before you leap!

In most process reengineering books, the section on actually designing the new process is short, containing guidance like "be creative" (Why didn't *we* think of that?) or the always helpful "think outside the box!" Sometimes, to aid in rethinking the process, you'll be treated to an exercise in creative thinking, like the infamous "try to connect all the dots in the following picture without..." People find this exercise entertaining or irritating, but utterly useless in rethinking the process. In BPR courses, the section on mapping the current process is typically followed by a segment on mapping the new, improved process, with a coffee break in between. How to get from the as-is to the to-be isn't explained, so we conclude that during the break, the famous ATAMO procedure is invoked—"And then, a miracle occurs."

This reflects the central problem of process redesign—it seems like a miracle really is required, because it's hard to pry people loose from their accumulated paradigms about the process. What will be done, by whom, when they will do it, and how, have been ingrained by years of experience.

In this chapter, we will substitute method for miracles with proven techniques that enable project teams to creatively invent ideas for the to-be process, assess them, and then select the ones that will actually work. When we select ideas, we will ensure that they are consistent, address the process goals, and are feasible with respect to culture and resources. As usual, the methods we'll describe are based on our experience with what works, and what doesn't.

Goals

The primary goals of "Characterizing and Designing the To-Be Process" are:

1. Produce a description of the important characteristics of the to-be process in terms of the process enablers—workflow design, IT, motivation and measurement, and so forth. Collectively, these are the specifications for the new process.

2. Develop swimlane diagrams at increasing levels of detail (handoff, flow, etc.) depicting the process workflow that supports the desired characteristics of the process or processes.

One way to look at this is that we're starting with conceptual process design—we will identify the main concepts and characteristics of the new process, and only then do we perform detailed process design by specifying the workflow.

Philosophy/approach

Two ideas characterize this approach. First, there are ways to generate creative ideas and to think out of the box. This is not a random, hit-or-miss activity—we can specify a methodology. It won't replace sheer brilliance and flashes of inspiration, but it might help you be more creative and look at your process in new ways. By the way, if you're interested in techniques for creative thinking, or lateral thinking, check out the works of the man who invented the term—Edward de Bono.

Second, a process improvement idea that looks great may not be so appealing when you look at it in context. Most ideas relate strongly to one of the six enablers, and when you look at the ramifications on the other enablers, you might be surprised—sometimes, an idea works synergistically with changes in other enablers, but other times, it turns out to be destructive or much more involved than originally thought. This approach hinges on generating ideas and assessing them with respect to all enablers (in context) before diving into workflow design or "leaping into solution space" by applying technology to the wrong problem.

The three core activities are done in sequence:

1. Generate ideas for the new process.

2. Assess those ideas (in context!) and select the ones that will work and meet the goals.

3. Develop the to-be workflow, one level of detail at a time.

Three techniques are central to this approach:

1. Generate enabler-specific ideas for each leverage point.

2. Generate process improvement suggestions by challenging the assumptions embedded in the as-is process.

3. Assess each suggestion in context by defining its impact on each of the six enablers.

Key steps

♦ Post and review key points from the sections on *framing the process* and *understanding the as-is process.*

♦ Collect ideas, using some or all of these techniques:

Review the improvement suggestions generated during as-is assessment;

Generate ideas that specifically address the leverage points identified during assessment;

"Steal" successful ideas by reviewing best practices;

Brainstorm—wide open;

Brainstorm—by enabler;

Apply the *challenge process* to discover and rethink implicit assumptions.

* Assess each idea by defining its impact on all enablers (workflow design, IT, human resources, etc.) in an idea versus enabler matrix.

* Select ideas that will become the characteristics (specifications) for the to-be process.

* Develop ideal to-be process flow.

* For each level of the to-be workflow (handoff, flow, etc.):

Develop new workflow;

Assess, and revise as necessary before proceeding to the next level.

* Road show—get feedback from a wider audience.

You don't have to go through all of the collect ideas steps, and you don't have to do them in the order listed. In fact, we struggled with the order because there is not a fixed sequence—it's up to you and the unique needs of your project. For instance:

* If you're concerned that your group is stuck in the status quo, start with the challenge process to shake them up.

* If you have an excitable group with no shortage of ideas, and your concern is focusing them, start by generating ideas that address the leverage points.

* If the process "ain't broke" in any particular way (i.e., there aren't distinct leverage points), then brainstorming by enabler will help the team take a balanced approach.

Caveats

This book covers process identification, modeling, assessment, and re-design, with the emphasis on identification and especially on modeling.

We won't spend a lot of time on redesign, but you'll find practical techniques that you can easily put to use on your projects.

We have organized these techniques into a process for process redesign, but there is no fixed process for design process any more than there is a fixed process for "paint masterpiece." Many of the famous process redesigns came about because of a critical insight or flash of inspiration, not finding and fixing flaws. The techniques in this chapter have helped generate their share of inspirations too, but don't be a slave to methodology. If you feel that the structured method described here is stifling some flash of brilliance, by all means experiment with alternate techniques.

Post and review key materials from previous phases

If you've done much facilitation, you know that people have an amazing ability to go off on tangents or to forget the points they agreed to the day (or the hour!) before. That's why facilitation has been compared to herding cats. As a facilitator, you need all the help you can get, which is why you must have the key findings from previous work posted during your session. By posted, we mean summarized on flipcharts that are visible to the group and easy for the facilitator to refer to. When it appears that the discussion is going off topic, the facilitator can ask (in a nonjudgmental way, of course) how the current points relate. The participants make the decision without the facilitator seeming heavy-handed.

The key materials to summarize and review are:

- The overall process map that shows related, but out of scope, processes.

- The scope (or frame) of the process being addressed, especially the event, result, and the milestones that must be achieved.

- Process vision and goals, to ensure we focus on the right things. In particular, have the group refocus on the improvement dimension—the facets of the process that *must* be improved to satisfy the key stakeholders.

- Key points of the stakeholder-based assessment (from framing) and enabler-based assessment (from "understand the as-is").

- Participants will need copies of the as-is process workflow models, as these are usually impractical to enlarge and post.

- You'll also be posting the improvement suggestions generated while assessing the as-is process, but there's a little more involved, so we will describe that shortly.

Collect ideas—getting started

A few points to remind the participants in your process redesign session:

- Just as landscape architects begin with the major structural elements—the "bones" of the landscape—we are after the central features of the new process. The details can be worked out later on when we develop the to-be workflow and the mechanics of individual tasks.

- We're not just gathering new ideas—we will also identify aspects of the current process to consider retaining.

- Finally, it's extremely important to remind participants not to judge the ideas while collecting them—they will be assessed in a separate step. Just as in brainstorming, we discourage criticism suggestions, because:

  Ideas that at first seem unreasonable often "improve with age."

  An idea that truly is impractical can nonetheless inspire other, useful suggestions.

Bring forward ideas generated during assessment

We will start with the work that's already been done—the ideas for the to-be process that were suggested while assessing the as-is (Chapter 13). They're probably already on flipcharts, so begin by hanging them on a wall. Then, invite the team to spend a few minutes looking them over with the intent of suggesting revisions or extensions, or capturing new ideas that they inspire. We do this because suggestions evolve, often unconsciously, during the downtime between sessions. What once seemed outlandish can seem practical after some settling-in time, and new ideas can sprout. You'll have to remind the group that suggestions will be assessed later, and so they must try not to be judgmental. You will also have to be strict about controlling the time spent because the upcoming steps are more important in terms of generating proposals.

Generate ideas that specifically address the leverage points

Unless you specifically focus the group on them, the leverage points will be forgotten and people, as they always do, will go off into the less important 80% instead of the crucial 20%.

One good way to accomplish this focus is to build a leverage points versus enablers matrix. This would be similar to the matrix we'll construct while assessing in context a little later on. It isn't so important that you do this in matrix form—what's important is that for each leverage point, the team specifically ask, "How could this leverage point be supported by a change within this enabler?" This is a good time to focus on the enablers that often get ignored:

- Motivation and measurement;
- Human resources;
- Policies and rules.

The review of common improvement practices in the next step might trigger additional ideas, so you might need to revisit this step.

Steal ideas by reviewing best practices

A best practice is a tactic or process characteristic that has been employed at one or more other organizations with excellent results. "Benchmarking," the companion term, takes a variety of forms but typically involves comparing one of your processes with the same or a similar process at other organizations, usually with metrics to quantify the relative performance. There has been much heated writing and discussion of best practices, with industry pundits either strongly pro or con. In general, the pro is that studying best practices can expand your horizons by exposing your team to ideas they wouldn't have thought of otherwise. The con is that they can contract your horizons when they are slavishly copied and misapplied. Note that after Michael Hammer described Ford's breakthrough "invoiceless accounts payable process" in his classic 1990 article on reengineering, it seemed that everyone was suddenly busy instituting the same, whether it addressed their problems or not.[1] Critics are right when they point out that by the time they're documented, "average practices" or "common practices" might be better terms. And benchmarking can degenerate into "industrial tourism" without concrete results. However, these criticisms miss the central points:

- Even the average practices may be better than what your organization does.

- The people you're working with may not be aware of what's possible because they are not all professional analysts or process consultants who live and breathe this stuff.

Depending on your assessment of the group you're working with, you could decide (as we often do) that a short presentation on common process redesign practices would be worthwhile. On the other hand, they may be well aware of current practices, or have been exposed to the ideas while you conducted the assess by enabler step. If you decide a presentation will help, you'll have to stress that the examples are food for thought, not dogma to be blindly implemented. In developing a presentation suitable for your team, there are many sources to draw on:

- A Web search on best practices (or benchmarking) and business process will yield lots of sites, including, of course, best practices consulting firms and benchmarking organizations. A good starting point is www.brint.com/BPR.htm.

- Books—a search of on-line booksellers for best practices and benchmarking will uncover many titles.

- Management and IT consulting firms often publish white papers (many industry-specific) on best practices.

---

1. In Chapter 13, we documented two examples of misapplying so-called best practices.

+ Consulting firms that specialize in this area, such as Best Practices, LLC (www.best-in-class.com).

+ Industry organizations or software vendors dealing with a topic of interest such as "supply chain optimization" or "customer relationship management" document best practices and success stories.

The previous chapter can provide material for a review presentation—the Assess by Enabler sections highlighted many *worst* practices, and either implied or stated an alternative. Below are some examples of common practices according to the primary enabler involved. These practices don't fit squarely under a single enabler. For instance, eliminating a management approval step is a change in policies and rules, but it also implies a change in workflow (the process proceeds without the handoff for review) and new information technology (to provide management information in lieu of the approval step).

During the review, or after each enabler has been covered, ask the group if any of the reviewed practices is relevant to the process, or if any ideas have been triggered. Capture all suggestions on your ideas list.

Process workflow design: actors, steps, and flow

+ Instead of having one complex process with many decisions based on the type of transaction, establish a reasonable number of distinct processes (say, three to five) each tailored for a particular type. Using available information to direct each case into the appropriate process is referred to as "triage," after the medical term for directing the initial treatment of injured persons. Once the type of case is determined, it flows through the appropriate process without unnecessary steps or decisions. An example is to have different problem resolution processes depending on the customer's history, or different purchasing processes depending on the value of the product or service.

+ Regarding approval or information steps, many organizations have eliminated them from the workflow, or have them take place "after the fact." In the case of escalating approval or inform steps, they can be done in parallel or directed immediately to the highest necessary level.

- Where serialization is a holdover from a paper-based process, IT can support shared access and therefore a parallel workflow. For instance, at an airline, the fleet maintenance, crew scheduling, and airport operations groups had to approve, in sequence, a new flight schedule. Any change late in the process meant the proposed schedule had to start all over again. Instead, each group simultaneously checked the first cut flight schedule for significant problems and got it "close" before the final approval, which still happened in sequence.

Application of information technology: applications, databases, computers, networks

Even in the popular media, we are so inundated with stories about leading-edge technologies that some of the basic, workhorse technologies are forgotten:

- The use of barcoding or self-identifying tags to eliminate error-prone, redundant data entry;

- In general, the use of shared databases (or data transformation middleware) to eliminate gaps and inconsistencies, and the errors introduced by rekeying data from system to system;

- In particular, shared databases that include full contact history to make all customer and case information is available to any sales or service representative.

You can no doubt find examples of the clever use of IT within your industry or process.

Motivation and measurement: "reward and punishment" schemes

Perhaps we shouldn't be surprised that this most-important enabler receives so little attention in the literature on best practices and benchmarking. This reflects a general obsession with technology, and with task, job, and process design, to the exclusion of the measurement schemes that motivate particular behaviors. We have made this point in Chapter 13, but to help fill the void, we'd like to describe a reference that might assist you in making the point at your organization.

It predates the reengineering revolution, but Wickham Skinner's article "The Productivity Paradox" [1] makes the point convincingly that what you measure matters, and it remains one the most-requested *Harvard Business Review* reprints ever. The article begins by outlining a massive productivity program at a large manufacturing organization that is representative of many organizations he studied. It sounds like a case study in reengineering, complete with operation-by-operation analyses to improve efficiency, retraining employees to work smarter not harder, and streamlined work flow. However, after three years the company netted an almost negligible 7% productivity gain, far short of the goal and not at all commensurate with the effort. Skinner then makes the point that by focusing on productivity and providing "daily performance reports on every operation, worker, and department," the company has inadvertently set up a cycle that ultimately does little for productivity because many other variables (especially the ones that matter to customers—product quality, meeting committed delivery times, order accuracy, etc.) are negatively impacted.

Some quotes will convey the feeling of the article, but do yourself a favor and obtain a copy:

"When low cost is the goal, quality often gets lost. But when quality is the goal, lower costs do usually follow. . . . A productivity focus inevitably forces management into a short-term, operational mind-set. The emphasis on direct costs, which attends the productivity focus, leads a company to use management controls that focus on the wrong target. . . . The reward system based on such controls drives behavior toward simplistic goals that represent only a small fraction of total costs. . . . When managers grow up in this atmosphere, their skills and vision never fully develop. . . . As long as cost and efficiency are the primary measurements of factory success, the manufacturing plant will continue to repel many able, creative people."

The good news: "...a number of companies have broken out of the bind with extraordinary success. Their experience suggests, however, that breaking loose from so long-established a mind-set is not easy. It requires a change in culture, habits, instincts, and ways of thinking and reasoning. And it means modifying a set of values that current reward systems and day-to-day operational demands reinforce. This is a tall order." Perhaps this is why we don't see enough attention placed on measurement and motivation as a lever to effect process change.

Although the article deals with manufacturing, the same phenomenon is demonstrated in all types of enterprises. A favorite recent example: If you measure customer service reps on short phone calls, that's what you'll get—short phone calls. Measures that focus instead on improving the quality of products or customer service, such as "recurring problems detected" or "problems solved on the first call," yield quite different results. An objection we've heard is that "we don't have the resources to provide each customer with that much time." Probably true, but in many fields (including customer service) it has been observed that it's more cost-effective to get it right the first time (i.e., on the first call) than to invest in scrap and rework.[2]

If you can't find examples of innovative measurement schemes that are suitable for your project, this could be a good time to reopen the discussion that began during assessment. Have the group identify current measures that are counterproductive, and new measures that would encourage the desired outcomes.

Human resources: organizational structure, job definitions, recruitment and placement strategies, skills, and training

- The most obvious and widely cited change is to recombine tasks into fewer job functions. (In general, as processes become simpler, jobs become more complex.) In some industries, more than 300 job titles have been reduced to 30. This is especially important where the customer is aware of the handoff. At an insurance company, a clerk recorded claim details, and then routed the claimant to an adjuster. The customer often had to go through the story twice, and good customers got the same treatment as everyone else. Now, the clerk takes on certain adjusting responsibilities. Within certain parameters such as claim type (e.g., vandalism), estimated value (e.g., under $1,000), and customer characteristics (e.g., five years or more with limited claims), the clerk can settle the claim on the spot. However, this also required new IT, workflow, and performance measures.

- Another common practice is an expanded role for front-line customer contact personnel, for instance, the integration of sales activities into customer service. For instance, customer service representatives fielding billing inquiries for a telecommunications company now sell calling plans that will reduce the customer's bill. Again, like most "enriched" jobs, staff must be supported with tools

---

2. We could also get into a discussion of using IT to identify high-value customers and give them higher service levels, but you get the idea.

(e.g., expert systems or operational data stores to present integrated customer history) and the whole thing can backfire if motivation and measurement isn't handled properly.

- Similarly, back-office specialists can receive additional training and be moved out to customer contact positions providing faster, more personal service. A useful guideline is that no one in a customer-facing process should be more than one actor removed from the customer. In other words, everyone either has direct contact with customers, or deals with others who do.

- Where work is too complex for a single person, and functional expertise is required, a cross-functional team organization can be adopted. As we noted in Chapter 13, this isn't a panacea, and has to be approached with caution.

Policies and rules: constraints and guidelines (whether self-imposed or external)

- Eliminate approval steps by providing regular information or audit reports to management. On the same topic, eliminate the delay inherent in review by allowing the process to proceed while review happens. This puts the onus on the reviewer to complete the review before the transaction gets too far into the process. It isn't suitable in life-and-death situations, but otherwise, if a high percentage of cases routinely pass the review anyway, it's worth considering.

- Eliminate delays due to credit history checks and proof of financial responsibility where a valid credit card or bond could cover any possible financial loss.

- Some organizations have gone so far as to eliminate volumes of policies and rules and guidelines and replace them with a simple statement of principles. These can be the ultimate examples of the oft-cited "empowered workforce." In general, the empowered workforce requires the following:

  Defined (and presumably greater) authority;

  Defined accountability for decisions, with consequences;

  Clear policies to guide front-line decision-making;

Tools and training;

A backup mechanism (a safety net) so individuals can delegate upwards in difficult cases.

Facilities design: workplace layout and equipment

This may not apply in your case, and can be substituted with some other more relevant category appropriate to your situation. The library example described during assessment is a good, simple example. Also, in organizations where there is a constant mix of collaborative and individual work, traditional fixed workstations (cubicles) are replaced by movable pods that can quickly be assembled in a way that each opens into a common area, sort of a twenty-first-century circling of the wagons.

Brainstorming

Most of you are familiar with the brainstorming technique, so we'll just provide a brief recap:

- The intent of any brainstorming session is to generate a *lot* of suggestions on whatever the topic or question is.

- It works because judgment is specifically held until later. Without the fear of immediate criticism, participants are more likely to join in and make suggestions. Many believe that brainstorming works because the human brain can't effectively be creative and critical at the same time.

- The guidelines are simple:

    Each participant makes one suggestion during their turn, or says "pass."

    The facilitator (or a scribe) records the idea without editing, except perhaps to have the participant restate it more briefly.

    No criticism or negative comment is given.

We always try to have the group arranged in a wide U or semicircle, and go around the group clockwise with each participant taking a turn in sequence. This may seem slower than random brainstorming, but it encourages participation from everyone and prevents anyone from taking over.

In most brainstorming sessions, we start out wide open to encourage unrestricted ideas, and then brainstorm within a framework to ensure coverage of the subject area. In brainstorming for process improvements:

- First, brainstorm for *any* improvement, tactic, or process characteristic that comes to mind.

- Then, brainstorm on each of the enablers in turn: workflow design, IT, and so forth. Note that many of the enabler-specific ideas may already have been identified during assessment.

As suggestions arise, they will be recorded on the ideas flipcharts for later assessment.

Apply the challenge process

The challenge process is simple and can be described quickly, but that doesn't reflect its importance—it is often the critical step in breaking people free from assumptions about how a process has to work, and generating those brilliant insights. The challenge process is all about not "paving the cowpaths," a popular phrase in the reengineering community that refers to blindly applying new technology to an old process. Examples abound: Many of the early imaging-based workflow applications "duplicated paper flow in silicon," and we have seen on-line, database applications handling financial transactions in batches of 25 for no other reason than that was how the paper-based process worked.

Here's how the challenge process works. Begin with a level 1 (handoff) or level 2 (flow) swimlane diagram for the as-is process. Participants might have their own copy, or post it on the wall if it's a manageable size. Before getting into the challenge process, you might eliminate some of the steps from further consideration, if the group has already decided that they are obvious flaws; we usually don't, because leaving the obviously wrong steps in can make the process even more fun (and it is usually fun, believe it or not). The central idea is to take each step (or linked series of steps) and its implicit assumptions, and restate it as hard and fast rules. For instance, in a claim handling process, the workflow might depict the following:

- The Customer initiates a Claim by telephone.

- The Claim is recorded by a Telephone Claims Representative (TCR).

- The TCR schedules an interview with the Customer at a company office.

- An Adjuster interviews the Customer.

Restating this as rules, we might come up with the following challenge statements:

- *Only* a Customer (beneficiary or policyholder) can initiate a Claim.

- Claims *must* be initiated by telephone.

- We will *never* consider compensation until a Claim is filed.

- The Customer *must* be interviewed in person *before* a Claim can be settled.

- The interview can *only* take place on company premises.

Note that we have overstated by using words like "only," "must," and "never." This makes it much easier for participants to challenge each of the statements by asking, "Is that *really* true?"

In some cases, the statement survives challenge, and so it is recorded on the list of ideas (characteristics) for the new process. For instance, the group might decide that a claim really can only be initiated by the beneficiary or policyholder ("no third parties, please") in which case the point will be recorded on the ideas list as a potential characteristic of the to-be process. (Remember, we haven't decided for sure yet—that comes later.)

In most cases, the statement can be challenged. For instance, the team might decide that initiating a claim via e-mail or the Web is an option to consider, or that interviews can take place at a location more convenient for the customer (home, place of work, etc.). These too would be recorded on the idea sheet.

You can even take one of the statements, and break it down word by word (or is that "bird by bird?"):

1. The *Customer* must be interviewed in person before a Claim can be settled.

2. The Customer must be *interviewed* in person before a Claim can be settled.

3. The Customer must be interviewed *in person* before a Claim can be settled.

4. The Customer must be interviewed in person *before* a Claim can be settled.

5. The Customer must be interviewed in person before a *Claim* can be settled.

6. The Customer must be interviewed in person before a Claim can be *settled*.

Some alternatives to each of the numbered points:

1. If we have a police report, do we need to talk to the customer?

2. Couldn't the customer complete an incident report form by mail or e-mail?

3. Even if the customer wasn't there? Could the interview be conducted by phone?

4. Couldn't we settle a small claim without actually going through the formality of a claim?

5. Does a claim have to be filed if the insured and victim are both customers and the insured admits fault?

6. Could we pay the customer the undisputed portion before settling? (It could reduce lawsuits.)

You may have noticed that this is an alternative to step-by-step assessment, which we suggested in Chapter 13 can be very tedious. The challenge process is a more effective way of addressing the kinds of questions we would answer if we were assessing each individual step:

*   Does this step yield a useful result?

*   Does it have to be done at all?

*   Does it have to be done by the actor currently doing it?

*   Does it have to be done in the sequence it is being done in?

- Does it have to be done where it is being done?

- Does it have to be done in the manner it is being done?

By this point, enough improvement ideas have surely been generated, so it's time to move on to assessment and selection.

Assess ideas in context and select

Like the challenge process, this step is so simple as to be almost obvious, but it has proven invaluable in practice. It involves taking each suggestion, and considering its impact on all enablers before deciding to proceed with it. Here's the process:

- Post (tape up) the idea lists that have been generated so far.

- Perform an initial review of the list to eliminate any ideas that are clearly not going to make it. They might be illegal, a poor fit with skills and culture, too resource-intensive (to implement or to operate), or not a contributor to the process's goals. (Set them aside, rather than tossing them out, because they may warrant reconsideration after the other ideas are assessed.) If there is disagreement on whether an item should stay or go, leave it in—the next steps should settle the discussion.

- Build an assessment matrix with seven columns—one for each enabler, and a seventh for "Notes/Conclusions." As with the leverage points versus enablers matrix, it isn't necessary that this be done in matrix form—we just find it convenient if there's enough whiteboard space. What is necessary is to have a checklist or matrix or whatever other device will ensure that you explicitly consider each of the enablers.

- Select an idea for assessment, and decide which enabler it most strongly relates to. Consider the example of "Customer Service Reps (CSRs) take on sales responsibilities." Because this is a significant change to job responsibilities, place this suggestion under the "Human Resources" column in a new row of the matrix. Don't agonize over which enabler to allocate an idea to, because all enablers will be considered.

• Now, the key step—fill in the rest of the columns in the new row of the matrix by asking what the consequences of the idea are for each of the other enablers. See Figure 14.1. Don't forget to consider other consequences for the enabler you placed the idea in. For the CSR example:

There are other consequences under "Human Resources"—the CSRs will have to receive training in sales techniques, and more training on the company's service options. Also consider the impact on the existing sales force, and on any CSRs who aren't comfortable with or able to perform sales duties.

The workflow will clearly change. If the client agrees, will the CSR set up the new service, or will a "closer" be brought in? What about clients who are interested, but don't have time right now—where will these leads be routed to? And many more...

Sophisticated IT solutions will be required to present a composite view of the client's business with the company, in real time, and suggest alternate service packages.

The motivation and measurement package for the CSR will have to change radically. Will they be paid more, now that they have increased responsibility and skill requirements? Will they be paid a commission? The primary current measure is call time, which will have to be changed.

Regarding policies and rules, will the CSRs have authority to offer special deals?

We could continue, but this is enough to make the point

• Assess the suggestion now that the consequences are visible—does the whole row make sense? Record impressions in the "Notes/Conclusions" column. You might decide at this point that the idea still has merit—the potential improvement isn't negated by other consequences. This may require research, though, to assess costs and other impacts versus benefits. Or, you might decide to revise the suggestion (and, of course, redo the assessment) or eliminate it.

- Continue with the next improvement idea. You can go through the list in sequence, or try to consider the "big ticket" items first, or consider similar ideas together.

- Once all of the plausible ideas have been assessed, go through the matrix and select ideas (rows) that will become the characteristics or specifications for the new process. This will involve judgment that can't be reduced to a step-by-step procedure, but the key elements are:

Impact on process goals;

Feasibility;

Consistency with other characteristics.

- Also, if you didn't select any "quick wins" or "low-hanging fruit" (discussed in Chapter 13) while assessing the process, the team might identify some at this time.

Here's a recap of some general principles to check for:

Workflow design	Information technology	Motivation and measurement	Policies and rules	Human resources	Facilities (or other)	Notes
Will the CSR or a "closer" set up the new service? Who follows up with interested customers not ready to commit?	System to present real-time view of customer's total business, and recommend alternatives.	CSRs paid more for additional responsibilities. Current measure is "call time"— must change. Commission? What impact on commissions for current sales force?	What will CSR's authority be for discounts, etc.?	Customer Service Reps (CSRs) take on sales responsibilities Sales training? Displacement of current sales reps?	CSRs may need more desk space for product catalogs that aren't on-line.	What will customer reaction be?

Figure 14.1   Using an enabler matrix to assess process improvement ideas.

- Ensure that every task is value-added. For every task, ask, "Would a reasonable customer pay for this if he or she knew it was being done?" Each task should accomplish a state change in the direction of completion, which usually excludes moving and checking.

- Measure outcomes, not tasks or handoffs.

- Information must be available when and where needed, unfiltered by layers of management.

- Eliminate or minimize approval or information steps that require a handoff to the approver, and then a handoff back into the flow. Instead, automate the production of information for management, especially exception/variance/excursion reports.

- Similarly, don't hand off to make a decision—push the decision to the front lines, where the work is being performed.

- Avoid cumbersome translations and interfaces such as rekeying data from one system to another (see next point).

- Seek straight-through processing (STP) and automate clerical activities, especially those that move a transaction from one system to another.

- As few people as possible should be involved in the process.

- Make individual jobs "rich" enough that people are working up to their potential.

- Parallelize wherever possible.

- Ensure that a work item can always be located in the process.

- Ensure that a work item can be maintained—revised, canceled, held—by the customer through the same mechanism they created it with. Don't implement a Web facility to allow customers to place orders that does not allow customers to access and modify these orders later.

When you're done, the new process is characterized—you have a matrix that describes the important (and probably some of the less important) characteristics of the to-be process. Many of the points will describe elements of the workflow—who does what, and when. So, armed with this information, it's time to express the new process as a workflow.

Develop ideal to-be workflow

Before starting on a swimlane diagram showing who, what, when, and how, it's useful to step back and express the essence of the process—the what and when. This is the ideal workflow, unconstrained by technology, human abilities, space, time, or other very real concerns. It's not an exercise in fantasy, though—such a model can provide a target for which our "real world" swimlane diagram should strive.

At the heart of this is the concept of "essential processes." Actually, "essential process step" would be a more accurate term, but we'll use the more common "essential process." The essential processes are the vital (essential) steps that remain after all references to "who" and "how" are removed, leaving only the essence of "what" has to occur. Imagine perfect database and communication technology, as if there were no barriers of space or time.

We like the way the concept was described by Daniel Whitney in an article [2] from our favorite publication, the *Harvard Business Review*. When designing robots (i.e., to automate manufacturing activities) too much focus is placed on *how* a person (the *who*) currently does the task, rather than the essence of *what* the task is. The goal is to understand "what, not who or how."

He explains: "I often ask beginning robotics students to design a robot to wash a stack of dishes. Usually the students conceive an expensive machine with two hands that lifts up each dish in turn, inspects it visually for dirt, picks up a brush, dips it in soap, scrubs the dish, and so on. After the discussion has gone on for a while, I remind the class that local department stores sell automatic dishwashers for about $250."

Whitney highlights the key point: "The mistake here—plausible as it might seem—lies in confusing what people do with how they do it. The goal in robotics should be to reproduce what's done (getting results), not how it's done (using certain methods)." When we use this article in our class on application process logic, this is the point at which we introduce the recurring chant "what, not who or how!" The identical goal arises in systems development (when we define the "modules" that make up the application logic layer) and in process redesign (when we define the "ideal" process flow).

That was a generalized example of the principle—here's a case from a process improvement assignment at a government agency. The subject matter was "issue business license," which included an inspection of the business premises. Here are the relevant steps from that phase of the process:

- The Inspector gets to the next inspection location.

- Inspector conducts inspection (these first two are repeated through-out the day).

- Inspector returns to Field Office.

- Inspector telephones Head Office (HO) Technician.

- Inspector reads each inspection report while HO Technician transcribes information onto HO transcription report.

- HO transcription reports are batched, and three times per week they go to data entry.

- Data Entry enters each HO transcription report into a minicomputer-based Inspection System.

- The Inspection System prints a three-part report on an impact printer detailing each inspection.

- An operator separates the three copies ("bursting and decollating," for you former machine room operators).

- Pink copies are attached to the corresponding original HO transcription report.

- All of the reports for an inspector are collected and mailed back to the correct Field Office.

- The Inspector matches the original inspection report with the printout from the Inspection System.

- If there is an error, the Inspector checks the HO transcription report to determine if the error occurred during transcription or data entry. (We won't get into the error-correction process, but trust us, it's a beauty.)

At a session to identify improvements to the process, suggestions included:

* The Inspectors could be equipped with cell phones so they could phone in each inspection report immediately.

* Inspectors could fax their reports so HO Technicians could transcribe them without tying up the phone or dealing with miscommunications.

* The batch update job could be run daily instead of three times a week.

* The reports could be printed on laser printers (three times) to eliminate the separation step.

You see the problem—participants were so locked into the current "who and how" that their improvement ideas were extremely limited. They really thought, for instance, that transcription was a fundamental part of the process. To be fair, this was a last-minute, "late in the game" engagement, so the participants hadn't been "opened up" by going through steps like identifying leverage points, assessing by enabler, or using the challenge process. Nonetheless, we encounter the same basic phenomenon all the time, and the idea of essential processes can help people break free of their current assumptions about what's really essential.

In the business licensing example, after being introduced to essential processes, participants were surprised to conclude that virtually all of the steps were "who and how." The essential process was simply "Record inspection results," or even better, "Conduct inspection," based on the principle that an essential process step should record its own results.[3] The focus then shifted to how inspection findings could be captured electronically in real time (or "real-enough time") with minimal intermediaries. Tablet computers or scannable forms were two options.

So, the essential processes (or process steps) are the "essence" of what the business does. They are the steps remaining after removing any reference to who (performer, that is, job function or organization) or how (technology, whether high tech, low tech, or no tech). They often

---

3. You could claim that completing each inspection item (checking for signage, office space, fire extinguisher, etc.) is an essential process, but let's not split hairs—the main point is the same.

correspond very strongly to "transactions" (units of work from the application process layer) that are introduced in Chapter 16.

Getting comfortable with the concept is the hard part; once you've got that, applying it is relatively easy.

- Identify the main essential processes using the as-is models and the process characteristics as a guide. Most essential processes will clearly be milestones or significant state changes.

- Recheck—if a change in performers or technology would change your essential processes, you're not done yet.

- Identify the dependencies among the essential processes: which *must* happen in sequence, and which can happen in parallel.

- Depict the dependencies graphically, as shown in Figure 14.2, just as you would if you were laying out a project plan.

This is a template for the ideal workflow. It's worth noting that certain e-commerce applications using enterprise application integration (EAI) tools to implement straight-through processing have achieved workflows that contain almost nothing but essential process steps. All human intervention, delays, batching, and transport have been wrung out of the process, with a process integration engine shepherding the transaction

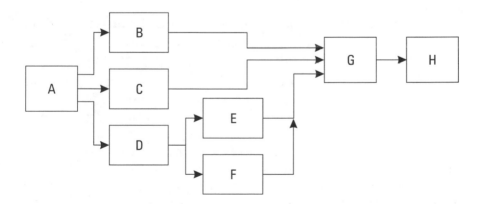

Figure 14.2 The dependency among essential processes is a template for the "ideal" workflow.

through various systems in real-enough time. This is especially prevalent in the financial services sector, where financial transactions (e.g., a stock exchange trade) that used to require multiday batch processing cycles are now completely processed instantly.

Next, we will consider the constraints of technology and the actors in our workflow and develop a swimlane diagram.

Develop to-be workflow

We are tempted to say, "and now, the easy part!" Admittedly, it still isn't easy to design a new workflow that meets your objectives. However, with all of the information you have assembled to this point, it will be much easier than it would have been if you'd just dived right in.

Using the characteristics matrix (to provide the "who" and "how") and your ideal workflow (to provide the "what") as guides, propose a handoff level first, then add detail in layers. You'll use exactly the same guidelines when developing each level of the to-be model that you used when you were developing the as-is model:

- Handoff (level 1) shows contiguous activities by the same performer;

- Milestone (level 2) adds significant milestones;

- Logic/Task (level 3) adds individual tasks and more indication of "how."

After your first effort at each new level of detail, assess whether the workflow still meets process goals, and is feasible. By "feasible," we primarily mean, "does each actor have the skills, resources, and information to carry out the designated process steps?" If not, revise or refine it. We also suggest treating each new level as an as-is model, and assessing it. Applying the challenge process to a to-be model can be an interesting exercise.

Figures 14.3 and 14.4 illustrate samples of handoff and flow to-be models. You should heavily annotate the diagrams to indicate what's noteworthy about the new process. Unless you highlight these points, many people won't notice!

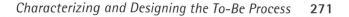
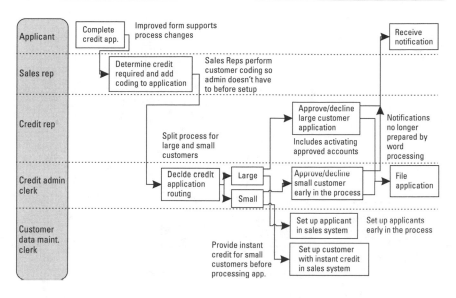

Figure 14.3 A handoff level diagram for a to-be process (compressed to fit on one page).

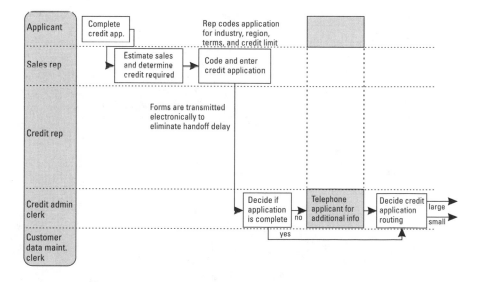

Figure 14.4a A milestone level diagram for a to-be process.

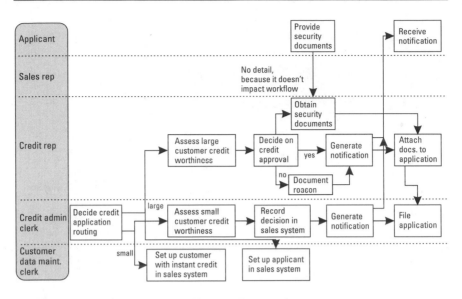

Figure 14.4b A milestone level diagram for a to-be process.

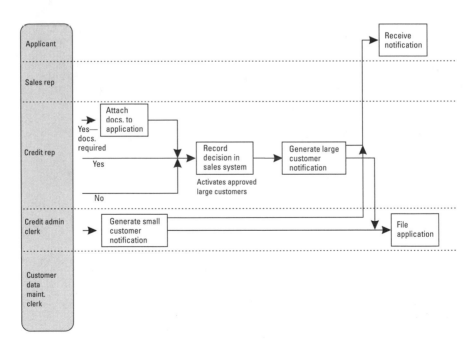

Figure 14.4c A milestone level diagram for a to-be process.

Road trip

At this point, you may want to take the new process on a road trip to review it with a wider audience. In addition to getting suggestions that might further improve the process, there are two reasons to do this.

First, especially if your organization is geographically distributed, you'll need to find out about any constraints due to local conditions or regulations. These may require changes to the version of the process operating at that location. However, before stepping out onto the slippery slope of local process versions, we'll caution you that (if you have the necessary executive support) it's best to vary the process *only* if there are legal issues. This eliminates all kinds of issues related to training, staff rotation, certification, and so forth.

Second, you can gather information for "force field analysis" which will help your preparations for training and implementation. Two topics need to be addressed:

◆ What aspects of the new process/systems are people positive about? These are your "drivers."

◆ What aspects are they negative about? These are your "barriers."

Armed with this knowledge, you can develop implementation strategies that promote/maximize the drivers and minimize the impact of the barriers.

Now that you have a new process and its supporting workflow designed, it's time to make a major transition into determining how information systems can support the actors in the new process. That is the purpose of use case scenario analysis—to move into the specifics of requirements determination. First, however, an introduction to data modeling is in order, because it is an important aspect of requirements definition, and is very helpful while working with use cases.

References

[1]   Skinner, W., "The Productivity Paradox," *Harvard Business Review*, July–Aug. 1986, pp. 55–59.

[2]   Whitney, D. E., "Real Robots Do Need Jigs," *Harvard Business Review*, May–June 1986, pp. 110–116.

15

Data Modeling

Data modeling—what it is, what it isn't

Data modeling is arguably the most widely used technique in modern systems analysis and design, but it isn't always used well. Too often, technically oriented "modelers" jump straight into excruciating detail, dense jargon, and complex graphics, incomprehensible to process-oriented participants and other mere mortals.

The root problem is a misconception—data modeling has been equated with database design. That's like equating architecture with the drafting of construction blueprints. Of course, the architect's work will eventually lead to precise, detailed blueprints, just as the data modeler's work will eventually lead to precise, detailed database designs, but it shouldn't start there. In fact, it can't start there, or the subject-matter experts will soon mentally "check out." Without their participation, the data model won't be a useful and accurate description of their business. And that's exactly how a data model should be regarded—not as a database design, but as a description of a business. Consider some ways to describe a business:

275

- An *organizational chart* describes an enterprise in terms of managerial structures and reporting relationships.

- A *financial statement* describes an enterprise in terms of its fiscal health.

- A *process workflow model* describes an enterprise in terms of the activities it must carry out.

Each of these is a model that helps people communicate about the subject matter it represents. A *data model* is no different—it describes a business in terms of the things it must record information[1] about, and the relationships among them. And just as we've seen with process modeling, data models must be simple and accessible during the early going. We will now cover the basic concepts, structures, and terminology of data modeling, and also help you get the most from this technique by reviewing practical techniques for developing a data model and managing detail.

Basic terms and concepts

Essentially, a data model depicts:

- The *things* of significance to an enterprise that it needs to maintain records about;

- The *facts about those things* that the enterprise needs to know.

"Thing modeling" wouldn't cut it as a discipline, so a *thing* of significance is referred to as an *entity*, hence the other common terms for data modeling—entity modeling and entity-relationship modeling. As in the earlier example, some of the main entities at a mail order retailer would be Product, Customer, Order, Warehouse, and Supplier. When a process is named in verb-noun format, the noun is almost always an entity.

There are two kinds of *facts* about entities in a data model—*relationships* and *attributes*. *Relationships* are associations or connections between

---

1. Strictly speaking, organizations maintain *data*—"the facts"—and from that data they can produce *information*—"data presented in answer to a specific request or query," or as Drucker put it, "data imbued with meaning and purpose."

one entity and another that must be recorded, such as Order "placed by" Customer. Relationships are always bidirectional, so the same relationship named in the other direction is Customer "places" Order. Other relationships could include Order "requests" Product, Product "stocked at" Warehouse, and Product "available from" Supplier.

Attributes are individual data items that describe an entity. For Product, they include Product Number, Description, and Unit Price. For Customer, the attributes could include Customer Number, Name, Customer Since Date, E-mail Address, Telephone Number, and so on.

Think of an *entity* as a standardized description for a set of essentially similar instances the business needs to keep track of. "Joe Smith," "Emily Dixon," and "Able Enterprises, Inc." are each a unique individual or organization, but if they all meet certain qualifications (as per the entity definition), then we consider them to be *instances* or *occurrences* of the Customer entity, and we record the same kind of facts (attributes and relationships) about each.

Strictly speaking, we should use the term *entity type* rather than *entity*. An entity type, such as Customer, is a standardized description of a whole set (or *type* or *class*) of instances, and an *entity* is a single instance—Joe Smith and Emily Dixon. Most modelers, for clarity, would simply refer to Customer as an entity, and Joe and Emily as *instances* or *occurrences* of Customer.[2]

A simple example

Shortly, we will provide guidelines and tips for entities, relationships, and attributes, but first we'll put this in context by illustrating the development of the two parts of the data model—the graphic and the narrative. The narrative part is the entity definitions, which clarify which instances qualify for "membership" in an entity. In the early stages of a process-oriented

---

2. If you're working within an object-oriented (O-O) methodology, the concepts are identical but the terms are different. An *entity* is referred to as a *class*, and a single instance is an *object*. In the O-O world, everything is a class (or an object), including transactions, screen widgets, and devices, so many distinguish the data-oriented classes that we call entities by prefixing them—"entity class" or "business class," and their corresponding instances, "entity objects" and "business objects." Terminology in the world of information systems can get confusing, but at least it's getting better—it's more standardized than it was 20 years ago.

project, this is the most important part of the data model, but explaining data modeling seems to be easier if we focus on the graphic part first.

Graphics: the entity–relationship diagram

The graphic is called an entity-relationship diagram, for obvious reasons, or E-R diagram or just an ERD. Figure 15.1 is a simple example—the entities are shown as labeled boxes, and the relationships as labeled lines between them. It shows the significant things—the entities—and how they relate to one another.

In Figure 15.2, the model has been revised to show an important property or "business rule" of relationships—*cardinality* or *multiplicity*. Cardinality is an arcane term for a simple concept—for a *single instance* of an entity, it shows the *maximum* number of instances of the entity at the other end of the relationship that it could be related to. The answer is either "one" or "many."[3] *Each* Customer could place a maximum of *many* Orders. They may have only placed one, or even none if our definition of Customer includes people who are on our mailing list but haven't ordered anything yet (see why definitions are important?), but our concern is with the potential maximum. The "many" is shown on the diagram by the "crow's-foot" adjacent to the Order entity, indicating that there could be multiple Orders for a single Customer.

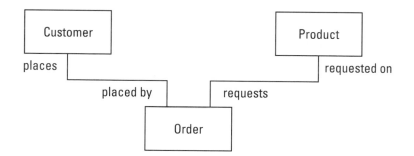

Figure 15.1 A simple entity-relationship diagram (ERD).

---

3. The other phrase used in place of "many" is "one or more," which gets around a potential source of confusion. "Many" implies "lots of them," but we don't actually care as data modelers whether it's a couple, a few, several, dozens, scores, hundreds, or a gazillion—in our simple counting scheme, the choices are "one" and "anything greater than one," which we reduce to "many."

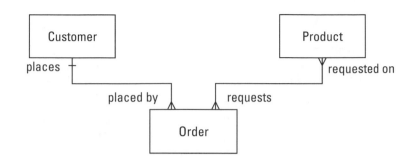

Figure 15.2 Adding business rules to the relationships on the ERD.

Now, we go to the other end of the Customer-Order relationship to determine cardinality. *Each* Order is placed by a maximum of *one* Customer. Note the emphasis on the word *each*. Even though we first agreed that a Customer places *many* Orders, we start again from one ("each") Order when asking how many Customers it could be related to. We stress beginning the statement with the word "each," because a common error with new data modelers goes like this—"Hmmm, a Customer could place many Orders, and if we have many Orders, I guess we must have many Customers." Wrong! The "one" is shown on the diagram by the hash mark (a small dash perpendicular to the relationship line) adjacent to the Customer entity, indicating that there could be at most one Customer for a single Order.

The Customer places Order relationship is described as a one to many (1:M) relationship. Order requests Product is a many to many (M:M) relationship—each Order requests a maximum of *many* Products (a shirt, a pair of socks, and a pair of slacks), and each Product is requested on a maximum of *many* Orders. The third type of relationship is one to one (1:1), but they are quite rare in practice.

With the basic structure laid out, we can add some attributes to the entities. At this stage, we don't try to identify every single attribute—just the main ones, to help clarify the meaning of the entity. Each of the attributes fits neatly into an entity except one—the Requested Quantity for each Product specified on the Order. At first glance, this seems like an attribute of Order, but there's a problem. A particular attribute should appear only once in an entity, but there is a Requested Quantity for each Product requested—if the Order specifies three different Products, there are three separate values for Requested Quantity. For instance, the Order might request one of Product Number 1719, a French blue dress shirt, but six of Product Number 4223, a pair of black dress socks, and two of Product Number 3764, a pair of khaki slacks. We could get around the problem by including multiple Requested Value attributes, but that introduces various difficulties. Which value of Requested Quantity goes with which Product? How many different values will we allow for? Five? Ten? Whatever we choose, someone will exceed it. There are other issues, but let's move on.

The key to the solution is that Requested Quantity is actually an attribute of the Order requests Product relationship, because it is the Requested Quantity of a particular Product requested on a particular Order. In this style of modeling, only an entity can carry attributes, so the solution is to introduce an entity in the "middle" of the relationship to hold this attribute and any others that might arise. As shown in Figure 15.3, this new entity is Order Line Item. This isn't unreasonable—each Order is made up of many Order Line Items and each Order Line Item requests one Product. Starting

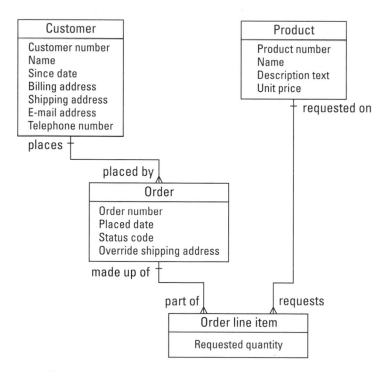

Figure 15.3 Resolving the M:M relationship.

in the other direction, each Product is requested on many Order Line Items, and each Order Line Item is part of one Order.

Note that this diagram is drawn following the "top-down dependency" convention, which vastly increases the readability when models get more complex. Some entities in a data model are *dependent*, because they can't exist unless they are related to one or more other entities that are referred to as their *parent(s)*. Order is dependent, because it can't exist unless there is a Customer that placed the Order, so it is drawn below Customer—that's top-down dependency. An Order Line Item cannot exist unless it is related to both the Order that it is part of, and the Product that it Requests, so it is drawn between and below these parent entities. Customer and Product are drawn at the top, because they aren't dependent on any other entity. They are referred to as *independent* or *fundamental* entities.

This example demonstrates a couple of key points about data modeling. The first is really *the* central point in data modeling—the data model *must* represent the "essence" or "natural structure" of the entities, not a particular physical implementation. We say it depicts "business reality," not a particular technology or record-keeping system. Our Order–Order Line Item model works whether the order is a "shopping cart" on a Web site, a paper order form with a header and multiple line items, or a list of items conveyed to a sales rep via the telephone. The importance of this is that from the data model we'll eventually derive the structure of the record-keeping system, usually a database of some sort. If the design of this database is based on the natural structure of things, it will be much more flexible in meeting new requirements and accommodating new technologies. Experience with "long-lived" databases has proved this absolutely. From the business process perspective, the importance is that the most successful business processes have a base of consistent, shared data from which all participants get the information they need. Clearly, an order fulfillment process will work more smoothly if sales, manufacturing, logistics, and accounts receivable all work from the same "picture" of Order.

The other point is a well-known pattern in data modeling—an M:M relationship is always "hiding" another entity, and it will be "resolved" by adding a new entity and a pair of 1:M (usually) relationships. This doesn't have to be done right away—M:M relationships are just fine while the model is at an overview stage, although the detail-oriented modelers we mentioned earlier tend to obsess about resolving the M:M relationships immediately. Don't worry about resolving the M:M relationship until the discussion turns to attributes that can only be captured in the new entity. Even very complex data models can be developed by applying a few basic patterns, like this one for handling M:M relationships.

One final point on the E-R diagram is that the symbols will vary slightly among the different data modeling "dialects." For instance, we've used the crow's-foot to indicate "many," while other notations will use a small circle or arrowheads. These are minor differences, easily learned, because the underlying meaning is constant. Over time, these differences will continue to disappear—currently, the symbols are much more standardized than they used to be.

The narrative component: the entity definitions

Just as important as the diagram is the accompanying entity definitions, which comprise the all-important glossary. This may seem like a strange thing to produce, but one of the most common sources of difficulty on projects is a failure to define common terms, especially the entities, on the assumption that everyone "knows" what they mean. After all, won't everyone working on an order fulfillment process agree what "order," "product," and "customer" mean? Surprisingly, no—even the most common terms will have different interpretations that will cause grief when they become evident (it's inevitable!) late in the game. Consider this moment of discovery—"Oh, no! You mean we're supposed to be able to handle *internal* customers, too? I assumed we were only talking about *external* customers, so that's how we designed the system. Maybe we can add dummy Customer records for external Customers, with some sort of a pointer to our legacy system—that's where Customer records are now. Of course, that involves a lot of reprogramming, we'll have to redesign the user interface, and our report generator will be blown out of the water...." This real-life example illustrates why a project should develop a glossary as soon as possible, whether it's treated as part of data modeling or a separate undertaking.

During the development of the definitions, things *invariably* get interesting—it's without question our favorite part of data modeling. Participants are surprised—even shocked—to learn the different interpretations that others have for terms they've been communicating with on a daily basis. Alec vividly recalls a marketing vice president being dumbfounded by accounting's definition of Customer (an account held by a corporation with more than $2,000 of business within the past six months), and then thinking out loud, "That's why those customer reports you've been sending us for all these years are so useless."

Think of the possible interpretations of "customer" at your organization. Is a customer an individual contact person, an operating location, or the customer organization (legal entity) itself? Is a "client" the same thing as a "customer?" Perhaps marketing will want to consider prospects or mailing list subscribers as customers, while accounts receivable will be convinced that "customer" means "someone who has purchased products from us and has a customer account" (even if many organizations have more than one customer account). If one part of the enterprise requests a product from another, does that mean the enterprise is its own customer? And we haven't even touched on the other entities. Is that internal request considered to be an "order," or something else? Does "product" imply goods only, or are services included?

A good definition comprises a few sentences, at most, and possibly some clarifying bullet points. It will answer the questions "What is one of these things, and are there any anomalies we all need to know about?" Here's a customer definition used by one of our clients:

"A Customer is a person or organization that is a past, present, or potential user of our products."

- This excludes cases where the company uses its own products.

- The Customer does not necessarily have to pay (e.g., a charity).

By the way, the definition of "product" clarified that both goods and services were considered to be products.

These distinctions aren't academic—consider the impact they have on the scope of a new Fulfill Order process, and the huge impact on the functionality of the supporting information system. If these ambiguities aren't dealt with early in the project, they will eventually surface, causing rework, delay, and expense. Data modeling, especially glossary development, should begin early in the project, paralleling the identification of business processes and development of workflow models.

Levels of detail

Earlier, we stressed that data modeling shouldn't start at the detail level. This is true of all types of models—they go through progressive levels of detail, each highlighting different aspects, each serving a different purpose and perhaps a different audience.

A house will progress through the following:

1.   Concept and features;

2.   Floor plan/front elevation (sketch);

3.   Detailed blueprints.

As we have seen, a business process progresses through the following:

1.   Identification and framing;

2.   Handoff level workflow diagram;

3.   Milestone level workflow diagram.

Similarly, data models have the following defined levels of detail:

1.   Glossary or vocabulary;

2.   Conceptual data model (an overview);

3.   Logical data model (the details).

A *glossary* or *vocabulary* lists the main entities (and other important things, such as transaction types) and the agreed-upon definitions. It's really an extract of the conceptual data model, but we treat it as a separate level of model to stress the importance of developing a common set of terms and definitions.

The order data model in Figure 15.3 is a *conceptual data model*, which serves to get the main ideas across (the main entities, attributes, relationships, and rules). In a conceptual data model, many of the M:M relationships are left unresolved. The main purpose of a conceptual model is to improve communication and clarify scope—the details needed for physical design are added while our conceptual model evolves into a logical model.

A *logical data model* contains all of the excruciating detail that is needed to actually build a database. This includes keys, every single attribute, the definition, data type, length, and validation rules for each of these attributes, and a host of other details. It will include many more entities (usually about four times as many) than the conceptual model—a conceptual entity may prove to be a whole collection of entities related to a subject that we hadn't yet discerned the details of. Customer, for example, may in the logical data model become many entities to record a Customer along with multiple Operating Locations, Contact Persons, Industry Groups, and so on. Eventually the logical model will become "physical" when the database administrator (DBA) uses it to produce a database design for the particular database management system (DBMS, e.g., DB2, Oracle, SQL Server, or Access) used by your computer system.

Much of the difference between conceptual and logical is in the handling of attributes. In a logical model, attributes are "atomic." For instance, Name is a legitimate conceptual attribute, but in the logical model it is broken down into its atomic components—the smallest parts of the attribute that would ever be handled independently. Name would become Prefix (Mr., Ms., etc., First Given Name, Second Given Name, Goes By Name, Last Name, etc.). Address could become Suite/Unit Number, Street Number, Street Name, City, State/Province, Country, and Postal Code, and so forth *if* there was a need to deal with these parts independently. Otherwise, it might become Address Line 1, Address Line 2, City, and so forth. If international addresses were to be handled, the simple attribute Address in the conceptual model could become a very complex data structure in the logical.

The other difference is that in the logical model, attributes are nonrepeating, as per our Requested Quantity example earlier. Returning to the Name example, if it turned out (as it often does) that the model must record a history of name changes, we would say that Name is a repeating attribute, because one Customer could have many Names. (The same thing would likely happen to Address as well.) In the logical model, this would be handled by creating a separate Customer Name entity connected to the Customer entity with a 1:M relationship (each Customer has had a maximum of many Names, but each Name is attached to a maximum of one Customer). Each Customer Name would record an effective date range during which the name was valid, as well as all of the atomic attributes described previously. Another wrinkle—a different format will be required for Customers that are organizations, not persons. We don't want to get bogged down too early, but eventually these details will have a major impact, not just on database internals but on the design of the user interface that actors in the business process will deal with. We'll look at that more closely in the following chapter on use cases.

There are other important differences between conceptual and logical models, but we've probably covered more than you wanted to know. However, we wanted to illustrate why both overview and detail models are necessary, what the main differences are, and why it's important not to get too detailed too soon. By the way, like many IS terms, "conceptual" and "logical" are a little strange—we would prefer to call these the "overview data model" and the "detailed data model," but we don't set the standards. Speaking of that, not everyone uses these terms consistently, and the detail-oriented folks we discussed earlier often don't even recognize the existence or need for the glossary or conceptual models.

A key point: As you add detail, your conceptual model will evolve into a logical data model, but don't lose the conceptual view! It will be an absolutely vital tool for presentations, training, and discussions about new requirements.

To summarize, here are the characteristics of each type of model:

Glossary/vocabulary

- Terms and definitions for the main entities (the ones that would be in the conceptual data model);
- May be the starting point, or may be an extract from your conceptual data model.

Conceptual data model

- "Overview" ensures everyone is on the same wavelength before diving into detail;
- Lots of M:M relationships;
- Relationships will show cardinality but not optionality;
- Main attributes only;
- Attributes will often be nonatomic and multivalued;
- Represents about 20% of the data modeling effort;
- *Save a copy before it evolves into the logical model!*

Logical data model

- "Excruciating detail" for physical design;

- "Fully normalized";

- Provides all of the detail needed for physical database design;

- Typically about four times as many entities as the conceptual model;

- No M:M relationships (all are resolved);

- Relationship optionality is shown;

- No multivalued attributes (all are moved into separate entities with a 1:M relationship);

- No nonatomic attributes (all attributes decomposed into their smallest component parts);

- All attributes completely documented (defined, data type and length specified, validation rules including allowable values documented, etc.);

- Primary keys, alternate keys (unique but nonkey attributes), and foreign keys all shown;

- Represents about 80% of the data modeling effort;

- *Save a copy before it evolves into the physical database design!*

The components—further guidelines and pitfalls

You can skip over this section for now, or forever, if you've learned as much about data modeling as you need. If you'd like to try it, we include some more specifics on the components of a data model—entities, attributes, and relationships.

Entities

An entity is a distinct thing the business needs to know about. It can be a person (Customer), place (Region), thing (Part), specification (Vehicle Make/Model), or even an event (Police Incident). It is always named using a singular noun meaningful to the content experts. Potential entities at a university include:

- Student;

- Instructor;

- Subject;
- Course;
- Class (or Section);
- Tutorial;
- Room;
- Scholarship Award;
- Residence;
- Residence Room.

From another perspective, an entity is a standard description for a set of similar instances. The main criteria for something to be an entity are that it is a distinct thing we need to maintain records about, it has multiple occurrences, there are facts that must be recorded about it, and there is a need (and the ability) to keep track of each individual occurrence. "Student" qualifies because there are multiple occurrences of it and all are essentially similar (i.e., have the same facts recorded), and the institution needs to keep track of each occurrence and can differentiate one from another.

You'll recall that a process must have a countable result, and you must be able to identify specific occurrences of that result. Entities are the same—you must be able to count the number of occurrences (not that you would necessarily want to), and you must be able to refer to individual instances when necessary. Look over the list of entities at the university and you'll see that all of them meet the "multiple occurrences" criterion. In contrast, the university may have departments called "Admissions," "Accounting," and "Facilities," but they wouldn't appear in a data model as separate entities, because there is only a single occurrence of each. Rather, there would be a "Department" entity, and these would be three of its instances. For that matter, if the university was Whattsamatta U,[4] we wouldn't expect to see the entity Whattsamatta U on one of its data models, because there is certainly only one Whatsamatta U!

Along with multiple, distinct instances, the criterion that it "has facts we need to record" is a simple and useful test for entities. Some of these

---

4.   Bullwinkle's alma mater.

facts are "attributes"—individual pieces of data, like the fields on a screen or report. Others are "relationships"—an association between two entities. For example, some Student attributes are ID Number, Name, Birth Date, and Grade Point Average (GPA), and some of its relationships are Student "majors in" a Subject, Student "enrolls in" a Class, and Student "currently occupies" a Residence Room.

Many potential entities will arise during your analysis, but you must select only those relevant to your scope and objectives. In a data model somewhere, Product and Order are surely entities, but they aren't relevant to this university example.

Perhaps the most common error is to confuse reports, forms, screens, and other ways of presenting or capturing information with the fundamental entities. For instance, "transcript" isn't an entity because it's really a report that presents data from other entities—a Student, the Courses the Student has taken, and so forth.

Each entity must be named and defined. The entity name should be a short phrase (one to three words) based on a noun. We use the singular form of the noun, and the convention is to capitalize the word when referring to it. It should be a phrase that business folks can relate to. The entity definition tells which instances in the real world are included within our understanding of that entity. Another term is "entity qualification." For instance, the world has hundreds of millions of people who are "students." Which ones would we expect to find in the Whattsamatta U Student database? Which ones would be excluded? Another way to look at it—are there any cases or anomalies that are likely to cause confusion? For example, is a person a Student as soon as he or she has applied for admission? Is he or she still a Student after graduation? And what about a Faculty Member (another entity) who takes classes? An example:

A Student is any person who has been admitted to Whattsamatta U, has accepted, and has enrolled in at least one class within a designated time. Faculty and staff members may also be Students, but up on graduation a Student becomes an Alumnus.

Note that the definition is always in terms of a single instance. If you can't name the entity in the singular, and define what a single occurrence is, you probably don't have an entity. We recall working at an insurance company where Weather was suggested as an entity, but it didn't seem to fit the bill. It wasn't named in the singular—the question "What is a Weather?" just didn't sound right. And it was hard to conceive of a singular instance of

Weather. By having the participants list sample instances, we were able to see that the entity was Weather Event—they were interested in recording particular events like Hurricane Floyd so they could tally the total damage due to each.

As that example illustrates, it's generally very helpful to get some examples—specific instances—as part of your definition of each entity. If you have only a vague notion of what the entity is, you'll be unable to come up with examples of specific instances. For instance, when you start listing examples of a Product, it may become evident that some participants are thinking about a product family, others are thinking about a base product, others assume that Product means a particular configuration of options and packaging, and still others are thinking about a specific unit (i.e., with a serial number) that must be tracked for warranty purposes. You might have four distinct but related entities—Product Family, Product, Product Configuration, and Product Unit. That's how models that start out small and simple become larger and more complex!

Attributes

Correctly identifying the entities is the difficult (and important!) part of data modeling. Once that's been accomplished, attributes are fairly straightforward. An attribute, also called a data element or data item, is a fact about (property of) an entity that can be expressed as a piece of data. The individual fields we see on screens, forms, and reports correspond to attributes in a data model. Traditionally, attributes in a data model are text strings, numbers, or alphanumeric strings that contain both characters and digits, as per the following examples for the university:

- Student Name;

- Course Description Text;

- Course Code;

- Admission Date;

- Special Admissions Flag;

- Fees Due Amount;

- Maximum Attendance Quantity.

New types of attributes are appearing in data models because of techni-cal advances in what can be recorded in a database, such as Student Portrait (a picture), Student Resumé (a word processing document), or Student Presentation (a video clip). Note that these were always "naturally occur-ring" attributes of the Student entity, but they wouldn't have appeared in the data model because there was no way to capture them in files or databases. This is one of the dilemmas of data modeling—we seek to produce a technology-neutral representation of the required data, but what gets included in the data model is always constrained by the available technology.

The basic criterion for an attribute is that it is a necessary fact, some-thing the enterprise needs to know. Student Shoe Size is a fact, but is unlikely to be a necessary fact, unless the Athletic department has a need to know.

The attribute should contain one and only one fact—otherwise, we say it's "semantically overloaded." The attribute Male Special Admissions Flag contains two facts—gender and admission status—and so should be split into two attributes. This is similar to guidelines we reviewed earlier—as the model progresses from conceptual to logical, attributes become atomic and nonrepeating.

The attribute should be a fundamental fact about the entity, not easily calculated from other attributes or relationships. Otherwise, it is referred to as a "derived" attribute. Student Age is derived, because it can be calcu-lated using Student Birth Date and today's date. Similarly, Section Current Enrollment could be derived (calculated) by adding up the number of Stu-dents currently enrolled in a Section. Even Student Grade Point Average is derivable. Eventually, you will get to the point where the calculation seems so onerous that it's more reasonable to include a derived attribute in the model. The classic example—your Bank Account Balance, which could be derived if you wanted to go right back to the opening balance and apply every deposit, withdrawal, fee, and adjustment that had ever happened. Where to draw the line isn't clear, demonstrating once again that data modeling is part science, part art. If you really want to show a derived attribute, be sure to record the calculation algorithm.

Finally, the attribute should be attached to the entity it's a fact about. This seems self-evident, but in practice, it's anything but. For instance, Instructor Name seems like a reasonable attribute of Section, but it isn't—it is a fact about Instructor, which is a related entity via the Instructor "is assigned to" Section relationship. This is an example of a common error—adding an attribute to an entity instead of creating a relationship to the entity that the attribute belongs in.

Relationships

A relationship is a named association between two entities. The relationship name will be verb-based (assigned to, located in, transported by, etc.), as opposed to an entity name, which is noun-based.

During conceptual modeling, you'll determine the *cardinality* of each relationship—the maximum number of one entity that another can be related to. The choices are one to one (1:1), one to many (1:M), or many to many (M:M). Eventually we will need to resolve all many-to-many relationships (databases can only store 1:1 and 1:M), but during conceptual modeling M:M relationships are fine.

Later, during logical modeling, you'll consider the *optionality* of each relationship, which answers this question—for each entity involved in the relationship, is it mandatory for every instance to participate in the relationship, or is it optional? Consider the 1:M relationship Course is offered by Section. (There may be many Sections of the Course English 100, each at different times and locations.) In the other direction, the relationship is: Section is an offering of a Course. Each Course *may be* (optional) offered by the scheduling of a Section. It is optional because a new Course may not have any Sections scheduled yet. Each Section *must be* (mandatory) an offering of a Course, because you can't have a Section unless there is first a Course to offer in that Section. Different data modeling dialects depict optionality in different ways, but the concept is always there in a detailed model.

Two common errors are redundant relationships and irrelevant relationships. A redundant relationship occurs when a "shortcut" relationship is added between two entities that are already connected via essential relationships involving another entity. For instance, Student enrolls in Section, and Section is an offering of Course are both fundamental relationships that the model must record. If we added a relationship directly connecting Student and Course (e.g., to make producing a transcript a little easier), that would be redundant, because the information is already available by going from Student to Section, and then from Section to Course. This may seem inefficient, but in the grand scheme of things, it's better to avoid redundancy. One reason—it's very easy to build an incomprehensible "spaghetti" model where every entity is connected to every other entity, the First Law of Ecology being that everything is ultimately connected to everything else.

Irrelevant relationships are those that, while true, don't contain information that must be maintained. For instance, it might be true that Student had coffee with Instructor, but if no one cares, why add it to the model?

There's a lot more to learn about data models—at the end of the chapter are references for two excellent books on data modeling.

Starting your data model

There are as many different approaches to starting a data model as there are data modelers. If you decide to give it a try, you will develop another data model, based on your abilities and preferences, and those of the people you work with. Treat this section as ideas, not prescriptions.

Starting with the glossary

The easiest way to begin data modeling in the context of a process-oriented project is to scan for the nouns in the verb-noun process, milestone, or step names. Ideally, this is done during framing the process, but certainly by the end of as-is modeling. If you leave it that late, though, you may discover you missed some important cases and have to go back to the drawing board. Some of the nouns will refer to things that are clearly central to the process, and you can say to the group, "Let's define some of these terms." This is the subtle approach—many participants will rebel if you suggest building a data model because they have suffered through the excruciatingly detailed data modeling we described earlier. The beauty of this approach is that you get started without referring to "data modeling." This is "guerrilla" data modeling, which beats "gorilla" data modeling every time! After the definitions are sorted out, a reasonable next step is to ask "What facts do we need to know about each of these things?" and then organizing the suggestions into a conceptual model as suggested in the next approach. You may even complete a substantial amount of data modeling before the detractors realize what you're up to!

Starting with a conceptual model

If your group doesn't have any problems with the idea of data modeling, it's often easier to build a first-cut conceptual model and then "extract" the glossary from that. In point form, here's an approach for developing the initial conceptual data model in a facilitated session:

- *Don't begin with a treatise on data modeling*—simply state that it's important to understand the information needs of the process, or words to that effect.

- Brainstorm for *anything* "data-related" needed by the process and the supporting applications:

   Things of interest (entities), information needs, facts, queries and re-ports, and so forth.

- For each item, ask, "Is this a thing, or a fact about a thing?"

   Circle "things";

   Cluster "facts" around the appropriate thing;

   Set aside "reports and other stuff" for later analysis.

- Check the validity of the entities.

   Consolidate obvious synonyms.

   Retain only those in the scope of your project.

   Ensure they meet the basic criteria: multiple occurrences, have facts, and the business needs to know about them.

   Is there any overlap (i.e., the same facts in two entities)? Overlap may indicate that a "report" has been listed as an entity.

- Starting with the fundamental entities, develop entity definitions.

- Draw an entity-relationship diagram.

   Fundamental entities at the top;

   Dependent entities below.

- Brainstorm important additional attributes for each entity, up to a maximum of seven or so.

- Validate the model, primarily by "playing it back" to the participants as a presentation, and asking if it sounds like a reasonable description of their business.

As an alternative to the first steps, do the brainstorm on index cards, and have participants arrange them. The use of index cards can have important benefits—participants take the model more seriously when they have been *physically* involved with creating and manipulating it.

Starting by reverse engineering

The majority of our current work involves going through the data modeling process in reverse! This is done when there is already a database in place, either for an existing (legacy or custom) application or for a piece of commercial software being evaluated. This requires a degree of technical skill and data modeling experience that we can't get into here, but it's worth knowing that this is a valid approach. Essentially, we study the physical database design and some real data to figure out what's going on, and then work backwards and represent the physical database as an entity-relationship diagram. (Some tools can automate this step.) This will approximate a logical data model. We then apply simplification heuristics, and turn it into a conceptual model. Finally, through a variety of techniques including interviewing developers and users, studying documentation, looking at screen shots and reports, checking with the vendor, and so on, we develop entity definitions. This leads up to a review presentation at which we unveil the model, and ask:

- "Is this what you expected?" (for current legacy or custom applications);

- Or, "Will this work for you?" (for commercial applications being evaluated).

This will provide important guidance on whether the database (and therefore, the application) will support the scope and objectives of the new business process.

From conceptual to logical

Techniques for developing the logical data model are well beyond the scope of this book, although we have provided some guidelines on what comprises a logical model. The basic principle of logical models is that they are primarily developed by discovering additional attributes.

These additional attributes are best discovered, surprisingly, by shifting our attention away from data and concentrating on other analysis techniques such as use case scenario analysis (in the next chapter), transaction specification (also in the next chapter), and report specification. While doing these, constantly check that all the necessary attributes are in the data model. If not, add new attributes according to rules such as the ones we covered earlier.

- ◆ If we need to record attributes of a relationship, create a new entity in the middle of the relationship.

- ◆ If one or more attributes repeats within an entity, create a new dependent entity to record them.

This is a lot of work—developing the logical data model takes roughly four times as long as developing the conceptual data model—and is probably going to require the assistance of specialists. We'll leave it at that, but there are many excellent books if you want to learn more. Two in particular stand out as excellent references. Graeme Simsion's *Data Modeling Essentials* [1] is eminently readable, and based on real-world experience—no idle theory here. David Hay's *Data Model Patterns* [2] isn't a book *about* data models, it's a book *of* data models—much can be learned by studying the generic (similar across enterprises and industries) data models the book presents.

We'll continue our whirlwind tour of related analysis techniques in the final chapter, where we consider the important role of use cases.

References

[1]   Simsion, G., *Data Modeling Essentials: Analysis, Design, and Innovation,* New York: Van Nostrand Reinhold, 1994.

[2]   Hay, D. C., *Data Model Patterns: Conventions of Thought,* New York: Dorset House, 1996.

16

Use Case Scenario Analysis

A time of transition

While characterizing and designing the to-be process, we identified where automation would be applied to support an actor completing a task or steps within a task. Now, we need to go down a level of detail and describe how an actor will interact with the system to complete process steps and how the system will behave from the perspective of that actor. The description must be clear and accurate enough that software developers can design a system (or prototype) that will support the process, and meet the needs and expectations of its users.

You could attempt to do this by adding detail to your to-be swimlane diagrams until you were describing every field entered on a screen, every time "enter" was pressed, and every system response. But what would be the point? You would be drawing a workflow diagram, but you wouldn't be diagramming the flow of work. Instead, you would be describing a procedure—the series of actions that an actor completes at a single time and place to accomplish a step in a process. The issue is no longer the flow of work among the various actors—it's determining how a system will help a specific actor complete a process task or step. In other words, it's time to make some important transitions:

1. From process workflow to individual procedures;

2. From process workflow to system requirements definition.[1]

Swimlane diagrams are, categorically, inappropriate for this purpose. We've seen it attempted, and it is not pretty. They become large, complex (imagine trying to show every decision point and path in an event driven interface), and fail to illustrate the central concern—system functionality and behavior. Instead, we make the transition to a variant of the popular "use case" technique[2] that employs "use case scenarios."

A *use case* describes a *case* in which an actor will *use* a system to complete a particular task (e.g., place an order) or obtain a service (e.g., view open orders). Use cases are an increasingly popular and widely used tool for discovering and documenting system requirements. They help us design an ideal set of interactions to accomplish a particular task or sequence of tasks in a process. This information is invaluable for the design of all sorts of user interfaces. That topic is beyond our scope, but many excellent books are available.[3]

People with a background in process redesign find that use cases are a great transition into the world of requirements specification; those having experience with use cases find that workflow process models provide an excellent framework for use case development. They are the focus of entire books, courses, and conferences, but in this chapter we can describe enough information for you to benefit from the technique. You will:

1. Be introduced to the terminology, concepts, and structures of use cases and use case scenarios;

---

1. Other terms include "software requirements definition," "requirements specification," or "requirements engineering." "External design" and "systems analysis" are also used, but have other interpretations as well, so may not be quite as accurate.

2. The book that propelled adoption of the technique was Ivar Jacobsen et al., *Object Oriented Software Engineering: A Use Case Driven Approach*, Reading, MA: Addison-Wesley, 1992.

3. A highly regarded text is Alan Cooper, *About Face: The Essentials of User Interface Design*, Foster City, CA: IDG Books Worldwide, 1995.

2. See how they fit naturally into a process workflow-driven project;

3. Look at a successful approach to applying use case techniques in determining system requirements.

Two warnings: First, if you're familiar with the use case technique as described in the earlier literature, you will find this approach quite different in two ways—using workflow models as a framework for discovering use cases, and exploring specific scenarios (like test cases) to uncover requirements. Many professionals, however, are independently arriving at the same set of methods. Second, whenever a technique is successful, someone will try to take it too far, and use cases are no exception. A notable example: They have been proposed as the core technique of a process reengineering methodology in which a process is viewed as a use case—a very large use case—that is progressively decomposed until it arrives at task-level use cases. This approach simply hasn't taken off, so if you're considering it, don't bother. Process framing and swimlane diagramming are better for dealing with complete business processes, just as use cases are better for determining how actors and systems will interact to complete tasks.

Now, let's get more specific about what a use case is.

Use case concepts

The notion of use cases is appealing in its simplicity—a unit of functionality offered by a system to an actor (a user)—but it requires clarification to avoid the common problems encountered. Here are some guidelines to keep in mind:

+ A use case will usually take place at a single place and time.

+ It is a unit of system functionality that is logically complete.[4] That is, it has business significance on its own and delivers measurable value to the actor or to the process. In the context of taking an order, recording the customer's name is not a use case, it's only part of one. "Take new order," which includes identifying the customer,

---

4. What it means to be "logically complete" is further explained in upcoming sections on events and transactions.

establishing delivery and payment terms, and recording the items being ordered would be an example of a logically complete use case.

♦ Use cases most commonly describe the steps by which an actor interacts with a graphical user interface, but they can illustrate any other type of interaction, such as the dialogues for an interactive voice response system or a keypad-based interface such as an automated teller machine. They can also show communication between systems or devices.

♦ Use cases are usually defined actor by actor. Some of the use cases for the actor "student" using a student registration system would include:

View semester schedule;

View course details;

Enroll in section;

Transfer section;

Drop section;

View account;

Submit payment;

View transcript.

♦ Generally speaking, a use case satisfies a specific query or information request, or invokes a single update transaction as defined in the application logic layer.[5]

♦ "Actor" has the same meaning that it does on a workflow process model—a person, job function, organization, system, or device playing a particular role.

♦ A use case will generally involve one actor, but could involve more (e.g., a customer, customer service rep, and credit specialist could all participate in the "order new service" use case). If you treat the system itself as an actor, a common practice, then two actors will typically be involved.

---

5. The connection to transactions will be expanded later in the chapter.

- There may be different use cases for the same service delivered to different actors. For instance, "student registers in section" and "departmental advisor registers student in section" would each behave differently and provide different capabilities. The latter might include student search capabilities, and more direct data entry (versus pick-list selection) to accommodate the more experienced user.

- Multiple use cases will often be employed in a single session or scenario. After accessing the student registration system, a student might use most of the use cases in the sample list. Similarly, use cases can be combined to extend basic capabilities. For instance, while carrying out "enroll in section," the use cases "view semester schedule" or "view course details" might be used.

There is a strong correspondence between use cases and workflow process models. Any time a step or a contiguous set of steps in a process receives automated support, there is probably a corresponding use case or linked series of use cases. Our swimlane diagrams therefore provide an ideal framework for discovering the important use cases.

Use case descriptions

Simply identifying all of the use cases has value, for instance, to define the scope of a system. Much more value emerges when we develop the use case description. This describes a generalized sequence of interactions between the actor and the system. Most importantly, it describes system behavior *from the perspective of the actor* interacting with the system. In terms of our three-tier systems model, the use case describes the *behavior* of the user interface (UI) layer, while shielding (at least initially) the actors from details of specific UI design elements, or "behind the scenes" activity involving the application logic and data management layers. Another way to put this is that use cases provide a "how used," not a "how built" view. This shielding is critical—the actors themselves provide the main input to the use case descriptions, and they must not be confused or misled by internal design considerations.

Figure 16.1 illustrates a typical format for a basic use case description. Some practitioners include much more, but these are the basic elements.

Use Case Name
Departmental Adviser enrolls student in section(s).
Description
When the student has submitted his/her enrollment form (by mail, fax, e-mail, etc.), his/her adviser will complete the enrollment process for him/her, including enrolling him/her in alternative sections or even courses as necessary. (Also see postconditions.)
Actor(s)
Departmental Adviser or certain other staff in the Registrar's Department. (Students have separate use cases for self-service enrollment.)
Preconditions
• The student must have completed the appropriate enrollment form • The student must be newly admitted or be a current student in good academic standing. • The student's account must not have any holds placed on it.
Normal sequence of steps
• Adviser signs on to system and provides password. • System validates adviser's sign-on and displays home screen. • Adviser enters student number and selects "enrollment". • System verifies student and account status and displays basic student data. • Adviser selects semester/session student is enrolling for. • System verifies that semester/session is available. • Adviser selects course code (e.g., "Math") for next course to enroll in. • System returns list of all courses for that course code available in selected semester/session that student has prerequisites for.
Postconditions
• The student will have a verified or waitlisted enrollment in each selected (section). • Available space in sections will be updated. • The student's account will be updated by either withdrawing funds electronically, or indicating an account due for handling by the A/R system. • A confirmation report will be produced for the student.
Alternate sequence of steps
If the student doesn't provide his/her student number: • If the desired section is full, "waitlist" can be selected for any number of sections (of the same course) in addition to enrolling in one. • If the student fails to provide his/her student number, then the adviser can enter any number of characters of the last name. The system will produce a list of matching students to select from.
Comments, issues, and design notes
• For student search, may need a mechanism for restricting the number of entries in the list. • For student search, need a way to indicate whether the whole name or a subset is being entered.

Figure 16.1   A use case description.

Your initial use case descriptions will be an approximation—they won't be complete or accurate until after you have developed the use case scenarios.

Use case scenarios

Now that you see the strength of use cases, you can also see the inherent challenges. One is ensuring that each use case includes *the right functionality* to handle not just the normal situation, but all of the errors, exceptions, and extensions that will surely arise. Use case scenarios deal with this concern. This extension of the basic use case technique addresses the major issues in requirements specification—completeness and accuracy—so this is no small improvement.

Essentially, a use case scenario depicts the dialogue or "back and forth" (*every single interaction*) between an actor and a system for a *particular scenario* (like a test case) that:

* Has named actors;

* Uses actual data values;

* Illustrates a specific sequence of interactions, including normal steps, errors, exceptions, extensions, or whatever the scenario is intended to illuminate;

* Illustrates a single scenario. *This is a critical point!* There is no branching ("If actor does X then…") because the scenario follows a single path. This manages complexity by ensuring focus on one case at time.

A use case scenario may cover multiple use cases, the classic example being a session at an ATM. This is a single use case scenario, but includes multiple use cases such as "customer deposits funds," "…pays bill," and "…withdraws cash," as well as "customer signs on," a use case fragment that can be reused in various contexts.

These are the critical aspects of use case *scenario* analysis that differentiate it from the more abstract or generalized use case analysis that is often employed. We say "abstract" because a use case is an abstraction of all of the ways an actor could use a particular unit of functionality. This isn't meant to be a criticism, because separately inspecting each significant function via its use case is a big improvement over the even *more* abstract or disconnected forms of requirements analysis that we used to rely upon. However, developing a perfect use case description without context is difficult. The use of scenarios provides the context that helps potential users relate to the example and provide much better feedback on how the system ought to behave. Important use cases might require several use case scenarios to uncover all of the requirements.

Note that a system has a finite number of use cases, but an infinite number of use case scenarios. Another challenge, then, will lie in defining a set of scenarios that is large enough to elicit all (or at least the great

Use case(s)	Scenario description/purpose
Department adviser enrolls student in sections. Department adviser searches for student by name.	Departmental Adviser "Ed Visor" enrolls Student "Stu Dent" in his selected sections. Normal flow with a few minor problems.
Precondition	**Impact**
• Stu Dent is a second year student. • Stu is in good standing, with no outstanding debts to the university. • Ed is already signed on to Registration Management application	• Already registered at the university with all student data in place. • None. • No sign-on for this scenario.
Condition	**Expected handling**
• Stu failed to provide student number. • Prerequisite to Math 210 is missing. • Section 3 of Chem 205 is full. • Successful enrollment in Phys 220, Span 200, and Math 221.	• Use student name search. • Prompt for waiver, which Ed grants. • Suggest alternate sections; one will be selected, but waitlist Section 3. • Successful enrollment in Phys 220, Span 200, and Math 221.
Dialog	**Notes**
When Ed selects "Enroll" from "menu" Then system presents a dialog box to select the student (either by number or by name).	
When Ed enters first five characters of last name Then system lists several matching students, showing student's full name, birth date, permanent residence city, and student number.	Should have option to display full information about any student in the list.
When Ed selects Stu from list and selects "enroll" Then system verifies Stu's academic and account status, displays Stu's basic personal/student data (to be determined), declared major, course history list, and department selection list.	
When Ed selects "Phys" from department list and enters "220" Then system checks that Stu has the necessary prerequisites, and lists all sections plus their current status (open, full, pending, …).	Should allow selection of department name either from pulldown list or direct entry.
When adviser selects "Phys 220, Section 3" Then system initiates transaction to enroll Smith in that section and displays confirmation.	
When Ed selects "Math" from deptartment list and enters "210" Then system checks that Stu has the necessary prerequisites—he doesn't—so system displays waiver dialog.	If Ed had just entered "Math", the system would list all of the courses that Stu had the prerequisites for—Math 210 would not be on the list.

Figure 16.2 A use case scenario description.

majority) of the requirements but not so large as to be impractical. This is addressed in the upcoming "how-to" section.

The example in Figure 16.2 conveys the important aspects of use case scenarios.

Developing use cases and scenarios

The concepts are simple enough that you could get started with use cases the same way we did—jump in and try it. The "just do it!" approach has its limitations, including moments of fear, uncertainty, and doubt, so we will provide a proven approach that organizes use case development into four phases:

1. Identify and describe use cases;

    a) Include name, actor, description, milestone steps, and sequence.

2. Prepare for use case scenario development;

    a) Identify process scenarios (scenarios that span the entire process, and therefore comprise many use case scenarios);

    b) Identify use case scenarios (specific conditions, major steps and sequence).

3. Develop use case scenarios—first-pass (dialogue only);

    a) Describe and iteratively refine dialogue;

    b) Don't dive for detail—move on to the next use case scenario.

4. Develop use case scenarios—second-pass (data, transaction points, and UI components).

Phase 4 gets into more detail than this introduction calls for, so it will be described with minimal detail. Well beyond the scope of this book, a full use case methodology would continue with subsequent phases such as refining and abstracting the use cases, constructing ideal object models, and developing object interaction diagrams. More extensive approaches go even further by describing archetypal actors or "personas" that embody characteristics of various types of system users, and ensuring that each of these will be satisfied with the system's behavior. Excellent books that explore these methods have recently come to market.[6]

---

6. Alan Cooper, *The Inmates Are Running the Asylum: Why High-Tech Products Drive Us Crazy and How to Restore the Sanity,* Indianapolis, IN: SAMS/Macmillan Computer Publishing, 1999; and Larry L. Constantine and Lucy A. D. Lockwood, *Software for Use: A Practical Guide to the Models and Methods of Usage-Centered Design,* Reading, MA: ACM Press/Addison Wesley, 1999.

Identify and describe use cases

Discovering the use cases

As with previous steps, use case development begins with facilitated sessions. Participants should include some of those who participated in the design of the to-be process, but *must* include experienced people who will use the resulting information systems.

The best results are obtained when multiple approaches are used to identify the required use cases. In any sort of discovery process like this, we begin with an open brainstorm, and then shift to structured approaches. The open brainstorm often uncovers the unusual situations ("departmental adviser calls in sick"), while the structured approaches ensure completeness by overlaying a framework on the subject area and then considering one perspective at a time.

The initial brainstorm can begin with the question "What functions must the system provide?" Optionally, this could be divided into two questions—"What transactions (updates) will the system be expected to handle?" and "What queries will the system be expected to satisfy?" We usually limit the time spent collecting suggestions to 20 minutes or so, because the purpose is mostly to get the participants warmed up and identify a few "outliers." After the flow of ideas has slowed, or time has run out, move on to the usual post-brainstorm steps:

1. Reduce the list by consolidating duplicate suggestions and eliminating those that are out of scope.

2. Group the remaining suggestions by the actor who will use the function (e.g., student, departmental adviser, etc.). A few more suggestions usually arise at this point.

This initial list of use cases won't be complete, but the structured approaches will address that. Don't be concerned if some use cases appear under multiple actors—later we'll decide if they are really different or can be handled as one, shared use case.

The next approach is to look at the needs of each actor in turn. Focusing on the actors is the essence of the use case approach, and will be helped tremendously by the work that has already been done—the core use cases have, for the most part, already been identified while characterizing the to-be process and modeling the to-be workflow. Begin by reviewing each actor's swimlane in the workflow model and listing the specific system functions they will require. Many of these will also have been identified in your matrix of to-be process characteristics. Add these to the "use cases by actor" list, and then extend it by asking four questions for each actor:

1. What other "normal" system functions will they require?

2. What error and exception situations will arise that require other functions?

3. What other maintenance functions (e.g., table or profile updates) will be needed?

4. What other supporting or recurring functions (e.g., help or search) will be needed?

Again, some ideas may have to be consolidated or eliminated. Annotating a version of the workflow diagram to relate use cases to steps will be helpful later on.

The final approach is to look for use cases by identifying the events that the system must be able to respond to. "Event" in this context has a broader meaning than when we considered events as triggers for business processes, so we'll begin with some definitions and guidelines for applying event analysis. This will take a couple of pages, but will be worthwhile because event analysis is so important to use cases and other types of requirements analysis.

An interlude on events

In the context of information systems, an event is an occurrence outside of the system's control for which a "planned response"—a system function—is necessary, such as "section is scheduled," "section enrollment is requested," or "section is canceled." These are not interface events or individual interactions like "mouse is clicked" or "pick list selection is made," but events which have business significance. They require a "logically complete response" in exactly the same sense that a use case represents a logically complete unit of functionality. The event "order is received" requires a logically complete response (a transaction) that validates the order and records all of the pertinent details. Events generally correspond one-to-one with the transactions that make up the application logic layer (the middle tier in the three-tier systems architecture). An upcoming section on transactions will further clarify the idea of logically complete.

A few events, like "order is received," are especially important because they initiate an entire business process, but we are considering *any* event (mainstream or exception) that happens *during* the course of a business process. We're not talking about every conceivable event, though, just those that will occur often enough and/or are important enough that they fall within the scope of the system.

The complete "planned response" provided by the system comprises user interface mechanisms (described in use cases) to get the necessary information about the event from an actor and convey the event to the system, and application logic (described in transaction definitions) to validate and process the event as well as to control database updates that record the outcome of the event. There is, therefore, a three-way correspondence—for each *event*, there will typically be a *use case* and a *transaction* in the application logic layer. Identifying any one of these leads easily to the identification of the other two, which explains our interest in events—identifying events generally identifies at least a few use cases missed by other approaches.

There are two main types of events, *action* and *temporal*. Action events occur when an actor (person, organization, system) takes an action or makes a decision that the information system must have a designed response for: "section is scheduled," "section enrollment is requested," "section enrollment is dropped," "final grade is posted," "transcript is requested," and so forth. We use the "object is verbed" naming format, which adds useful rigor. Note that the object of the event is very often an entity from the data model. Some analysts separately consider internal and external events, depending on whether or not the actor triggering the event works within the organization responsible for the process. This is a less useful distinction now that processes frequently span multiple organizations, but if you think it will help focus attention, use it.

Temporal events occur when a predetermined time arrives that the information system must have a designed response for (e.g., scheduled events, such as "time to produce account statements," "time to publish semester results," "time to produce payroll," and "time to submit government financial statements"). These generally correspond to the system functions that are part of the batch processing schedule. They are important for complete requirements definition, but aren't usually of interest in use case identification.

One or more descriptive data items always accompany action events. The event "section enrollment is dropped" must have an associated "student number" and "section identification." The role of the user interface is to provide a means of capturing these data items, and signaling the event to the system by invoking the correct transaction by passing it a message containing the data items. A temporal event, on the other hand, is essentially like an alarm going off, and any required parameters are already somewhere in the database, although there may have been an event and use case to set them.

Variations of "who, how, and why" are avoided when identifying action events. This keeps the number of events manageable, and encourages focus on the essential functions that must be provided. For instance, for "section enrollment is requested" we don't indicate whether the request came from the student, or on their behalf from the departmental adviser ("who"). Similarly, the request may have been transmitted via the Internet, EDI, or fax ("how"). "Section is canceled" may have happened because enrollment was too low, facilities were unavailable, or the budget was cut ("why"). In all cases, what is important is the essence of "what" happened, not the particulars.

Returning to use case identification

With the theory in hand, applying event analysis is straightforward. We generally begin with a short, open brainstorm on events—"What happens that the system must respond to?" You might narrow the focus by looking only for events not covered by the use cases already identified, but this restriction might defeat the purpose of brainstorming. Instead, we just keep it short so we can quickly move on to brainstorming by entity, which tends to be more productive.

Focusing on one significant entity from the data model at a time, brainstorm for events targeting that entity. Surprisingly, this works best if you begin with dependent entities at the bottom of the entity-relationship diagram and work your way up to the independent entities at the top. For instance, consider "section enrollment," then "section," then "course." If you start with an entity at the top, there's a tendency to try to cover all of the events for its dependent entities at the same time.

Another useful technique is to first trace the normal sequence of events—the "entity life cycle"—which makes missing events more obvious. For instance, "section enrollment is requested," "section enrollment midterm grade is posted," and "section enrollment final grade is posted." Next, look for the exception events, such as "waitlisted section enrollment is confirmed," "section enrollment is dropped," or "section enrollment is transferred."

The brainstormed list of events will require some cleanup. Some of the suggested events might be eliminated (with caution!) because they are beyond the expected scope of the system. Others will have to be made more "essential" by removing references to who, how, and why. Temporal events that don't require any action on the part of an actor, such as "time to finalize enrollment," can be set aside. These won't require a use case, but are part of your overall requirements specification.

Finally, check that each remaining event is covered by a use case. If not, decide which actor(s) will own the use case, and add it to that actor's list of use cases.

A closing note on using event analysis—for many analysts, this is the preferred starting point for use case identification and requirements specification. A particular strength of the approach is that it is both straightforward and thorough, especially in combination with a data model, because your subject matter experts will have no trouble identifying events. Also, by stressing the *essence* of the business, it leads to systems that are stable in the face of changes to the who and how. Event analysis can also validate and extend the to-be process model— you might want to check that it is able to handle all of the expected events.

Describing the use cases

A use case description must now be completed as per the outline provided earlier. We'll just provide some tips, because the outline is very self-explanatory.

Like framing the process, this works best from the outside in. First, describe the main postconditions (results) of the use case—the value the actor or the enterprise receives from the use case, and the major updates to stored data. This is essentially the same as the use case description some approaches specify. Then, go to the beginning and determine the significant preconditions. This typically includes the pre-use case status of the actor and any other involved parties, as well as the status of the affected entities.

Next, identify the milestones within the use case, but not each individual step in the dialogue. For enrolling a student in a section, the milestones might be simply "student is identified," "section is selected," "course prerequisites are verified," and "enrollment is confirmed." Consider and note any mandatory sequence. For example, could a section be selected and checked for available space before the student is identified? This can have a significant impact—for instance, some retail sites on the Internet promote browsing through flexible dialogues that allow customers to fill up electronic shopping carts before identifying themselves.

For a use case that serves multiple actors, this is a good time to check if it should be the same for each actor. If so, add the other actors to the list for this use case. If there's any doubt, leave them separate—they can be consolidated later if the details prove to be the same.

Once the milestones are listed, flesh them out by identifying the sequence of steps that the actor and the system would go through to achieve them. This can involve some "intermingling" of milestones. For instance, some of the steps could be "system defaults to current semester," "student selects course," "system verifies prerequisites," and "student selects from available sections." Next, identify the sequences of steps for alternate conditions along with any significant rules. For instance, "If the desired section is full, system will allow waitlisting in any number of sections in addition to enrolling in one." Any other significant requirements, unresolved issues, or ideas can also be captured at this time.

Remember, this isn't the final use case description. Only after one or more use case scenarios have been explored will we have the confidence to finalize the description. Key to this is identifying a representative set of scenarios, which we will now move on to.

Prepare for use case scenario development

The goal of this phase is a set of use case scenarios that represent useful variations on the basic use cases. We begin by inventing *process scenarios* that help us use the process workflow model as a framework for discovering use case scenarios. Just as a use case scenario illustrates a particular variation of one or more basic use cases, a process scenario illustrates a particular variation of the overall process, or a plausible series of events for more transaction-related projects. Each process scenario has a named cast of characters, and demonstrates a unique combination of conditions by tracing a specific path through the process.

Creating these scenarios is an iterative, trial-and-error process. You could begin by asking the participants to identify a reasonable set of scenarios based on their experience. We have never used less than three, or more than ten. For the student enrollment process, there might be four scenarios:

1. A scholarship-winning student who is given early registration and gets into all of her chosen sections;

2. A returning student in good standing, who encounters the usual problems of missing prerequisites and full sections, but is generally satisfied;

3. A problem student on academic probation who also has financial issues, and requires various waivers and other special handling;

4. A mature student requiring extensive appeals and life experience credit to meet the prerequisites for the sections he wants.

Then, trace the path each scenario takes through the process workflow by identifying the branch taken at each major decision point. Sometimes we use a different colored pen to show each scenario's path. The intent is to ensure that each branch containing significant steps is exercised at least once, and more if it is a core piece of the process that most real-life cases would go through. You might find it easier to start with tracing the paths and then proposing a likely scenario for each unique path.

Once you're satisfied that you have a representative set of process scenarios, describe each, including the actors' names and characteristics, the preconditions, the main conditions and events to be demonstrated, and the outcome of the scenario. We often separate the group into sub-teams, with each working on a specific process scenario. Whatever you do, don't split into subteams until the overall set of use cases and process scenarios has been defined, otherwise you'll never get all the different ideas reconciled.

Each process scenario will involve several use case scenarios, which will be identified next.

Establish use case scenarios

Again, this is not a mechanical step—it requires imagination, trial and error, and iteration. However, the process scenarios and the path traced by each through the process workflow will provide useful structure. Each process scenario could include just a few use case scenarios, or many, depending on how complex the path is and how many actors are involved. Don't be surprised if you end up with 40, 50, or more use case scenarios— after the first few, they go fairly quickly. If this seems overwhelming, don't despair—our experience is that time spent on use case scenarios results in a net time savings as well as a higher-quality product.

We'll develop the use case scenarios for one process scenario at a time. Choose a simple process scenario, and begin by following its path in the workflow. Each contiguous (done "all at a time") sequence of steps by an actor represents a probable use case scenario, as long as it involves use of the information system. Note that contiguous steps by an actor are represented as a single step in the to-be handoff level workflow model, so that can be a useful aid.

Using the annotated (with use cases) workflow diagram, the process scenario description (especially the conditions list), and the actor's use cases list as guides, decide which use cases should be demonstrated in this scenario. Have the group refine the scenario by identifying the conditions, with basic data values, and expected handling. Some of these conditions will demonstrate "out of context" and "extends" use cases (search, help, print, etc.) that will appear in many use cases. Without getting into the actual dialogue, refine the scenario description by describing the order of the main steps or milestones. You might even discover a few new use cases.

After going through all of the process scenarios, check the "by actor" lists for use cases that haven't been covered yet. These will likely be error and exception cases that didn't appear in your basic workflow model. They can be worked into the appropriate process scenarios, either by creating additional use case scenarios, or adding them to existing ones.

Develop first-pass use case scenarios

The first pass of detailing the use case scenarios focuses entirely on the dialogue between actor and system. This usually goes smoothly because of the structured preparation you have done—the process scenario provides context, and for each use case scenario you have a description specifying the actors, main steps, and specific conditions to be demonstrated. This keeps the process orderly, and the group focused, which is also helped by working through one process scenario at a time, and within that, going through the use case scenarios in sequence.

Start with a review of the process scenario description, and then the description of the first use case scenario. Keep it low tech, using flipcharts and handouts—using a projector can be distracting at this point, and the facilitator will use the flipcharts later to keep the group on track. Having the conceptual data model available at this point helps, because the relationships and dependency among the entities often constrain the path the dialogue can follow.

Next, have the group identify the first step in the use case, which the facilitator writes up, such as:

- When client telephones the Service Center;
- When customer inserts bank card into ATM;
- When student accesses the university's URL.

We generally develop use case scenarios on the whiteboard, because it is easier to make changes as the use case scenario evolves. Note that the scenario would use actors' names rather than "client" or "student." Have the group complete the first clause, for instance:

- Then IVR system routes call to next available Service Rep;
- Then ATM prompts for password;
- Then system displays the university home page including a student sign-on box.

From that point on, simply work through the rest of the dialogue, using the steps and conditions in the scenario description as a guide. *Always* use the form "when action, then response," for example,

- When Joan (customer) calls the Service Center,

   Then IVR routes call to next available Service Rep (Adam).

- When Adam greets Joan and asks for Customer ID,

   Then Joan provides last name.

- When Adam selects Customer Search,

  Then System displays Search Window.

- When Adam enters "Johnson" and selects "Phonetic,"

  Then System retrieves all customer records with last names that sound like "Johnson" and displays them including last name, first name, telephone number, street address, and city.

Each when-then clause extends from an action by an actor through to control returning to that actor. After we first read about this form and began using it, we were surprised at how much more useful the use case scenarios became. When-then forces explicit dialogues that drive out ambiguity about use case behavior. This is because every action is essentially a decision point—did the actor provide the right information for the system to proceed, and did the system provide the right information or choices for the actor? For instance, if the actor is choosing which account to withdraw cash from, then the system must have provided the ability to make this choice by displaying the options. It's surprising how many important points like this can be missed, so when-then helps the facilitator ensure the group considers the following:

- For each actor step:

  Do they have the right information to proceed?

  What choices will they make and what information will they provide?

- For each system step:

  What data (in general) will it access/store, and what rules or validations will it perform? Check the conceptual data model—are the basic entities available, and can you get to them in the desired sequence?

  What will it display (visible to user) and what choices will it offer?

For some clauses you'll want to capture notes such as operational needs and wants or explanatory points, for example: "Matching names are listed with exact matches first, then alphabetically."

Be sure to start at the real beginning of the use case scenario, or at least early enough to demonstrate how the actor will see things. A common mistake is to begin at the desired system function without showing how the actor gets there. For instance, in a Web-based application, it's a good idea to be sure that some scenarios begin with the actor accessing the appropriate home page or portal URL. Some "friendly" dialogues will allow the actor to immediately enter his or her account ID, password, and selected function, while others require a ridiculous number of back and forth interactions—for example: select customer area, enter account ID, enter password, and select function—each requiring a separate interaction (when-then clause).

While developing the dialogue, differences of opinion will naturally arise. Don't waste time wrangling about which option is best—develop the dialogue for each alternative, and then let the appropriate actor representatives decide. Don't let system considerations dominate, either—this first pass is intended to produce a satisfying dialogue for the actors, and the second pass ensures that it's feasible with respect to system considerations.

Once the end of the use case scenario is reached, walk through the dialogue from the beginning, refining it until the team is satisfied with the flow. You will also have to ensure that the use case will support the goals of the process, and that the actors have the skills, information, and incentive to use the system as described by the use cases. Most important of all—Will it actually work in the actor's environment, which might include stringent performance measures and difficult clients?

Some guidelines to consider when assessing the scenario dialogue:

* Have you made the actor go through multiple steps when fewer (even one) would do? Many systems (especially interactive voice response systems) force people through cascading menus for technical reasons, or out of sheer design laziness. You should never have to navigate hierarchical menus to access common cases—they should be instantly accessible.

* Good e-commerce sites are easy to do business with the first time, and "instant" thereafter. (Think of Amazon.com and "one-click" ordering.)

* Consider different types of actors ("archetypes")—the "normal" user, plus nervous, first-time users, and impatient, experienced users.

As you progress through the use cases for the first process scenario, and then through the other process scenarios, you will find that conventions emerge and you'll need to refine earlier dialogues. This might seem a little discouraging, but it actually demonstrates a benefit of the approach—you're improving the design before going to the expense of detailed analysis or prototyping. Now, we'll move on to the second pass, which considers how data model navigation and transaction invocation will fit with the use case dialogue. First, we need to look at transaction concepts in more detail.

An interlude on transactions

Why bother?

Before going any further, let's acknowledge that "transactions" is a topic warranting an entire book, not just a section within a chapter on a topic that in turn warrants an entire book. So, for those of you with knowledge in this area... "Yes, we know we've omitted important concepts and details." For the rest of you who might ask, "Why bother?" some reasons are:

- We have introduced techniques for the other two layers of the three-tier architecture (UI and data management), so for completeness we'll cover transaction basics.

- Developing transaction requirements makes business rules visible, so they can be rethought as appropriate. Sometimes, rethinking a rule is better than redesigning the workflow to support it.

- The definition of transactions and their boundaries can have a significant impact on use cases and therefore on the support the process actors receive.

- Transactions are extremely important for system integrity and flexibility, which in turn impact the business, so analysts should understand the concepts and be able to gather the main requirements.

Even experienced analysts and technical specialists can struggle with the concept of transactions and the specific details. It's hard to get the idea across in a few well-crafted sentences. We suggest you read through the section, which includes concepts, benefits, examples, and specific guidelines, and then reread it—it will make more sense the second time through.

Terms and definitions

Transactions are the main units of functionality in the application logic layer. Other names include "application process," "elementary process,"[7] and "essential process." In component-based development (CBD), each service offered by a component will often correspond to a transaction.[8] In object-oriented terms, a transaction corresponds to a "control class," or to the "public methods" associated with a "business class" (an entity). In all cases, user interface facilities are required to make the function usable by process actors.

Earlier, we defined an event as an occurrence outside the system's control for which a logically complete response—a transaction—is required. A transaction, in a somewhat circular definition, is a "logically complete unit of work" that a system provides in response to an event. Building on what we know about events, we will clarify this business of being "logically complete."

At its core, a transaction is an information systems concept for packaging control logic (the code your programmers write) in a way that provides a complete response for an event, assures the integrity of updates to the database, and achieves a measure of reusability. They're not purely a technical concept, though—they must be defined with respect to the business. A transaction is a discrete unit of work, initiated in response to an event (as defined earlier), with significance to the business, that can't be broken down into smaller units and still be meaningful—it's said to be "atomic" or "indivisible." Examples will clarify this.

Concepts and examples

In the student registration environment, three transactions (following the usual verb-noun naming format) are:

---

7. The "elementary process," a concept in the information engineering methodology is documented in: Texas Instruments, *A Guide to Information Engineering Using the IEF: Computer-Aided Planning, Analysis, Design*, Plano, TX: Texas Instruments, Inc., 1988, pp. 171–174.

8. "Component" means many things these days, but in this context we mean a functional "chunk" or "repackaging" of a system that offers a related set of services. An order-management component would provide services (corresponding to transactions) such as create order, revise order line detail, add order line, drop order line, cancel order, and so forth.

- Enroll student in section;
- Drop enrollment;
- Transfer enrollment.

Note that each is a response to a discrete event: "Section enrollment is requested," "section enrollment is dropped," and "section enrollment is transferred." Think about how you would expect the system to properly and completely respond to each of these events. For "enroll student," you would expect the system to ensure the student had the prerequisites, check for available space in the section, create an enrollment record attaching the student to that specific section, lower the number of available spaces in the section, and update the student's account due. This description of the "expected actions" is the essence of the transaction definition.

Consider what would happen if the transaction definition was "sub-atomic," only going as far as creating the enrollment record, but not updating the number of available spaces or the student's account. The system's databases wouldn't be in a state of integrity—the number of available spaces in the section would be out of synch with the number of enrollment records attached to the section, and the account due would be inaccurate. In other words, the system wouldn't reflect the business's expected handling of the event, because the indivisible was divided. Our responsibility as analysts is to ensure that the complete, indivisible set of expected actions is documented.

Once these actions are programmed into a transaction, transaction processing (TP) monitors or application servers provide a variety of implementation services, one of which is ensuring that transactions are *all or nothing*. This means that if a transaction successfully completes, *all* of the database updates are "committed," meaning they become permanent. On the other hand, if the transaction fails part way through, for any reason, all of the database updates to that point are "backed out" and *nothing* is changed, as if the transaction never even started.

Other lessons are provided by "transfer enrollment," which responds to the event "section enrollment is transferred" by ending one enrollment in a section and creating a new enrollment in a different section. You might think you could handle this by simply having the appropriate actor invoke two transactions—first "drop enrollment" and then "enroll student in section"—but that would eventually cause problems. For instance, if the actor completed the "drop" transaction and then went for coffee, the "from" and "to" sections might both get filled before the "enroll" transaction happened. Now the student is in neither section, which certainly wasn't the intended result of the transfer event. The rule is that for each discrete event, there must be a single, discrete transaction.

Another way of looking at this example is that transactions are complete *business* operations, not single *database* create, update, or delete operations, and must implement the business's complete, expected response to an event.

Worth the effort?

Three key benefits ensue from packaging control logic into well-formed transactions. The first is integrity. If business rules and updates are documented and implemented in one place, in a transaction that has precisely one function, the odds of getting it right are much higher than if the logic was scattered around in little pieces, or jammed into huge, multipurpose programs. This becomes even more important when you consider maintenance of the transactions by future generations of programmers. Related to process redesign, focus on "what" (business rules and expected actions) rather than "who or how" often leads to new insights about what the rules *should* be.

The second benefit is flexibility. This requires that we first cover another important rule for transactions—they are completely independent of the user interface. Earlier, we noted that the role of the user interface is to provide a means of capturing data about an event, and then invoking the correct transaction by passing it a message containing the data items it expects. The transaction doesn't know or care whether the user interface was on a personal digital assistant (PDA), a Web browser, or an IVR system, as long as the UI can send the right message. (This is possible because the TP monitor or application server isolates the transaction from the UI, and manages the communication between them.) The benefit of this isolation is huge, as it provides the flexibility to use new interface technology, or modify existing interfaces, without recoding the transactions. Organizations with their application logic packaged into transactions had a much easier time going to client/server computing, and then providing access via the Web.

The third benefit, reuse, is closely related. Transactions are like building blocks that can be reused as needed when new applications require services that are already coded as transactions. Not only does this save development time, it ensures that there is one version of the business rules.

Most important in the context of this book, it supports the design of new business processes with the rapid development of "assemble to order" applications. This is a major driver behind CBD.[9]

A few more guidelines

- Each transaction does exactly one type of thing. It's tempting to create multipurpose transactions that can handle a number of related events (enroll, transfer, drop, etc.), but the imagined efficiency of combining multiple transactions into one doesn't materialize because of the extra effort decoding different message formats, deciding what to do, handling different security requirements, and so on. Besides, "small is beautiful."

- All editing that takes place at the user interface is redone—the transaction trusts no one. (We still need the UI to do some validation, of course, so it can "hand hold" the user to correction.)

- The transaction could be newly coded, or it could be a legacy transaction "wrappered" and made available through a component interface, or it might be a "composite transaction" constructed out of existing transactions (legacy, custom, packaged) using EAI tools or application server technology. Be sure to check with your IT staff on the availability of tools and techniques like these—you might be able to make more use of your existing applications than you thought.

Discovery and documentation

Like use cases, transactions are discovered iteratively using a variety of perspectives including direct identification ("What system functions are needed?"), inspecting the workflow model, event analysis, and use case description. Documentation follows the universal input-process-output framework for documenting system processes:

- Input—message from the UI, validation and reference data retrieved from databases;

- Process—the expected actions and rules;

- Output—message back to the UI, updates to the databases.

---

9. If this topic interests you, the Component-Based Development and Integration Forum at www.cbdiforum.com is a good place to start.

The first pass at transaction documentation includes simply the name and result, just like a business process, and optionally the main expected actions.

The second pass adds input and output message formats, and expands on the expected actions using this framework:

- Validation—business rules, further divided into:

  Entity existence and state;

  Attribute or relationship values.

- Operations and calculations (more business rules);

- Updates—entities created, updated, or deleted.

Figure 16.3 provides an example to this level of detail—it's not rigorous, but it illustrates the intent.

The third pass gets into complete, excruciating detail such as attribute-level validation and setting, algorithm details, error and exception handling, and handling complex or long-running transactions. Documenting the detailed logic will require other techniques such as state-transition diagrams, flowcharts, decision trees, truth tables, and pseudocode. How fully you document transactions before turning them over for development depends on the environment in your organization, and how involved the designers and programmers are in the analysis.

Want more?

There's much more to learn about transactions—the ACID test, two-phase commits, reusable data services, techniques for business rule specification, long-running transactions, and so on. If the topic interests you, we encourage you to check into these references:

- *The Client/Server Survival Guide* [1] is a wonderful, readable book that includes a section of transaction processing, along with many other topics. If you need an introduction or update on modern distributed computing, this is definitely the place to start.

Transaction name
Transfer Enrollment
Result (description)
A Student's Enrollment in one Section of a Course is ended, and a new Enrollment in a different Section of the same Course is established.
Input message
Student Number, From Section ID, To Section ID
Output message
Result Code, Confirmation Number
Actions—validation
• Student must be in "registered" state. • From Section must be in "filled" or "available" state. • From Section Enrollment must be in "active" state. • To Section must be in "available" state. • To Section Enrollment must not exist. • Transaction date must be on or before Semester last drop date.
Actions—operations and calculations
• If start date has passed, calculate transfer fee and new student account balance. • Calculate new enrollment count for From Section, and set state to "available" if it was "filled" before. • Calculate new enrollment count for To Section, and set state to "filled" if enrollment count is at maximum. • Set Result Code. • Set Confirmation Number (as per rules in data model).
Actions—updates
• Set From Section Enrollment to "ended" state, and set state change date. • Create To Section Enrollment in "active" status. • Update From Section as determined. • Update To Section as determined. • Update Student Account balance due.
Notes
• Investigate need to provide transfer fee exemption number • Investigate need to provide late transfer approval number.

Figure 16.3   A transaction description.

* *Transaction Processing* [2] is the bible on this subject, but isn't for the casual reader. If you *really* need to understand the theory and the practice, this is the book for you.

* *Essential Systems Analysis* [3] is hard to find now, but is worth the search for anyone serious about requirements analysis. It was the first book to cover topics like events and essential processes. Even though it's over 15 years old, it still provides useful insights—many of our friends say their dog-eared copy is the most important book on their "analyst" bookshelf.

This section on transactions was primarily included because the second pass of use case scenarios focuses on ensuring that transactions can be invoked, and that their expected behavior is documented. Now we will return to use case scenarios, and put the transactions in context.

Develop second-pass use case scenarios

As noted at the beginning of this chapter, things get significantly more detailed and technical at this point, so this section is intended only as an overview. The main point of the second pass is to capture the expected behavior of transactions invoked during the use case, which the preceding section has described. If the first pass is complete when a satisfying dialogue has been developed, then the second pass is complete when we have ensured that the dialogue will work given the constraints of the system. Specific goals for the second pass are:

- Identify the data items (attributes) required by each clause of the dialogue, and the points at which transactions will be invoked.

- Document each transaction as per the guidelines in the previous section.

- Confirm that the dialogue will work given the constraints of the data model and transaction definitions.

In documenting the second pass, it's usually more convenient to set up a matrix where the columns are the dialogue, the data requirements, and the transaction points. Optionally, add a column for notes. Each row is a single when-then clause, but we consider the "when" and the "then" separately. Proceed by filling in the matrix, row by row.

1. In the dialogue column, fully describe the validations being performed at each clause.

2. Next, in the data column, list the individual data items (attributes) that are being captured from the UI or displayed on it.

3. Ensure that data items being used for validation are either in the data model (update it as necessary) or are captured from the UI. If the data comes from the data model, check that the keys are available and that the navigation will work. Note that this second pass is driving the refinement of the logical data model.

4. Identify points in the dialogue where transactions should be invoked.

5. Ensure that the data necessary for the transaction has been gathered.

At this point, note that the dialogue can change the transaction boundaries and vice versa. However, exercise caution—don't let convenience for the programmer disproportionately drive the behavior of the application. This is a central point from Alan Cooper's *The Inmates Are Running the Asylum*, referenced earlier. We don't want to unnecessarily restrict the dialogue, just make sure it's feasible.

- Will the dialogue support the task in the intended environment, and be satisfying and usable for the actor?

- Will interface technology support the intended dialogue? That is, are functions like "display" and "select" supported appropriately?

- Does the UI gather the right information to support transaction invocation?

- Are data model accesses and transaction sequences valid with respect to dependency? For instance, do we ever try to create a dependent entity without confirming that the parent(s) exist?

If further confirmation of usability is required, prototypes can be developed from the information gathered so far.

Closing thoughts

More uses of use cases

Use case scenarios are typically developed only for the to-be process, to guide the design of systems that will provide the best support for process performers. They are used in the design of prototypes and production applications, and later in the systems development process; they are invaluable for system testing and acceptance testing. It's usually overkill to get down to the details of individual use cases when describing the as-is process. However, if your existing systems provide poor support, use case scenarios can expose particular deficiencies so improvement resources can be efficiently targeted. Similarly, some of our clients are using use cases and use case scenarios for existing applications as system documentation, as training tools, and for use in on-line help functions.

For many years, we have used scenarios and data models as tools for evaluating purchased applications. We are now extending this approach to include use case scenarios. Seeing a scenario dialogue clearly laid out, whether it is clean and elegant, or convoluted and primitive, is a powerful evaluation tool. It helps clients get past flashy GUIs and performance promises and see the support an application will actually provide to their people. Some clients have said they would have handled their ERP software implementation very differently if they'd had use case scenarios to see how the system actually behaved.

But why do they work so well?

After diving into the details, let's resurface and remind ourselves why use case techniques work so well. This isn't to convince you, but to point out the specific strengths so you get the most from use case techniques.

The first reason is simply that use cases deal with the user interface, which is where the interests of the business representatives (managers and process actors) and the IS representatives (analysts and developers) most strongly intersect. Throughout this book, we have used our five-tier framework, which comprises:

- Mission, strategy, and goals;

- Business process;

- Presentation (user interface);

- Application logic;

- Data management.

The top three tiers are primarily the realm of business professionals, the bottom three the realm of systems professionals. The two groups meet most comfortably at the tier they have in common—the presentation. Subject matter experts from the business can see, via the use case, whether the behavior evident at the system's presentation layer will support their tasks and processes. System developers can gather requirements from the use cases, not just for user interface design, but for application logic and data management as well.

The second is almost self-evident, but it bears pointing out—a use case scenario is better than the traditional bland list of requirements because it's a story, and everyone loves a story. By working within the context of a scenario that includes specific situations and conditions, participants are much more effective at visualizing the new system in operation and describing how it should behave. They involve clients in a real and meaningful way in specifying requirements, giving them confidence that their true requirements are understood and documented in a form that easily lets them decide whether the delivered system conforms to those requirements.

Compared to these strengths, use case techniques are disproportionately simple and cost-effective, so their adoption as a fundamental requirement analysis technique is increasingly widespread. No doubt, interesting applications and variations of this powerful technique will continue to emerge.

References

[1]   Orfali, R., D. Harkey, and J. Edwards, *The Client/Server Survival Guide, Third Edition*, New York: John Wiley & Sons, 1999.

[2]   Gray, J., and A. Reuter, *Transaction Processing: Concepts and Techniques*, San Francisco, CA. Morgan Kaufmann Publishers, 1992.

[3]   McMenamin, S., and J. Palmer, *Essential Systems Analysis*, New York: Yourdon Press, 1984.

Afterword

And so it ends—not your project, but this book's contribution. We have covered the intended topics, from discovering your processes up to using data modeling and use case scenario analysis to make the transition to requirements definition. Looking back, refer to Chapter 3, "The Approach in a Nutshell," and to Figure 3.4, "A workflow-driven approach," for a summary. Looking ahead, other sources can provide guidance on completing requirements specification and dealing with other issues such as training or managing change.

We hope this book has made a solid contribution to getting your project to this stage. Good luck, and remember: start with the end—the result—in mind.

About the Authors

Alec Sharp is the founder and senior consultant of the Damex Consulting Group Ltd., in West Vancouver, British Columbia, Canada. He is a founding member and a past president of the British Columbia Data Administration Management Association (DAMA) chapter, and has served as a director of the Vancouver Information Systems Training Association (VISTA).

Patrick McDermott is the president of McDermott Computer Decisions, Inc., in Oakland, California. He received his B.A. in economics from California State University at Sacramento. He has served as director of the Data Management Association (DAMA).

Index

Multimedia Database Management Systems, Guojun Lu

Practical Guide to Software Quality Management, John W. Horch

Practical Process Simulation Using Object-Oriented Techniques and C++, José Garrido

Secure Messaging with PGP and S/MIME, Rolf Oppliger

Security Fundamentals for E-Commerce, Vesna Hassler

Security Technologies for the World Wide Web, Rolf Oppliger

Software Verification and Validation: A Practitioner's Guide, Steven R. Rakitin

Strategic Software Production with Domain-Oriented Reuse, Paolo Predonzani, Giancarlo Succi, and Tullio Vernazza

Systems Modeling for Business Process Improvement, David Bustard, Peter Kawalek, and Mark Norris, editors

User-Centered Information Design for Improved Software Usability, Pradeep Henry

Workflow Modeling: Tools for Process Improvement and Application Development, Alec Sharp and Patrick McDermott

For further information on these and other Artech House titles, including previously considered out-of-print books now available through our In-Print-Forever® (IPF®) program, contact:

Artech House
685 Canton Street
Norwood, MA 02062
Phone: 781-769-9750
Fax: 781-769-6334
e-mail: artech@artechhouse.com

Artech House
46 Gillingham Street
London SW1V 1AH UK
Phone: +44 (0)20 7596-8750
Fax: +44 (0)20 7630-0166
e-mail: artech-uk@artechhouse.com

Find us on the World Wide Web at:
www.artechhouse.com